THREE NUANCES
of the PERFECT INDICATIVE
in the GREEK NEW TESTAMENT

THREE NUANCES
of the PERFECT INDICATIVE
in the GREEK NEW TESTAMENT

Hanbyul Kang

WIPF & STOCK · Eugene, Oregon

THREE NUANCES OF THE PERFECT INDICATIVE IN THE GREEK NEW TESTAMENT

Copyright © 2021 Hanbyul Kang. All rights reserved. Except for brief quotations in critical publications or reviews, no part of this book may be reproduced in any manner without prior written permission from the publisher. Write: Permissions, Wipf and Stock Publishers, 199 W. 8th Ave., Suite 3, Eugene, OR 97401.

Wipf & Stock
An Imprint of Wipf and Stock Publishers
199 W. 8th Ave., Suite 3
Eugene, OR 97401

www.wipfandstock.com

PAPERBACK ISBN: 978-1-6667-1529-3
HARDCOVER ISBN: 978-1-6667-1530-9
EBOOK ISBN: 978-1-6667-1531-6

09/21/21

Scripture quotations marked (ESV) are from The ESV® Bible (The Holy Bible, English Standard Version®), copyright © 2001 by Crossway, a publishing ministry of Good News Publishers. Used by permission. All rights reserved.

Scripture quotations marked (NASB) are taken from the (NASB®) New American Standard Bible®, Copyright © 2020 by The Lockman Foundation. Used by permission. All rights reserved. www.lockman.org"

Scripture quotations marked (NIV) are taken from the Holy Bible, New International Version®, NIV®. Copyright © 2011 by Biblica, Inc.™ Used by permission of Zondervan. All rights reserved worldwide. www.zondervan.com The "NIV" and "New International Version" are trademarks registered in the United States Patent and Trademark Office by Biblica, Inc.™

Scripture quotations marked (KJV) are from The Authorized (King James) Version. Rights in the Authorized Version in the United Kingdom are vested in the Crown. Reproduced by permission of the Crown's patentee, Cambridge University Press

CONTENTS

Abbreviations | ix
Tables | xi
Introduction | xiii

1 HISTORY OF RESEARCH: DIVERSE VIEWS OF THE GREEK PERFECT INDICATIVE | 1
   History of Research of the Greek Perfect Indicative | 1
      Jakob Wackernagel (1904) and Pierre Chantraine (1927) | 1
      Kenneth L. McKay (1965) | 2
      Stanley E. Porter (1989) | 4
      Buist M. Fanning (1991) | 6
      Daniel B. Wallace (1996) | 8
      Mari Broman Olsen (1997) | 8
      Rodney Decker (2000) | 10
      T. V. Evans (2001) | 12
      Thomas R. Hatina (1999) | 13
      Constantine R. Campbell (2007) | 16
      David L. Mathewson (2010) and Wally V. Cirafesi (2013) | 20
      Robert Crellin (2012) and Michael Aubrey (2014) | 20
      Randall Buth (2016) | 21
   Conclusion | 22

2 THE FIRST STAGE: RESULTATIVE-STATIVE | 24
   Introduction | 24
      Perfecta Praesentia | 25
   First Stage of the Greek Perfect | 29
      Resultative-Stative Perfect | 29
      Persistent Situation of the Perfect | 37
      Summary | 39
   Ancient Intransitive Perfect | 40

  Perfect of Intransitive Verbs | 41
  Perfect of Transitive Verbs | 43
  Summary | 48
 Ancient Perfect and Middle Voice | 48
  The Innovation and Spread of the Perfect Middle | 49
  Perfect Middle/Passive in the Greek New Testament | 53
  Γέγονα (γεγένημαι) | 63
  Perfects with Stative Nuance | 65
 Intensive Perfect | 68
  Intensive Perfect in the New Testament | 70
  Permanent (Inalterable) State | 74
 Conclusion | 77

3 STAGE TWO: FROM RESULTATIVE TO ANTERIOR | 79
 Introduction | 79
 The Second Stage: Transitive Anterior Perfect | 82
  Resultative Perfect of Wackernagel and Chantraine | 83
  Semantic Change: From Resultative to Anterior | 87
  Summary | 96
 Anterior Perfect in the Greek New Testament | 97
  Selected Texts from the Book of Revelation | 98
  Πεπίστευκα | 101
  Ἀκήκοα | 102
  Texts with Anterior Perfects in the New Testament | 104
  Anterior Perfects Having a Simple Past Nuance Occasionally | 112
  Perfect Middle with Anterior Sense | 122
 Conclusion | 124

4 THE THIRD STAGE: PERFECT AS SIMPLE PAST | 126
 Semantic Change from the Anterior to Simple Past | 127
 Aoristic Perfect Problem and Remedy from the Traditional Approach | 134
  Selected Texts from the Book of Revelation | 134
  The Dramatic Historical Present Perfect | 136
  Conclusion | 141
 Greek Perfect as Simple Past | 141
  Εἴληφας | 142
  Πέπρακεν | 144
  Εἴρηκα | 145
  Ἑώρακα | 150
  Ἀπέσταλκα | 154

    Δέδωκα | 157
    Second Corinthians | 159
    Book of Hebrews | 161
    Μεμαρτύρηκα | 164
    Γεγέννηκα | 165
    Γέγονα | 166
  Conclusion | 169

5 CONCLUSION | 171

APPENDIX 1 | 177
CHART OF THE PERFECT INDICATIVE WITH THREE NUANCES
IN THE GREEK NEW TESTAMENT | 177

APPENDIX 2 | 178
PERFECT INDICATIVE WITH THREE NUANCES
ACCORDING TO EACH BOOK IN THE NEW TESTAMENT | 178

Bibliography | 181

ABBREVIATIONS

AC	*Acta Classica*
BAGL	*Biblical and Ancient Greek Linguistics*
BBR	*Bulletin for Biblical Research*
BDF	Friedrich Blass and Albert Debrunner. *A Greek Grammar of the New Testament and Other Early Christian Literature*. Translated by Robert W. Funk. Chicago: University of Chicago Press, 1961
BECNT	Baker Exegetical Commentary on the New Testament
BICS	*Bulletin of the Institute of Classical Studies*
CC	Concordia Commentary
CEC	Critical Exegetical Commentary
CSB	Christian Standard Bible
CP	*Classical Philology*
EAGLL	*Encyclopedia of Ancient Greek Language and Linguistics*. Edited by Georgios K. Giannakis. Leiden: Brill, 2014
ECNT	Exegetical Commentary on the New Testament
ESV	English Standard Version
ICC	International Critical Commentary
IITSC	Invited Inferencing Theory of Semantic Change
IJL	*Italian Journal of Linguistics*
JBL	*Journal of Biblical Literature*
JETS	*Journal of Evangelical Theological Society*
JGL	*Journal of Greek Linguistics*
JSNT	*Journal for the Study of the New Testament*
JSNTS	Journal for the Study of the New Testament Supplement
KJV	King James Version
LCL	Loeb Classical Library

LI	*Linguistic Inquiry*
LXX	Septuagint
NAC	New American Commentary
NASB	New American Standard Bible
NET	New English Translation
NICNT	New International Commentary on the New Testament
NIGTC	New International Greek Testament Commentary
NIV	New International Version
NLT	New Living Translation
NovT	*Novum Testamentum*
NT	New Testament
NTL	The New Testament Library
OT	Old Testament
PS	*Philological Society*
PIE	Proto Indo-European
RSV	Revised Standard Version
TB	*Tyndale Bulletin*
TLG	Thesaurus Linguae Graecae
TPS	*Transactions of the Philological Study*
WBC	Word Biblical Commentary

TABLES

1. The percentages of Perfect Indicative with three nuances in the NT
2. Perfect Indicative with three nuances according to each book in the NT
3. English perfect and simple past

INTRODUCTION

AT THE 2013 ANNUAL meeting of the Society of Biblical Literature, debate about the Greek Perfect created the "perfect storm." The session featured Stanley E. Porter, Buist M. Fanning, and Constantine R. Campbell, discussing tense and aspect of the perfect. The debate rages on with a volume of essays derived from the SBL meeting.[1] Nevertheless, before we enter into the current debate, it is important to first understand the traditional view to which scholars are reacting. This traditional perspective was nicely articulated by Moulton and Turner, who state, "It [the Greek perfect indicative] is therefore a combining of the *Aktionsarten* of aorist and present" (emphasis original).[2] Blass and Debrunner (again reflecting the traditional view) define the Greek perfect as a combination: "The perfect combines in itself, so to speak, the present and the aorist in that it denotes the *continuance of completed action*" (emphasis original).[3] Another traditional proponent, Zerwick, asserts that the Greek perfect is not a past tense but a present one indicating a present state resulted from a past event.[4] Smyth similarly states, "The perfect denotes a completed action, the effects of which still continue in the present."[5] In sum, the traditional understanding of the perfect indicative can be summarized as: an ongoing state from a completed action. Nevertheless, difficulty lies in merely accepting this definition of the perfect since many exceptional cases exist in the Greek New Testament.[6]

1. Campbell et al., *Perfect Storm*.
2. Moulton and Turner, *Syntax*, 82.
3. BDF, 175.
4. Zerwick, *Biblical Greek*, 96.
5. Smyth, *Greek Grammar*, 434.
6. They are apparent stative perfects such as οἶδα and ἕστηκα, and the contested aoristic perfect. Thus, scholars have made a variety of endeavors in order to elucidate the Greek perfect. Mussies and Rademacher focus on the completed action more (Mussies, *Morphology*, 227, 261–65). Wackernagel and Chantraine pay more attention to "resultative perfect," that is, the perfect describing a state of the object (Wackernagel,

In more recent years, debates over the perfect have tried to resolve perceived tensions in the traditional understanding and bring outlying grammatical phenomena into the orbit of a unifying theory. Yet, rather than unity, we find a variety of conflicting views about the Greek perfect. For example, Stanley E. Porter argues that Greek does not grammaticalize absolute tense and maintains that the Greek perfect conveys a stative aspect.[7] Buist M. Fanning, on the other hand, adheres to a nuanced traditional definition of the Greek perfect.[8] Constantine R. Campbell introduces spatial concepts of the proximity and the remoteness, maintaining that the Greek perfect encodes an action's *heightened* proximity.[9] In this book, however, I will show that these new theories are not satisfactory to explain the complex behaviors of the various Greek Perfects found in the Greek New Testament.

In the midst of this cacophony of scholarly voices, Rutger J. Allan has perhaps provided the most helpful, succinct, and cogent explanation of the variegated uses of the Greek perfect found in the New Testament. In his article, "Tense and Aspect in Classical Greek," Allan traces the historical semantic development of the Greek perfect.[10] Allan suggests the three stages of the development of the Greek perfect: (1) stage one (resultative-stative) in Homer; (2) stage two (current relevance perfect or anterior)[11] in Classi-

---

"Griechischen Perfektum," 3–24; Chantraine, *Histoire du parfait grec*. McKay argues that the perfect represents the responsibility of the subject along with resulting state ("On the Perfect," 296).

7. Porter, *Verbal Aspect*, 98, 251–81. Porter states, "*Stative aspect is the meaning of the perfect tense, including the so-called pluperfect form* (not always augmented but with secondary endings): *the action is conceived of by the language user as reflecting a given (often complex) state of affairs.* This is regardless of whether this state of affairs has come about as the result of some antecedent action or whether any continued duration is implied" (*Idioms*, 21–22; emphasis original). Along with Fanning, on the other hand, Porter is the one who yields the verbal aspect theory. Porter defines the verbal aspect as "a synthetic semantic category (realized in the forms of verbs) used of meaningful oppositions in a network of tense systems to grammaticalize the author's reasoned subjective choice of conception of a process" ("Defence of Verbal Aspect," 32).

8. Fanning, *Verbal Aspect*, 109–20. On the other hand, Fanning's contributions to verbal aspect is that he accepts the theory of Vendler and Kenny who divide verbs into four categories: (1) states; (2) activities; (3) accomplishments (focus more on the durative result of the event rather than its activity); and (4) climaxes. Fanning believes that the types of the verb significantly affect the verbal aspect (Fanning, *Verbal Aspect*, 129–63; Vendler, "Verbs and Times," 143–60).

9. Campbell, *Indicative Mood*, 161–211; Campbell, *Verbal Aspect*, 46–51.

10. Allan, "Tense and Aspect," in Runge and Fresch, *Greek Verb Revisited*, 81–121.

11. Slings, "Geschiedenis van het perfectum," 242. Bybee defines anterior as the situation occurring prior to reference time, which is "relevant to the situation at reference time." English perfect is a good example of anterior (Bybee et al., *The Evolution of Grammar*, 54, 61. Similarly, Bentein calls this perfect "the perfect of current relevance," citing the example of Gerö and Stechow, "I have lost my glasses" which implies the

cal Greek; and (3) stage three (past/perfective) in the Koine period. Allan argues that all three of these historically-developed uses are found concurrently in the Koine period and that grammarians are likely misguided to search for one core non-cancelable meaning or discourse function of the perfect.

Allan's view of the perfect does not arise out of the thin air. As a predecessor of the proponents accepting the semantic changes of the Greek perfect, Martin Haspelmath in 1992 wrote the article "From Resultative to Perfect in Ancient Greek" and provided three diachronic stages of the Greek perfect.[12] Afterwards, scholars like Haug and Bentein supported this perspective.[13] Therefore, it is worth studying three distinct uses of the Perfect in the Koine period on the basis of a careful diachronic analysis: the resultative-stative perfect, the perfect of current relevance with anteriority, and the perfect as simple past. There is a necessity, however, of testing this thesis more rigorously on all the instances of the perfect throughout the New Testament.

The Greek New Testament shows the perfect with these three nuances. Perfect indicative forms occur 839 times in the New Testament. Out of 839, the perfect with stativity appears 461 times (55 percent). The anterior (current relevance) perfect occurs 289 times according to my research, consisting of 34 percent of occurrences. The aoristic perfect occurs 89 times (11 percent). Several debatable passages exist. I will scrutinize those texts in this book.

Table 1. The percentages of Perfect Indicative with three nuances in the NT

	Resultative-Stative	Anterior (Current Relevance)	Perfect as Simple Past	Sum
Occurrence	461 (55%)	289 (34%)	89 (11%)	839

The entire occurrences of the perfect with three nuances according to each book in the New Testament (including pluperfect) appear as below. The determination of which category the perfect should belong to is on a careful study of the surrounding literary contexts (including debatable passages

---

ongoing state of the past event (Bentein, "Periphrastic Perfect," 178; Gerö and Stechow, "Tense in Time," 251–94).

12. Haspelmath, "From Resultative to Perfect," 185–224. Haspelmath states the three periods of Greek: (1) Homeric; (2) Classical Greek; and (3) post-Classical Greek.

13. Haug, "From Resultatives to Anteriors," 285–305; Bentein, "Periphrastic Perfect," 175–209; Bentein, "Perfect," 46–49; Bentein, *Verbal Periphrasis*, 114–16, 153.

with asterisk in the table below). This book will analyze these debatable passages in detail.

Table 2. Perfect Indicative with three nuances according to each book in the NT[14]

	Resultative-Stative	Anterior (Current Relevance)	Perfect as Simple Past	Pluperfect	Sum
Matthew	37	11	4	8	60
Mark	31	15	1	8	55
Luke	38	18	4	16	76
John	81	106*[15]	19*[16]	34	240
Acts	26	23*[17]	7*[18]	17	73
Romans	46	8	3	1	58
1 Cor	55	11	2		68
2 Cor	26	10	8		44
Galatians	11	3	4		18
Ephesians	1				1
Philippians	9	2			11
Colossians	4	2	1		7
1 Thess	10	2	1		13
2 Thess	3	1			4
1 Timothy	6	2	1		9
2 Timothy	7	5			12
Titus	2	1			3
Philemon	1				1
Hebrews	8	13	24		45
James	12	1	1		14
1 Peter	2	1			3
2 Peter	5	2			7
1 John	19	39	2	1	61
2 John		1			1
3 John	1	2			3

14. The asterisk mark (*) indicates the inclusion of debatable passages.
15. John 20:18.
16. John 3:32.
17. Acts 22:15.
18. Acts 9:17.

INTRODUCTION   xvii

Jude	2	1			3
Revelation	18	9	7	1	35
	461	289	89	86 (Pluperfect)	Total 925 (839 Perfect)

THESIS

The three stages of the Greek Perfect in the historical development of the Greek language provide the most convincing explanation of all the actual occurrences of the Perfect Indicative, with the co-existence of the three nuances in the Greek New Testament.

METHODOLOGY

This book will analyze the three nuances of the perfect tense occurring in the Greek New Testament: resultative-stative, anterior (current relevance) perfect, and perfect as simple past. Every occurrence of the perfect indicative in the NT will be analyzed. I will also touch on some of the texts outside of the NT, such as Classical Greek or the Septuagint, if necessary. In analyzing every perfect indicative, dominant opposing theories will be tested and found wanting. Instead, we will find in each instance that seeing the Perfect as variegated in meaning with three possible distinct nuances makes the most sense of the NT authors' usages.

So far I briefly introduced the verbal aspect debate and the historical development of the Greek perfect. In chapter 1, I will present the main arguments of scholars about Greek perfect (including temporality, aspect, and any other issues) with accompanying evaluations. In chapter 2, I will explore the first stage of the development of the Greek perfect, from Homer to Koine Greek. During this stage, the archaic perfect active conveyed a resultative-stative nuance. In chapter 3, I will investigate the anterior (current relevance) perfects in the Greek New Testament, as well as selected examples from Classical Greek literature and the Septuagint. In chapter 4, I will address the thorny issue of the aorist perfect and the semantic change of the perfect from the anterior to simple past. Then I will apply major theories to these debatable perfect forms in order to seek solutions to these challenges.

1

HISTORY OF RESEARCH
DIVERSE VIEWS OF THE GREEK PERFECT INDICATIVE

THE TRADITIONAL CONCEPT OF the Greek perfect is that it is a combination of the present and the aorist (preterite). As mentioned above, many scholars support this definition. However, in recent years, some scholars have deviated from this view and have begun promoting different views of the Greek perfect.

HISTORY OF RESEARCH OF THE GREEK PERFECT INDICATIVE

Jakob Wackernagel (1904) and Pierre Chantraine (1927)

Wackernagel states that the Greek perfect in Homer connoted a present *result* of the subject and was purely intransitive.[1] After Homer, the perfect referred to the present result of the *object* rather than to the subject. In Classical Greek, the perfect represented a state out of a past action that perpetuates the impression of the object. Wackernagel says, "the perfect [is] the past

---

1. Wackernagel, "Griechischen Perfektum," 4–6.

action whose value persists in the object up to the present."[2] He terms it the resultative perfect (*Resultativ-perfektum*).[3]

Like Wackernagel, Chantraine argues that in the Homeric era the Greek perfect denoted the state of the subject out of a past event.[4] In Classical Greek, Chantraine says, "The perfect still expresses a state; but it is not the state of the subject, it is the state of the object."[5] Accepting Wackernagel's term "resultative perfect," Chantraine importantly notes that the Greek perfect shifted from the intransitive in Homer—focusing on the subject—to the transitive in Classical Greek—denoting the state of the object.[6] Chantraine provides a great number of examples from Classical Greek and the New Testament. Chapters 2 and 3 will handle Chantraine's work in detail.

Kenneth L. McKay (1965)

McKay's writings are an important precursor to the verbal aspect debate occurring today. McKay claims that "the perfect tense expresses the state or condition of the subject of the verb, mostly in present-time contexts . . . and in some circumstances it has an added strong reference to an event which is already past."[7] Although Porter accepts McKay's stativity notion and develops it further, McKay does not fully exclude time in Greek verbal

---

2. Wackernagel, "Griechischen Perfektum," 4. Wackernagel says, "bei der das Perfekt von einer vergangenen Handlung gebraucht wird, deren Wirkung im oder am Objekt noch in der Gegenwart fortdauert."

3. This book will follow the general linguistic term "resultative perfect" defined by Nedjalkov, which expresses "a state implying a previous event" (Nedjalkov and Jaxontov, "Resultative Construction," 6–9). According to Bentein, it is unfortunate that the term "resultative perfect" of Wackernagel and Chantraine means differently from "resultative" used in cross-linguistics studies (Bentein, "Periphrastic Perfect," 177n14; Bentein, *Verbal Periphrasis*, 38n177).

4. Chantraine, *Parfait grec*, 4–7, 20.

5. Chantraine, *Parfait grec*, 122. Chantraine says, "Le parfait exprime bien encore un état; mais ce n'est plus l'état du sujet, c'est celui de l'objet."

6. Chantraine, *Parfait grec*, 6, 253–54.

7. McKay, *New Syntax*, 49; McKay, "Perfect and Other Aspects," 296. McKay offers several examples: ἤγγικεν denotes "the kingdom of heaven is [*has come*] near" (Matt 3:2); γέγραπται refers to "for so it is written" (Matt 3:2). For pluperfect, McKay states, "The pluperfect tense expresses the state or condition of the subject of the verb, mostly with reference to past time when it is used in past narrative contexts, but in excluded potential statements and unreal conditions it as readily has reference to present time if the context requires." For future perfect, he says, "The future-perfect tense expresses the state or condition of the subject of the verb in future time, and sometimes possibly as intention. It combines the perfect and future aspectual nuances" (McKay, *New Syntax*, 51; McKay, "Perfect and Other Aspects," 296).

system. McKay describes, "the state or condition of the subject of the verb, as a result of an action (logically a prior action)."[8] McKay claims that for some verbs the Greek perfect stands for a pure state. McKay regards οἶδα as "I am *in a state of* knowledge."[9] In John 8:55, (καὶ οὐκ ἐγνώκατε αὐτόν, ἐγὼ δὲ οἶδα αὐτόν) McKay reads the text as "and you do not (have not come to) know him, but I know him."

McKay notes that in Greek perfect, the subject sometimes expresses the "responsibility" of the stativity. He offers examples detailing the responsibility: (1) κεκοίνωκεν τὸν ἅγιον τόπον τοῦτον, "he has defiled (is guilty of defiling) this holy place" (Acts 21:28); (2) ἐν δὲ εἰρήνῃ κέκληκεν ὑμᾶς ὁ θεός "God has called (it is God who is responsible for having called) you in peace" (1 Cor 7:15); and (3) ἡ πίστις σου σέσωκέν σε, "your faith has saved you (is the basis of your healing)" (Matt 9:22).[10] Further, in John 19:22 Pilate responds to Jesus ὃ γέγραφα, γέγραφα ("what I have written, I have written") in which McKay renders it as "Pilate accepts responsibility for what he has written."[11]

McKay's concept of "responsibility" of the subject for stativity might not be completely inappropriate because in virtually any action, the subject is responsible for an action performed. In fact, many passages appear awkward if this notion of "responsibility" is forcibly applied to the translation in context.[12]

---

8. McKay, *New Syntax*, 49.

9. McKay, *New Syntax*, 49. In John 8:19 εἰ ἐμὲ ᾔδειτε, καὶ τὸν πατέρα μου ἂν ᾔδειτε ("if you did know me, you would know my father too"), he focuses on the "existing state" of knowledge (McKay, "Perfect and Other Aspects," 299–302). On the other hand, McKay distinguishes οἶδα from ἔγνωκα. While he regards the former as a pure state being irrelevant to contexts, McKay refers the latter to the knowledge added to the stativity with "having come to know." He claims that ἔγνωκα is only employed in contexts of the acquisition of knowledge. McKay sees ἐγνώκατε having some added nuance even though its translation will not be able to become other than "know."

10. McKay, *New Syntax*, 32.

11. McKay, "Perfect and Other Aspects," 317–18n68.

12. Campbell criticizes McKay's view of "responsibility," pointing out that the origin of this "responsibility" is not certain whether it is from the perfect per se, or from the contexts.

John 1:18	θεὸν οὐδεὶς ἑώρακεν πώποτε ("No one is *responsible* for having seen God")
John 1:41	εὑρήκαμεν τὸν Μεσσίαν ("We are *responsible* for having found the Messiah")
John 7:22	διὰ τοῦτο Μωϋσῆς **δέδωκεν** ὑμῖν περιτομήν ("because of this Moses is *responsible* for having given you circumcision")

In John 1:18, Campbell sharply points out the awkwardness of McKay's notion of

Stanley E. Porter (1989)

In 1989, Porter published his dissertation *Verbal Aspect in the Greek of the New Testament*. Not only is the enormous quantity of the research striking, but also his comprehensive presentation of the Greek verbal system is stunning. Porter avers that the Greek verbal system does not inherently contain temporality.[13] The Greek verb does not grammatically function to denote temporality, but rather time is expressed by a speaker according to contextual factors, such as adverbs, prepositional phrases, or simply the literary genre.[14]

Porter maintains that the Greek perfect denotes the stative aspect. Porter claims that Greek has three aspects: perfective, imperfective, and stative.[15] Compared with McKay, Porter states a slightly different version of the stative aspect, which he describes as "a general state of affair." Porter describes the perfect as denoting the stative aspect for the whole affair conceived by the speaker.[16]

---

responsibility. It sounds awkward that "no one" is responsible for seeing God. In McKay's thesis, the subject plays an important role to denote the stativity of the verb. This passage violates McKay's argument, so that Campbell criticizes the absence of the subject, i.e., "no one" in the text. Secondly, in John 1:41 Campbell says that Andrew is not really responsible for finding the Messiah. It was John the Baptist who identified Jesus Christ. Thus, McKay's "responsibility" language does not work here. Thirdly, Campbell shows the passages which denote the oxymoron of McKay's notion. According to Campbell's language John 7:22 should say literally, "Moses is *responsible* for having given you circumcision." The author of the Gospel of John adds a statement that the circumcision is not from Moses, but from the patriarchs. McKay's model of the perfect does not function perfectly. Therefore, McKay's argument that the Greek perfect emphasizes the responsibility of the subject does not fully work (Campbell, *Indicative Mood*, 168–69; Campbell, *Verbal Aspect*, 48).

13. Porter, *Verbal Aspect*, 78. Runge criticizes Porter's "contrastive substitution" to justify timelessness of Greek verbs. See Runge, "Contrastive Substitution," 154–73.

14. Porter, *Verbal Aspect*, 98–99, 264; Porter, *Idioms*, 25–26; Porter, "Prominence," 58. Porter says, "The verbal aspect as 'a synthetic semantic category (realized in the forms of verbs) used of meaningful oppositions in a network of tense systems to grammaticalize the author's reasoned subjective choice of conception of a process'" (Porter, "Defence of Verbal Aspect," 32).

15. Porter, *Verbal Aspect*, 107; Porter, "Prominence," 59. Fanning notes that Porter does not seem to comprehend the semantic distinction between *Aktionsart* and aspect. According to Fanning, there is a general consensus that "stative" should be *Aktionsart* among scholars. Fanning asserts that *Aktionsart* must be differentiated from aspect because the aspect is subjectively chosen by a speaker or writer. Fanning critiques Porter who confuses the objective *Aktionsart* with the subjective aspect (Fanning, "Approaches to Verbal Aspect," 59).

16. Porter, *Verbal Aspect*, 259; Porter, *Idioms*, 21–22. Unlike McKay, Porter focuses more on the general state of the verb rather than the subject. Porter follows Louw, who

Porter argues that the Greek perfect encodes a stative aspect. This argument of Porter especially appeals to stative perfect verbs: οἶδα, γέγονα, δέδωκα, ἔγνωκα, εἴωθα (be accustomed), ἔοικα, ἑστάναι (stand), ἥγημαι, κέκραγα, κέκρικα, μέμνημαι, πέποιθα, σεσίγηκα (be still), τέθνηκα and so on.[17] On the basis of these perfect verbs, Porter hastily concludes that the Greek perfect is stative without further investigation of the details and its complexity.[18] For example, Porter reads John 6:69, "we are *in a state of* (πεπίστευκα) faith and knowledge; we are *in a state of* recognition (ἐγνώκαμεν) the truth and hold it."[19] Porter denies the perfect of anterior nuance.[20]

Many criticize Porter, in that Porter's thesis is based on exceptional cases. Fanning opposes Porter's view that the Greek verbal system does not convey temporality. Fanning regards time as playing an important role in Greek verbal system even though the concept of time in Greek is not the

---

says that stative aspect denotes the whole affairs, not the event described by the perfect (Porter, *Verbal Aspect*, 258; Louw, "Perfektum," 27).

17. Porter, *Verbal Aspect*, 254; Porter, *Idioms*, 40-42. Many grammarians recognize that these verbs often convey a stative notion: Robertson, *Grammar*, 894-95; BDF §341, §343; Moulton, *Prolegomena*, 143-48; Goodwin, *Syntax*, 19; Burton, *Syntax*, 37, 39-40; Turner, *Syntax*, 82.

18. Porter, *Verbal Aspect*, 259.

19. Porter, *Verbal Aspect*, 255. Porter criticizes Barrett's reading of the second half ("have recognized") of the verse as unnecessary while he agrees with Barrett's rendering "in a state of faith" of the first half of the verse (Barrett, *Gospel according to St. John*, 306).

20. See more examples Porter quotes (*Verbal Aspect*, 255, 269, 278):

John 1:18	θεὸν οὐδεὶς **ἑώρακεν** πώποτε ("No one has ever seen [sees] God")
John 6:63	τὰ ῥήματα ἃ ἐγὼ **λελάληκα** ὑμῖν πνεῦμά ἐστιν ("The words that I have spoken [speak] to you are Spirit")
Acts 6:11	**ἀκηκόαμεν** αὐτοῦ λαλοῦντος ῥήματα βλάσφημα ("We have heard [hear] him speak blasphemous words")

In John 1:18 Porter renders John 1:18 θεὸν οὐδεὶς ἑώρακεν πώποτε as "no one ever sees God." His translation is not appropriate according to the context. Here, the apostle John is witnessing the incarnated God for the first time whom no one has ever encountered within the Old Testament period. Secondly, in John 6:63 (ἃ ἐγὼ λελάληκα)v Porter translates this phrase as "which I speak." However, the whole context of John 6 is Jesus Christ's explaining the spiritual truth after he miraculously distributed bread to the crowds. After teaching the crowds, Jesus Christ utters the final comment in John 6:63, "what I have spoken (λελάληκα) is the spirit, because the flesh is useless." Hence, even the context connotes that it is not a plausible translation of λελάληκα as "which I speak." Thirdly, Porter refers the perfect in Acts 6:11 to present time. However, the context denotes that the current accusation is based upon the anterior event of their hearing "blasphemous" words.

same as in English.²¹ Olsen also criticizes Porter as his system is too simple; the Greek verb does not include a time reference.²² Runge points out that "even though the perfect is an aspect, it nevertheless has a logical temporal ordering that cannot be ignored."²³

Decker supports Porter's view, saying that his system is not substantiated only by an assembly of the exceptional cases, but rather it is the most robust explanation.²⁴ However, Porter's view is still a minority among scholars.

Buist M. Fanning (1991)

Fanning adheres to the traditional perspective of Greek verbs in that he accepts grammaticalized time in the verbal system. On the basis of this idea, he does not reject the traditional notion of the Greek perfect, which regards the perfect as subsequently related to precedent event.²⁵ Fanning considers the perfect with its state as combination of the present and aorist senses.²⁶

Fanning maintains that the meaning of the perfect tense form incorporates the combination of three elements: (1) stative *Aktionsart*;²⁷ (2) *anterior* tense; and (3) summary viewpoint (perfective) aspect.²⁸ Fanning

---

21. Fanning, "Approaches to Verbal Aspect," 58. See Evans, *Verbal Syntax*, 40-50.

22. Olsen, *Semantic and Pragmatic Model*, 202, 232. Olsen says that Porter often utilizes the examples of the stative verbs.

23. Runge, "Discourse Function," 462.

24. Decker, *Temporal Deixis*, 38.

25. Fanning describes the perfect: "the perfect denotes the *completion* of the action and a *state* or condition which is the consequence of the action" (Fanning, *Verbal Aspect*, 112, 119, 159; emphasis original).

26. I believe that the "aorist" senses Fanning means would represent the past tense. I do not agree with the identification of the aorist with the past tense. See Stagg, "Abused Aorist," 222-31.

27. Until 1920, *Aktionsart* and aspect were employed exchangeably, indicating the nature of the action such as duration, punctiliar, inception, or repetition (Fanning, *Verbal Aspect*, 31). *Aktionsart* in itself stands for objective inherent meaning, i.e., "kind of action" (Moulton, *Prolegomena*, 108) such as durative, punctiliar, or iterative. On the other hand, the aspect represents a free choice of speaker's viewing the event, whether it is *inside* or *outside* (of the parade, for example). The external viewpoint is perfective just like seeing the street parade from a helicopter. The inside perspective is called imperfective just like being in the street parade (this analogy is from Campbell, *Basics of Verbal Aspect*, 20). Therefore, Fanning and Campbell critique that Porter's argument that the perfect encodes the stative aspect results from confusion between *Aktionsart* and *aspect*. Fanning and Campbell state that Porter confuses *Aktionsart* with aspect. Porter responds to them that *Aktionsart* category itself is substantiated on.

28. Fanning, *Verbal Aspect*, 112-20, 290-91; Fanning, "Approaches to Verbal

states, "Put together, these result in a sense usually described as denoting 'a condition resulting from an anterior occurrence.'"[29] However, Fanning tries to hold too many diverse elements together.[30]

Although Fanning's analysis is insightful and each element is substantiated on the basis of correct understanding of the perfect, his analysis suffers from lacking the coherence to hold these three elements together. For example, the stative *Aktionsart*, indicating the elapsed time between the present and the past, is able to elucidate οἶδα. However, the anterior tense, the second element, does not fit in the stative perfect such as οἶδα. Likewise, the second and third elements can explain the aoristic perfect which denotes the past event, but the first element—stative *Aktionsart*—does not cohere with it. Although Fanning's analysis is correct and insightful on a micro-level, it suffers from lack of coherence on a macro-level. Lumping together all attested characteristics of the perfect (*Aktionsart*, anteriority, aspect) does not necessarily yield a coherent product.[31] Fanning's view is a form of "illegitimate totality transfer" with potential nuances of the perfect.

Aspect," 48–50. Unlike Porter, Fanning maintains that a theoretical distinction between aspect and *Aktionsart* is necessary. While Porter refers the Greek perfect to the stative aspect, Fanning notes that "stative" should be in an objective category of *Aktionsart* rather than in a category of aspect that connotes more subjectivity. Porter argues that the perfect conveys the stative aspect. According to Fanning, since the stativity is a category of *Aktionsart*, it should be distinguished from the aspect (Fanning, *Verbal Aspect*, 31–32). Aspect does not have anything to do with the sequence of time (Fanning, *Verbal Aspect*, 85). According to Porter, to put more emphasis on aspect does not necessarily lead to the preclusion of the time. These two should be separated and dealt with respectively. According to Campbell, it is the most important that most linguists regard stativity as *Aktionsart* rather than as aspect (Campbell, *Indicative Mood*, 172–75). Porter responds back to Campbell, saying that the linguists have not done a popular vote for this and the consensus Campbell maintains is not found (Porter, "Greek Linguistics and Lexicography," 48). On the other hand, Campbell summarizes well the distinction between *Aktionsart* and aspect: "Aspect is a semantic value. The aspect of a particular tense-form doesn't change. An aorist will always be perfective in aspect. This will be the case no matter which word (lexeme) is used as an aorist or in what context it is used. Aspect is uncancelable. . . . *Aktionsart*, on the other hand, is a pragmatic value. The *Aktionsart* of a particular tense-form can change. Sometimes an aorist will be punctiliar in *Aktionsart*. Sometimes it will be iterative, sometimes ingressive. It all depends on which lexeme is used as an aorist, on the context, and on what actually happened. *Aktionsart* is cancelable" (Campbell, *Basics of Verbal Aspect*, 23).

29. Fanning, *Verbal Aspect*, 119–20, 290–91. Campbell criticizes this definition, on the grounds that Fanning merely provides "a modern restatement of the classic view."

30. Evans, *Verbal Syntax*, 29, 50; Cirafesi, *Synoptic Parallels*, 41.

31. Despite the beauty and neatness of the theory, Silva rightly critiques Fanning in that he is too generous "to salvage what he can out of the traditional grammar" (Silva, "A Response," 75, 77). Campbell criticizes that Fanning's view of the perfect allows too many exceptional cases such as οἶδα or ἕστηκα (Campbell, *Indicative Mood*, 190).

Daniel B. Wallace (1996)

Wallace preserves a traditional perspective of Greek verbal aspect. Wallace states that the perfect tense is a combination of external (action) and internal (continuous).[32] With the basic notion of the traditional perfect, Wallace introduces categories of resultative perfect, aoristic perfect, and perfect with a present force.[33] For example, he put οἶδα, ἕστηκα, and πέποιθα into the category of perfect with a present force.[34] Although Wallace attempts to clarify the exceptional cases of the perfect by introducing categories of "aoristic perfect" or "perfect with a present force," his presentation is still vulnerable to criticisms.

Mari Broman Olsen (1997)

Olsen analyzes Koine Greek a little differently from both Porter and Fanning. She views the indicative as mixed tense and aspect system. Olsen maintains that tense is still communicated in the Greek verbal system. She criticizes Porter by stating that his system is too simplistic. Olsen does not eliminate the time relevance as a whole. For example, Olsen states that the imperfect denotes past time with imperfective aspect.

For the Greek perfect, Olsen maintains that the perfect form denotes perfective aspect. Unlike Fanning, however, she claims that the Greek perfect conveys present time. Olsen does not follow the traditional definition of the perfect, but maintains that the perfect denotes the present time. She nuances this assertion further in asserting that there may be an interaction in the Greek perfect between tense and grammatical aspect and lexical aspect.[35]

Olsen's Greek perfect communicates perfective aspect with present time. She claims that the Greek perfect represents a present tense.[36] Some

---

32. Wallace, *Beyond the Basics*, 573.
33. Wallace, *Beyond the Basics*, 574–80.
34. Wallace, *Beyond the Basics*, 579.
35. Olsen, *Semantic and Pragmatic Model*, 202. However, Olsen's definition of the Greek perfect is not completely clear. Olsen's Greek verbal system:

	Past	Present	Future	Unmarked
Imperfective	Imperfect			Present
Perfective	Pluperfect	Perfect		Aorist
Unmarked			Future	

36. Olsen, *Semantic and Pragmatic Model*, 232. Campbell points out the problem of

of her analysis appears plausible because the perfect tense denotes a present status from the past event. However, Olsen denies the stativity of the Greek perfect.[37] Moreover, her system cannot explain a perfect denoting simple past time. The perfect behaving like the aorist, the so-called "aoristic perfect," occurs many times in the NT.

Nevertheless, Olsen observes important characteristics of some perfects, focusing on their present relevance with perfective aspect.

[John 16:28] ἐξῆλθον παρὰ τοῦ πατρὸς καὶ ἐλήλυθα εἰς τὸν κόσμον.
I came from the Father and *have come* into the world.

In John 16:28, Porter regards the aorist verb as denoting past time and the perfect verb highlighting the past event.[38] Olsen basically agrees with his statement in that the perfect marks a perfective situation with present time. Olsen pays attention to the present relevance of the perfect, and then its perfective aspect from a completed situation.[39] Thus, she seems to be able to render the perfect above as "have come." Olsen states that the perfect semantically includes the present relevance, and it is not cancelable.[40]

Table 3. English perfect and simple past

The baseball strike *has canceled* the 1994 postseason	The baseball strike canceled the 1994 postseason

Interestingly, she illustrates the English perfect contrasting the simple past. Olsen concludes that compared to a simple past tense rendering in English, the perfect delivers the statement during 1994 more felicitously. She notes that the perfect asserts a present situation.[41] In sum, Olsen's concept of the perfect does not fully clarify behaviors of the Greek perfect such as the aoristic perfect, but her analysis and description of the perfect is worthwhile.

Olsen's approach in that not every perfect does refer to the present time as in John 5:33, ὑμεῖς ἀπεστάλκατε πρός Ἰωαννην, καὶ μεμαρτύρηκεν τῇ ἀληθείᾳ ("You sent to John, and he has borne witness to the truth") (Campbell, *Basics of Verbal Aspect*, 49).

37. Olsen, *Semantic and Pragmatic Model*, 250.
38. Porter, *Verbal Aspect*, 262.
39. Olsen, *Semantic and Pragmatic Model*, 234.
40. Olsen, *Semantic and Pragmatic Model*, 233.
41. Olsen, *Semantic and Pragmatic Model*, 233–34.

Rodney Decker (2000)

In his book *Temporal Deixis of the Gospel of Mark*, Decker appropriates Porter in that he systematically demonstrates his system.[42] Against those who charge Porter with founding his system on the exceptional cases, Decker refutes them, saying that Porter's work is much more "extensive and rigorous" than merely utilizing exceptional cases to bolster the argument.[43]

Decker emphasizes that a view of the Greek verb as temporally ungrammaticalized does not mean that Greek cannot convey temporality. Instead of grammaticalizing the temporality in verbs, Greek employs a variety of means to deliver the concept of time. If the traditional approach is correct, according to Decker, it allows too many exceptional cases. Decker remarks that surprisingly no one has ever refuted Porter, and no one has suggested major obstacles to Porter, in spite of criticism.[44] Although there is no 100 percent perfect system, says Decker, Porter's system is more consistent and adequate than others.[45]

Decker divides the perfect verbs into four time-reference: (1) present time; (2) past time; (3) future time; and (4) temporally unrestricted. Decker

---

42. Decker defines temporal deixis as "the grammaticalization of temporal relationships of events to the coding time. Lyons defines deixis as "the location and identification of persons, objects, events, processes, and activities being talked about, or referred to, in utterance (Lyons, *Semantics*, 637). Decker regards deixis as one area of pragmatics (Decker, *Temporal Deixis*, 54–56). Decker insightfully analyzes all the deictic indicators in Mark: nominal indicators (the nominal indicators are genitive, dative, accusative, and nominative that are employed to indicate time reference such as genitive of time or dative of time); adverbial indicators (ἐγγύς, ἐπαύριον, ἔτι, νῦν, ἤδη, ὀψέ, πάλιν, πάντοτε, πρωΐ, σήμερον, τότε, εὐθύς, etc.); prepositional indicators (ἀπό, διά, εἰς, ἔπι, μέτα, etc.); conjunctive indicators (ἕως, ὅτε, καί, πρίν, ὡς, etc.); and lexical indicators (*Temporal Deixis*, 66–90).

43. Decker, "Verbal Aspect," 4; Decker, *Temporal Deixis*, 38.

44. Decker, "Verbal Aspect," 5; Decker, *Temporal Deixis*, 38, 49.

45. Decker, *Temporal Deixis*, 37.

offers several perfect forms in Mark according to these four cases.⁴⁶ Then he attempts to apply Porter's model to the Gospel of Mark.⁴⁷ For example,

> [Mark 13:19] ἔσονται γὰρ αἱ ἡμέραι ἐκεῖναι θλῖψις οἵα οὐ **γέγονεν** τοιαύτη ἀπ' ἀρχῆς κτίσεως .
> For in those days there will be such tribulation as *has not been* from the beginning of the creation.
>
> [Mark 13:23] ὑμεῖς δὲ βλέπετε· **προείρηκα** ὑμῖν πάντα.
> But be on guard; I *have told* you all things beforehand.

In Mark 13:19, Decker notes that γέγονεν should refer to past time because of the temporal preposition ἀπο ἀρχῆς.⁴⁸ Decker disregards the possi-

---

46. Decker, *Temporal Deixis*, 52 (perfects in bold).

Perfect (Past Time)	John 6:32	οὐ Μωϋσῆς **δέδωκεν** ὑμῖν τὸν ἄρτον ἐκ τοῦ οὐρανοῦ ("Moses *did* not *give* you the bread from heaven")
	Rom 16:7	οἳ καὶ πρὸ ἐμοῦ **γέγοναν** ἐν Χριστῷ ("who also *were* in Christ before me")
Perfect (Present Time)	John 1:26	μέσος ὑμῶν **ἕστηκεν** ὃν ὑμεῖς οὐκ **οἴδατε** ("in the midst of you he whom you do not *know stands*")
	2 Tim 4:6	Ἐγὼ γὰρ ἤδη σπένδομαι, καὶ ὁ καιρὸς τῆς ἀναλύσεώς μου **ἐφέστηκεν** ("the time of my release *is imminent*")
Perfect (Future Time)	John 17:22	κἀγὼ τὴν δόξαν ἣν **δέδωκάς** μοι **δέδωκα** αὐτοῖς ("I *will give* them the glory)
	James 5:2–3	ὁ πλοῦτος ὑμῶν **σέσηπεν** καὶ τὰ ἱμάτια ὑμῶν σητόβρωτα **γέγονεν** ("your riches *will rust* and your garments *will become* moth-eaten")
(Temporally Unrestricted)	John 1:18	θεὸν οὐδεὶς **ἑώρακεν** πώποτε ("no one ever *sees* God")
	Rom 7:2	ἡ γὰρ ὕπανδρος γυνὴ τῷ ζῶντι ἀνδρὶ **δέδεται** νόμῳ ("for the married woman *is bound* to her husband by law")

These perfect forms are tough to give a clear explanation. This book will plumb the issues concerning these perfects such as stative perfect or aoristic perfect. Decker claims that the perfect can denote the future time as well. However, just like the usage of a futuristic perfect in Hebrew, the perfect indicates the disaster coming upon the rich in the future judgment according to context (See McKnight, *Letters of James*, 386). It is not because the perfect is free from temporality. Even Porter says that "only a few uses of the perfect with future implication, and even these are not altogether clear" (Porter, *Verbal Aspect*, 266–67).

47. The perfect οἶδα occurs nine times in Gospel of Mark (out of forty-six occurrences of the perfect) (Decker, *Temporal Deixis*, 109).

48. Decker, *Temporal Deixis*, 134. For example, Decker explains that the articular

bility of inherent temporality in γέγονεν but supposes that the prepositional phrase entails the temporality of the verb according to context. In Mark 13:23, Decker describes the temporal prefix on the verb as indicating antecedent time. Rejecting the inherent temporality of the verbs, Decker puts much emphasis on the external markers such as adverbs or prepositional phrases.

However, Evans significantly points out,

> He [Porter/Decker] reverses the normal approach, that temporal adverbs take their precise semantic flavor from context and that an influential factor within that context is the temporal reference of the verbal forms which they modify. For Porter, as noted above, it is the adverb which furnishes the temporal reference of the context. It seems impossible to accept the new limitations this interpretation imposes on the lexical semantics of temporal adverbs.[49]

The role of the temporal deixis is crucial. However, adverbs and prepositional phrases should not be the sole determiner for temporality. Moreover, it is not certain that the temporal deixis such as adverbs or prepositional phrases should affect the verbs enough to determine their time. Fanning importantly notes that the internal or inherent time element of the Greek perfect should be distinguished from the *external* time markers in the indicative mood.[50] Thus, not only the inherent time of the verb, but also the temporal deixis should be considered for correct interpretation of the text.

T. V. Evans (2001)

Evans analyzes the Greek verbal system in his book *Verbal Syntax in the Greek Pentateuch*. Concerning the perfect, Evans criticizes the traditional approach of the perfect. He states that the traditional definition of the perfect cannot explain all the examples such as a stative verb, saying: "it [the traditional interpretation of the Greek perfect] operates only on

---

νῦν refers to the present.

49. Evans, *Verbal Syntax*, 44. With the example νῦν, Evans goes on to say that Porter pays attention to its semantic flexibility ("its temporal reference encompasses a broad span, from the immediate moment to a large stretch of time") but disregards its conventionally recognized application to the past time. For example, in John 11:8 (λέγουσιν αὐτῷ οἱ μαθηταί, ῥαββί, νῦν ἐζήτουν σε λιθάσαι οἱ Ἰουδαῖοι, καὶ πάλιν ὑπάγεις ἐκεῖ;) Porter renders it, "Rabbi, the Jews are now seeking to stone you," instead of "Rabbi, just now the Jews were seeking to stone you." Porter says that the deictic indicator νῦν represents the present time (Porter, *Verbal Aspect*, 210).

50. Fanning, *Verbal Aspect*, 113.

the pragmatic level and does not adequately describe the grammatical category."[51] Nevertheless, Evans holds the traditional view of the Greek verbal system, in which the tense is expressed by the verbal system (such as an augment communicating past time).[52] Evans treats the Greek perfect as stative, like Porter. Evans is not in favor of Fanning's view of the perfect in which the perfective aspect is combined with stativity in *Aktionsart*, along with past tense.[53] Evans criticizes Fanning's mixing the aspect, along with two other elements—*Aktionsart* and temporality. Evans concludes that the perfect tense is aspectually imperfective, expressing stativity.[54]

However, Evans's view of the perfect as conveying imperfective aspect is not able to explain the case of the "aoristic perfect." Evans's view that the Greek perfect encodes imperfective aspect will be refuted in detail in the next section, because Campbell also claims imperfective aspect for the Greek perfect.

Thomas R. Hatina (1999)[55]

In his article "The Perfect Tense-Form in Colossians," Hatina attempts to show that Porter's system works better and functions well in a larger spectrum of contexts. Hatina accepts Porter's markedness theory and applies it to his interpretation of Colossians and Galatians.[56] Following Porter's

51. Evans, *Verbal Syntax*, 27–28.

52. Evans, *Verbal Syntax*, 45–49. Evans describes, "The augment is found as a feature of IE [Indo-European] verbal systems in Indo-Iranian, Armenian, and doubtfully in Phrygian, as well as Greek. . . . In my view the introduction of the augment signposts introduction of an additional value—which is interpreted here as temporal reference—to the semantic baggage of indicative forms."

53. Evans, *Verbal Syntax*, 50.

54. Evans, *Verbal Syntax*, 32.

55. Hatina is introduced a little out of the chronological order to compare him with Campbell in the following.

56. Hatina, "Perfect Tense-Form," 229. Porter introduces "markedness theory" between tenses. He claims that the perfect/pluperfect is the most heavily marked due to its morphological bulk—stem, reduplication, and tense formative. According to Porter, the perfect/pluperfect (reduplication + tense formative) is "heavier" than the present (nothing), imperfect (augment), and aorist (augment + tense formative). He asserts that the perfect, as the heaviest form, plays a role in the frontground to highlight the most significant part of the sentence. The least heavy form, the aorist, represents the background. Porter states that the aorist describes the background, the present the foreground, and the perfect indicates the frontground. Porter argues that the heavier morphological tense entails more prominence (Porter, *Verbal Aspect*, 246; Porter, "Defence of Verbal Aspect," 35). However, Steven Runge points out a setback of Porter's markedness theory especially with regard to the reverse rank between the present and

markedness theory, Hatina argues that the perfect plays a role of highlighting the event.

> [Col 1:17] καὶ αὐτός ἐστιν πρὸ πάντων καὶ τὰ πάντα ἐν αὐτῷ **συνέστηκεν**.
>
> And he is before all things, and in him all things *stand together*.
>
> [Col 2:1] Θέλω γὰρ ὑμᾶς εἰδέναι ἡλίκον ἀγῶνα ἔχω ὑπὲρ ὑμῶν καὶ τῶν ἐν Λαοδικείᾳ καὶ ὅσοι οὐχ **ἑόρακαν** τὸ πρόσωπόν μου ἐν σαρκὶ.
>
> For I want you to know how great a struggle I have for you and for those at Laodicea and for all who *have* not *seen* my face in the flesh.

In Colossians 1:17, Hatina is skeptical of rendering συνέστηκεν as "having stood" with traditional translation of the perfect. Rather, he argues that συνέστηκεν fits better with a stative notion. The perfect συνέστηκεν in 1:17 seems to be best translated as a present tense in English. Then, asks Hatina, why does the author not merely use a present form? Hatina maintains that Paul emphasizes the divine creation with perfect form.[57]

In Colossian 2:1, Hatina rejects reading ἑόρακαν as "have seen," with an ongoing state from the past. The context is that Paul is writing a letter to the Christians in Colossae who already know Paul. In addition, Paul talks to those who have not seen his face yet.[58] Hatina concedes that the context allows "anteriority and result." Nevertheless, he avers that it does not lead to the conclusion that the perfect has a semantic implication of temporality.

---

the aorist. The problem occurs between the present/imperfect and the aorist. Providing statistics, Porter maintains that the present/imperfect is slightly heavier than the aorist. However, Runge sharply notes that the aorist should be bulkier than present because of the augment and tense formative sigma. Runge criticizes Porter in that he manipulates the result in order to confirm his claims. Although Porter builds a plausible and logical argument, Runge points out a lack of linguistic support. Porter, according to Runge, selectively omits aspectually vague verbs such as perfective (εἶδον) or stative (οἶδα). Including them will overturn his statistical result, so that the number of the imperfective exceeds that of the perfective. Runge states that Porter seems to artificially create "ranks" and "prominent" among tenses in order to put the aorist tense into the least heavy level as a default (Runge, "Markedness," 43–56).

57. Hatina, "Perfect Tense-Form," 232–33.

58. Commentators have a general consensus for the implied anteriority that Paul had a relationship with Colossian Christians and struggles with those who have not met him personally. See Dunn, *Epistles to the Colossians and to Philemon*, 129–30; Pao, *Colossians & Philemon*, 136; Sumney, *Colossians*, 113; Melick, *Philippians, Colossians, Philemon*, 244.

Rather, Hatina claims that "dual temporality" is a pragmatic feature of the Greek perfect.[59]

Moreover, Hatina criticizes the traditional view of temporality in the perfect with the evidence of perfect participles in Colossians. Translating the perfect participles according to the traditional view does not seem to work.

> [Col 1:21] Καὶ ὑμᾶς ποτε ὄντας ἀπηλλοτριωμένους καὶ ἐχθροὺς τῇ διανοίᾳ ἐν τοῖς ἔργοις τοῖς πονηροῖς.
> And you, who once were alienated and hostile in mind, doing evil deeds.
>
> [Col 1:23] εἴ γε ἐπιμένετε τῇ πίστει τεθεμελιωμένοι καὶ ἑδραῖοι.
> If indeed you continue in the faith firmly established and steadfast.
>
> [Col 1:26] τὸ μυστήριον τὸ ἀποκεκρυμμένον ἀπὸ τῶν αἰώνων καὶ τῶν γενεῶν.
> The mystery which has been hidden from the past ages and generations.
>
> [Col 2:7] ἐρριζωμένοι καὶ ἐποικοδομούμενοι ἐν αὐτῷ καὶ βεβαιούμενοι τῇ πίστει.
> Rooted and built up in him and established in the faith.

Hatina states that ἀπηλλοτριωμένους and ἐρριζωμένοι do not fit the traditional concept of the perfect. The perfect participle τεθεμελιωμένοι does not necessarily convey the notion of "having been established."[60] Likewise, ἐρριζωμένοι does not fit with rendering "having been rooted" either.[61] In Colossians 1:21, ἀπηλλοτριωμένους likewise does not fit a traditional understanding of the perfect.[62] Similarly, ὄντας ἀπηλλοτριωμένους is a periphrastic construction, which grammarians generally agree describes an existing state.[63] Hatina notes that only ἀποκεκρυμμένον has a possibility of conveying anteriority, "having been hidden."

---

59. Hatina, "Perfect Tense-Form," 237. Hatina goes on to say, "When a stative aspect is the only semantic feature ascribed to the perfect, one can account for temporal flexibility on pragmatic grounds and thus eliminate a number of so-called exceptions." However, his suggestion could become to put the cart before the horse.

60. Hatina, "Perfect Tense-Form," 234.

61. Hatina, "Perfect Tense-Form," 237–38.

62. Hatina, "Perfect Tense-Form," 233.

63. Hatina, "Perfect Tense-Form," 233. For periphrastic participle construction, see Robertson, *Grammar*, 902–3; Burton, *Syntax*, 40; Levinsohn, "Functions of

However, Hatina's employment of perfect participles to criticize the traditional interpretation is not persuasive. The traditional view does not consider non-indicative moods to convey temporality. Hatina's critiques against the traditional approach based on perfect participles are vacuous because even traditional scholars do not regard time as absolute in non-indicative moods.[64]

In addition, Hatina describes Paul as employing ἀποκεκρυμμένον in order to denote the mystery hidden in the past. He states that the perfect here points out past time, not an ongoing result. Hatina says that there is a contrast between the mystery hidden in the past and the present revelation of it. The mystery has been kept from ancient times, but it is now being made manifest. Hatina concludes that ἀποκεκρυμμένον conveys a state of affairs in the past and that Paul may have selected the perfect form in order to express the "long duration" of the hidden mystery.[65] Based on the immediate context, however, it seems better to render ἀποκεκρυμμένον using the "traditional interpretation" Hatina criticizes—"having been hidden."

Constantine R. Campbell (2007)

Campbell published his books *Verbal Aspect, the Indicative Mood, and Narrative* and *Verbal Aspect and Non-Indicative Verbs* in 2007 and in 2008 consecutively. Campbell follows Porter's verbal aspect theory in that Greek verbs do not contain grammaticalized time.[66] Campbell asserts imperfective aspect for the perfect.[67] Campbell suggests that the acceptance of the imperfective aspect of the perfect would solve many textual conundrums.

> [2 Tim 4:6–7] Ἐγὼ γὰρ ἤδη σπένδομαι, καὶ ὁ καιρὸς τῆς ἀναλύσεώς μου **ἐφέστηκεν**. τὸν καλὸν ἀγῶνα **ἠγώνισμαι**, τὸν δρόμον **τετέλεκα**, τὴν πίστιν **τετήρηκα**.
>
> For I am already being poured out as a drink offering, and the time of my departure *is coming*. I *am fighting* the good fight, I *am finishing* the race, I *am keeping* the faith.

Copula-Participle," 307–26.

64. BDF §339; Picirilli, "Meaning of the Tenses," 544; Mounce, *Basics of Biblical Greek*, 255–58; Köstenberger et al., *Going Deeper*, 229; Ellis et al., "Greek Verbal System," 42.

65. Hatina, "Perfect Tense-Form," 235.

66. Campbell, *Basics of Verbal Aspect*, 36–39. Campbell makes an exception for the future.

67. Campbell, *Basics of Verbal Aspect*, 50; Campbell, *Indicative Mood*, 193–95.

First of all, Campbell states that the perfect is normally translated as "have + past perfect." This usual translation of the perfect implies the nuance of 2 Timothy 4 that Paul's journey of faith in life is over. Paul is reflecting on his life of ministry on the point of time before death. Yet Campbell suggests that if the perfect conveys the imperfective aspect, the translations of those perfects are, "I am fighting . . . I am finishing . . . I am keeping." With these changes, the translation is nuanced to convey that Paul is still fighting and his race is continuing. These changes of translating the perfect, according to Campbell, can deliver the meaning that Paul's ministry is not finished yet and he continues to serve the Lord.[68] Even without Campbell's suggestion, however, there is no doubt that Paul's faith is continuing and he keeps serving God in this context.

Moreover, 2 Timothy is almost certainly written at the last point of Paul's life. Most commentators support this view.[69] Paul is reminding Timothy of his life of ministry and is now facing impending death. Second Timothy 4:8 seems especially clear: "Henceforth there is laid up for me the crown of righteousness, which the Lord, the righteous judge, will award to me on that day." Campbell does not deny that this letter is written at the end of Paul's life. Nevertheless, he argues that the perfect forms put an emphasis on Paul's continuance of fighting and keeping faith, rather than an ongoing state rooted in a past event.[70] The general context of 2 Timothy does not support merely an ongoing event of Paul keeping his faith. In this letter, Paul reflects on his whole life and ministry, and stresses his keeping the faith throughout his life.

---

68. Campbell, *Indicative Mood*, 194.

69. Mounce, *Pastoral Epistles*, 577–79; Collins, *1 & 2 Timothy and Titus*, 273; Lea and Griffin, *1, 2 Timothy and Titus*, 247–48; Towner, *The Letters to Timothy and Titus*, 611–15. Towner notes that the verb σπένδω ("offer a libation/drink-offering") does not refer to bloody sacrifice. Nevertheless, its usage is for the drink offering that would complete the sacrificial ceremony. In the same vein, the word ἀνάλυσις ("departure, loosing, releasing, retirement, death") does not indicate death directly, but in 2 Timothy 4:7, Paul assesses his life and ministry on the whole so that the context implies his impending death. Crellin critiques Campbell's handling of the text and doubts whether it is sufficient or necessary to regard the perfect as imperfective aspect (Crellin, "Greek Perfect (2013)," 157–60; Crellin, "Basics of Verbal Aspect," 201–2).

70. Campbell, *Indicative Mood*, 195. Campbell cites Prior whose work of the phrase "being poured out as a drink offering" (2 Tim 4:6; Phil 2:17) does not refer to Paul's death. Prior notes that the noun (ἀνάλυσις "departure, loosing, releasing, retirement, death") does not mean death but rather refers to "Paul's expectation of release" following a good outcome for his case (Prior, *Paul the Letter-Writer*, 92–110). However, the context of 2 Timothy indicates Paul's last moment of his life.

Heightened proximity

To explain the Greek verbal system, Campbell argues for the notion of proximity and remoteness.[71] He maintains that the present tense denotes *proximate* imperfective aspect while the imperfect represents the *remote* imperfective aspect.[72] Campbell defines the "remoteness" as "the metaphysical value of distance." This remoteness often expresses the past tense with the aorist (85 percent).[73] The remoteness is applied to the imperfect as well, since the imperfect shares remoteness with the aorist tense, while it shares imperfective aspect with the present tense.[74]

Proximity is equal to the absence of remoteness. The present tense denotes proximity, which means "it portrays actions with a view from the inside."[75] Moreover, the present tense encodes imperfectivity, that is, an ongoing process. The *heightened* proximity, on the other hand, means that the spatial relationship between the event and the viewpoint is much closer than regular proximity.[76] Campbell regards the perfect as conveying heightened proximity, which is "super-present." He makes an analogy that a reporter is very close to the parade so that he or she can watch the parade more vividly.[77]

In sum, Campbell argues that the perfect is an "enhanced" imperfective tense-form paralleled to the present indicative that is a "basic" imperfective tense-form.[78] In addition, Campbell asserts that his notion of heightened proximity not only fits with the concept of intensive perfect of Curtius and Sauge,[79] but also has a relevance to Hatina's perfect which highlights the action in the frontground.

---

71. Campbell, *Basics of Verbal Aspect*, 51.

72. Campbell, *Basics of Verbal Aspect*, 37–44. Campbell refers the aorist to the remote perfective aspect.

73. Campbell, *Basics of Verbal Aspect*, 37.

74. Campbell, *Basics of Verbal Aspect*, 41–44.

75. Campbell, *Basics of Verbal Aspect*, 40.

76. Campbell, *Indicative Mood*, 197.

77. Campbell, *Indicative Mood*, 199–201; Campbell, *Basics of Verbal Aspect*, 51.

78. Campbell, *Non-Indicative Verbs*, 28.

79. To clarify the heightened proximity of the perfect, Campbell draws attention to the concept of the intensive perfect of Georg Curtius. Curtius states that the perfect indicative was originally a particular kind of present. Curtius says, "It seems to me hardly to admit of a doubt that the perfect indicative was originally nothing but a particular kind of present formation. As a reduplicated present with an intensive meaning this form separated itself from the present-stem and became by degrees an independent member in the system of verbal forms, with a distinctive stamp of its own" (Curtius, *Greek Verb*, 354–55, 376, 382). On the basis of this description, Campbell prescribes

Summary

Campbell states that the perfect is closer to the present than the aorist.[80] The notion that the perfect shares its aspect with the present, however, has some problems. The Greek perfect sometimes clearly denotes past time, occurring in the midst of aorist forms.

Secondly, Mathewson rightly points out that Campbell pays too much attention to "proximity." He criticizes Campbell who elaborates extensively on the spatial concept of remoteness and proximity rather than on aspect.[81] Campbell's view of the perfect as being in parallel with the present is not able to clarify the "aoristic" perfect.[82]

---

that the original intensive perfect went through a development supposedly into the traditional understanding of the perfect—past event and present result.

Campbell also cites Sauge who argues for the intensive perfect. Sauge maintains that the notion of intensive perfect can explain most of the perfect forms. He states that the original sense of the verb is intensified in combination with the Greek perfect. Campbell introduces Sauge's statement that the two major alternatives to the intensive model of the Greek perfect, i.e., the resultative perfect and the stative perfect, are not helpful. On the resultative perfect, according to Sauge, to speak of the resulting state of an anterior event is to acknowledge an experience, but it is not an appropriate analysis of a process in a language. On the stative model of the perfect, Sauge also asserts that the concept of the state of the subject is not an adequate description of the perfect because it does not explain all cases of the perfect. Instead, Sauge maintains that the notion of the intensive perfect can explain the full range of employments of the perfect (Sauge, *Les degrés du verbe*, 23, 43, 104). Campbell summarizes Sauge's thought: "Sauge posits that the Greek verbal system is able to express verbal events or actions in two degrees. The first degree is the normal sense of a verb; this may be the sense expressed by, say, the combination of a verbal lexeme with the present indicative tense-form. The second degree, however, intensifies the original sense of the verb; this is what happens when the same verbal lexeme is combined with the perfect indicative." Campbell supposes that this intensification of the perfect is ultimately equivalent to the heightened proximity.

80. Campbell, *Basics of Verbal Aspect*, 50.
81. Mathewson, *Verbal Aspect in Revelation*, 32–33.
82. Mathewson points out that Campbell fails to show a substantial argument how a heightened proximity applies to perfect and present participles or infinitives. Campbell states that non-indicative verbs do not encode "remoteness" and "proximity" (Campbell, *Non-Indicative Verbs*, 28–29). Mathewson points out that it creates a problem in handling perfect participles and infinitives, saying, "[Campbell] must maintain the semantic feature of heightened proximity for these forms, otherwise the duplicate aspectual form would be unnecessary and would presumably drop out." In other words, Campbell's language of remoteness and proximity is vulnerable when it comes to non-indicative perfect participle forms. Mathewson points out that Campbell ought to provide compelling evidence of the notion of heightened proximity in perfect participle forms (Mathewson, *Verbal Aspect in Revelation*, 32–33).

David L. Mathewson (2010) and Wally V. Cirafesi (2013)

Mathewson accepts Porter's system and applies it to the book of Revelation. Mathewson insightfully analyzes a variety of issues in the book of Revelation such as shifting tenses. Like Porter, Mathewson rejects the temporality of the perfect. Similar to Hatina, Mathewson utilizes Porter's markedness theory for his argument. He argues that the perfect, as the most heavily marked form, functions as a frontground for highlighting.[83]

Cirafesi is also one of those who advocates Porter's system. Accepting Porter's view of verbal aspect, he applies it to the Synoptic Gospels.[84] For instance,

> [Matt 21:4] τοῦτο δὲ **γέγονεν** ἵνα πληρωθῇ τὸ ῥηθὲν διὰ τοῦ προφήτου.
> This took place to fulfill what was said by the prophet.

Just like Mathewson, Cirafesi's arguments are based upon the assumption that Porter's markedness theory is correct. According to Cirafesi, γέγονεν is the most heavily marked form. He maintains that Matthew marked γέγονεν most heavily, in conjunction with τοῦτο, in order to highlight the present scene.[85]

However, γέγονα is a perplexing perfect, as Moulton and Robertson state. Γέγονα denotes not only a traditional meaning of the perfect but also the present time in the Greek New Testament. Robertson and Moulton express the difficulty of the cases of γέγονα conveying the past time.[86] In relying on Porter's model, Cirafesi's solution that the perfect entails the most marked form is open to the charge of oversimplification.

Robert Crellin (2012) and Michael Aubrey (2014)

In 2012, Crellin wrote his dissertation, "The Greek Perfect Active System: 200 B.C.–A.D. 150." He notes that the Greek perfect does entail temporality, in spite of the exceptional cases.[87] Crellin summarizes the Greek perfect as (1) past reference or anterior, "where an event is presented as terminating prior to reference time and there is no resultant state"; (2) resultative,

---

83. Mathewson, *Verbal Aspect in Revelation*, 41–45.
84. See Cirafesi, *Synoptic Parallels*.
85. Cirafesi, *Synoptic Parallels*, 86–87.
86. Moulton, *Prolegomena*, 145–46; Robertson, *Grammar*, 900. Chapter 4 will introduce the cases of γέγονα as a simple past.
87. Crellin, "Greek Perfect (2012)," 11–18.

where an event is presented with a resulting state from the past; and (3) pure state.[88] Crellin points out that in some cases the perfect denotes anteriority while in others the perfect represent a pure state. He attempts to illuminate the various behaviors of the perfect by investigating the lexeme and dividing verbs into groups such as transitive and intransitive, telic and atelic, pure state, change of state, and change of nature.[89]

Crellin rejects the "stative aspect" of the perfect. He says that "the stative readings which are regularly attributable to the perfect are due to its combination with verbs of particular semantic types, and not to its own function." Moreover, Crellin is not satisfied with the traditional approach to the perfect because it does not explain the many cases with no prior event.[90]

In his thesis, Aubrey views the perfect as having more in common with the imperfective aspect by providing background information, past happenings, and dialogue to show the context.[91] Nevertheless, his view is not the same as Campbell's in that the perfect is different from the imperfective aspect. Aubrey claims that the imperfective aspect does not have an intrinsic end-point while the perfect contains the completion of the event from one time to another.[92]

Aubrey's argument is that "the Greek perfect should be viewed as functioning within the domain of aspect rather than tense."[93] He tests whether the perfect is closest to anterior, resultative, or completive. Aubrey concludes that the perfect semantically conveys both resultative and completive, and it is almost impossible to differentiate them.[94]

Randall Buth (2016)

Buth argues for three aspects on the basis of semantic features: perfective, imperfective, and perfect. He maintains that the perfect aspect is a combination of perfective and imperfective aspect.[95] Buth defines the Greek perfect as "continuing an achieved state."[96] For example, the perfect ἐμήμεκα ("I have vomited") denotes a completed action of vomiting, but its ongoing

---

88. Crellin, "Greek Perfect (2012)," 69.
89. See Crellin, "Greek Perfect (2012)."
90. Crellin, "Basics of Verbal Aspect," 201.
91. Aubrey, "Greek Perfect," 91.
92. Aubrey, "Greek Perfect," 92.
93. Aubrey, "Greek Perfect," 92.
94. Aubrey, "Greek Perfect," 131.
95. Buth, "Verbs Perception," 191–92.
96. Buth, "Perfect Greek Morphology," 422–23.

effect still continues. On the other hand, the aorist ἤμεσεν "he vomited" does not show a current relevance.[97]

Buth opposes regarding the Greek perfect as "stative."[98] He notes that the term "stative" is an objective lexical and semantic feature of a verb rather than "a subjective, deictic, morpho-syntactic aspect category." Buth sees the notion of the perfect as: (1) temporally, a past event with current relevance; and (2) aspectually, a completed event with continuing relevance. Buth concludes,

> I think that this complexity is a reasonable generalization and that Greek morphology iconically reflects the history of that complexity. The Greek perfect is not a simple stative, the Greek perfect is not a simple perfective, and the Greek perfect is not a simple imperfective. Only a complex semantics does justice to the synchronic use of the perfect in Classical and Koine Greek, and that complexity is iconically mimicked by the complex anomalous morphology.[99]

Buth's statement is notable in that he attempts to define the Greek perfect by negating it—not a simple stative, not a simple perfective, and not a simple imperfective. Instead, he suggests that this complexity itself is a trait of the Greek perfect.

CONCLUSION

The Greek perfect behaves in a complicated way. Many scholars have attempted to elucidate its perplexing behaviors. McKay's view of the perfect shows the limitation of his interpretation of the perfect as "responsible." With a tremendous contribution to verbal aspect study, Porter maintains that the perfect highlights a main action in the frontground. However, his theory is very radical because of the extent to which the Greek verbal system does not grammaticalize time. Moreover, Porter's markedness theory tends to confuse and hinder correct exegesis of the perfect.

Wallace adheres to the traditional concept of the perfect but still faces difficulties regarding how to clarify stative and aoristic perfects. To overcome the traditional interpretation of the perfect, Fanning's perspective

---

97. Buth, "On the Greek Perfect."

98. Similarly, Ellis rejects the term "stative aspect" for the Greek perfect but prefers to use "combinative aspect" which reflects the perfective nature and the imperfectivity of its ongoing relevance (Ellis, "Aspect-Prominence," in Runge and Fresch, *Greek Verb Revisited*, 142–43).

99. Buth, "Perfect Greek Morphology," 423–25.

thus is innovative: the perfect with stative *Aktionsart*, anterior time, and perfective aspect. Unfortunately, this system is too complicated to facilitate grasping the notion as a whole. Olsen's view of the perfect is fresh: perfective aspect and present time. Evans argues that the perfect conveys stativity, with imperfective aspect. However, neither Olsen nor Evans is able to account for the aoristic perfect.

Campbell presents the perfect of "heightened proximity" on the basis of ancient Greek's notion of intensiveness. His explanation of the intensive perfect is noteworthy, but it leads to an awkward conclusion: the perfect as imperfective aspect with "heightened proximity." In the midst of this grammatical cacophony, scholars like Mathewson and Cirafesi merely follow Porter's system, while Buth and Crellin attempt to overcome the setback and find a better explanation of the Greek perfect.

In this chaotic scene, Allan states that the perfect may be a "chain of related meanings, a polysemous network of family resemblances, a complex layering of variant meanings that resulted from a long historical process of semantic extensions."[100] The following chapters will study and test the historical development of the Greek perfect to see if it will shed light on the unique characteristics of the perfect in the NT.

---

100. Allan, "Tense and Aspect," 113.

2

THE FIRST STAGE
RESULTATIVE-STATIVE

INTRODUCTION

THE PREVIOUS CHAPTERS INTRODUCED the three diachronic stages of the perfect. We found that the Greek perfect fails to show a unified core meaning. Homeric perfects do not convey a typical nuance of the English perfect. For example, the perfect τεθάρρηκα [τεθάρσηκα] in Homer denotes a present state (*Iliad* 9.420: τεθαρσήκασι λαοί "people *are* confident").[1] The perfect frequently functions this way in the Greek New Testament.

This chapter will demonstrate that the ancient Greek perfects are mostly resultative-stative. In Homer the perfect actives were often intransitive and subject-affected, just like the middle voice. Moreover, perfect middle forms, with the same meaning, were innovated and spread successfully. They also appear frequently in the NT, where most of them are resultative-stative. But, some of them show a stative nuance. The final section of this chapter will deal with the intensive notion of the perfect and how that relates to the reduplication.

---

1. Homer, *Iliad*, 412–13. This example is found in Sicking and Stork, *Two Studies*, 168.

Perfecta Praesentia

The perfect οἶδα and ἕστηκα are considered the main representatives of the Greek perfect with a stative meaning.[2] Monro calls this kind of perfect as *perfecta praesentia*, "the perfect denoting a lasting condition or attitude."[3] Most scholars regard οἶδα as expressing a present time.[4] For example, Mussies maintains that οἶδα has lost its perfect meaning and functions as a virtual present.[5] Robertson states that in οἶδα "the punctiliar idea drops out and only the durative remains."[6]

The perfect ἕστηκα also conveys a present state "standing," rather than "having stood." The traditional "past action/continuing result" interpretation of ἕστηκα does not satisfactorily elucidate these perplexing "stative" perfects:[7]

[Rev 3:20] ᾽Ιδοὺ, ἕστηκα ἐπὶ τὴν θύραν καὶ κρούω.
Behold, I *stand* at the door and knock.

In Revelation 3:20, ἕστηκα is not rendered "I have stood," but conveys the present state of Jesus Christ's standing and knocking on the door. The perfect ἕστηκα, located in parallel with κρούω, seemingly reinforces this

---

2. Trotter, "Perfect Tenses," 63; Moulton and Turner, *Syntax*, 82. Moulton and Turner state that more stative perfect verbs are ἐκκέχυται, τέθνηκεν (be dead), πέποιθα, πέπεισμαι (Rom 2:19), μέμνημαι, δέδεται, ἥγημαι (I believe), κέκραγα, ὄλωλα (from ὄλλυμι), πέφηνα, κατήργηται (Rom 7:2), ἔοικεν ἔγνωκεν, etc. They have become independent presents, each one divorced from its own present stem; BDF §341, §343; Fanning, *Verbal Aspect*, 112n74, 136. Fanning treats οἶδα and ἕστηκα as exceptional cases derived from historical development, saying that in Homer οἶδα and ἕστηκα are employed as a present state. Fanning categorizes οἶδα into verbs of state, such as "live," "have" or "be full of."

3. Monro, *Homeric Dialect*, 31.

4. Goodwin, *Greek Grammar*, 270; Robertson, *Grammar*, 881; Gildersleeve, "Stahl's Syntax," 395; Monro, *Homeric Dialect*, 31, 32; Trotter, "Perfect Tenses," 63; Mussies, *Morphology*, 347; McKay, "Non-Literary Papyri," 25; Wallace, *Beyond the Basics*, 580; Moulton, *Prolegomena*, 109. Moulton states that the meaning "I know" of the primitive perfect οἶδα comes from the root *weido* "I discover."

5. Mussies, *Morphology*, 347.

6. Robertson, *Grammar*, 898.

7. Olsen notes that five verbs only show stative readings in the perfect and pluperfect: οἶδα ("I know"), ἵστημι ("I stand"), εἴωθα ("I am accustomed"), πείθω ("I persuade"), and παρίστημι ("I bring; I am present") (Olsen, *Semantic and Pragmatic Model*, 211). Thompson states that the perfect form ἕστηκα may be derived from the Hebrew niphal נצב ("stand"). For example, Exodus 17:9 [LXX] employs ἕστηκα in place of the Hebrew נצב ("Tomorrow I [Moses] will stand on top of hill with the staff of God in my hands"). However, Thompson does not offer substantial arguments for his claim (Thompson, *Apocalypse*, 44–45).

present reference. Many commentators observe that ἕστηκα is equivalent to the present here, having a "durative" sense in relation to the present κρούω.[8] Similar stative perfects include βέβηκα, ἕστηκα, μέμνημαι, οἶδα, ἔοικα, and πέποιθα.[9] Moulton and Smyth accept the category *perfecta praesentia* for perfect tense with present meaning. Similarly, Wallace defines these perfects as "perfects with a present force."[10] However, these explanations fail to provide an answer as to *why* these perfects deliver a present nuance.[11]

In order to solve this thorny question, traditional grammarians argue for a special category, "the intensive perfect."[12] Robertson gives examples of these "intensive perfects": ἕστηκα, ἔοικα, ἀνέῳγεν, οἶδα, ἐνέστηκα, πέποιθα, and κέκραγεν (John 1:15).[13] Concerning the intensive perfect, Rijksbaron states,

> In the case of verbs whose present stem forms already to some degree express a state, the perfect expresses the highest degree of that state (so-called *intensive* perfect). Examples are ἥγημαι "be firmly convinced" (ἡγοῦμαι "believe, think"), τεθαύμακα "be surprised" (θαυμάζω "wonder, marvel"), πεφόβημαι "be terrified" (φοβοῦμαι "be afraid"), σεσιώπηκα "maintain complete silence" (σιωπῶ "be silent").[14]

Rijksbaron maintains that the perfect conveys the highest degree of the state when its lexical meaning is a state semantically. However, closer

---

8. Beale, *Book of Revelation*, 309; Osborne, *Revelation*, 212; Smalley, *Revelation to John*, 101; Köstenberger et al., *Going Deeper*, 301.

9. Monro, *Homeric Dialect*, 31. More examples are δαίω ("I kindle"), ὄρωρε ("is astir"), ὄλωλε ("is undone"), βέβρυχε ("roars"), etc.

10. Wallace, *Beyond the Basics*, 574–80. Wallace provides another category, "intensive perfect" but confusingly adds that it is also known as "resultative perfect." What he says literally is "The perfect may be used to *emphasize* the results or present state produced by a past action."

11. Smyth, *Greek Grammar*, 434; Moulton, *Prolegomena*, 147; Wallace, *Beyond the Basics*, 579–80. Mathewson criticizes this view because this perspective confuses semantics and pragmatics, and incorrectly assumes temporal implicature applying to semantics. He maintains that the perfect ἕστηκα denotes a state, probably present time in the context, but grammatically it does not point to a duration of the state (Mathewson, *Verbal Aspect in Revelation*, 102–3).

12. Dana and Mantey, *Manual Grammar*, 202; Wallace, *Beyond the Basics*, 574–76; Köstenberger et al., *Going Deeper*, 298. Chantraine rejects the intensive notion of the perfect, saying: "Nothing authorizes to establish a class of intensive perfects . . . the distinction is artificial" (Chantraine, *Parfait grec*, 17).

13. Robertson, *Grammar*, 895. Robertson notes that most of these verbs have an inchoative or conative or iterative sense in the present.

14. Rijksbaron, *Syntax and Semantics*, 38.

scrutiny reveals that this description is not satisfactory to explain the "abnormal" stative perfect.

The notion of *perfecta praesentia* or the "intensive perfect" category does not clarify the puzzling "stative perfects." More delicate investigation is necessary to apprehend their subtle nuances. Chantraine strongly opposes the category "intensive perfect," saying that nothing authorizes this artificial category.[15] Agreeing with Chantraine, McKay also rejects this category.[16]

Another passage from Revelation includes the Greek perfect occurring alongside two present tense verbs:

> [Rev 3:17] πλούσιός εἰμι καὶ **πεπλούτηκα** καὶ οὐδὲν χρείαν ἔχω.
> I am rich, and *have prospered* and have no need.

The perfect πεπλούτηκα does not necessitate the translation "have prospered." The context rather favors a translation in the present state, "I prosper." Dougherty argues that the perfect tense is synonymous with the present tense only when the perfect tense is truly a present perfect (οἶδα / ἵστημι).[17] However, this argument is not persuasive.

Wackernagel and Chantraine

Wackernagel and Chantraine defend the view that the perfect in ancient Greek expresses a state. Wackernagel asserts that the Homeric perfect denotes the present state of the subject.[18] He offers an example τέθνηκα, which renders in German "er ist todt" ("he is dead").[19]

Following Wackernagel, Chantraine argues that the ancient perfect expresses the state of the subject.[20] Chantraine provides twelve categories of the perfect in Homer (bold-font perfects occurring in the NT):[21]

1. Mind: **οἶδα, μέμνημαι**

2. Joy: γέγηθα ("I am joyful"), **κέχαρισμαι** ("I am pleasant")

---

15. Chantraine, *Parfait grec*, 17. See Sicking and Stork, *Two Studies*, 126.
16. McKay, "Ancient Greek Perfect," 6.
17. Dougherty, "Syntax of the Apocalypse," 407, 424, 426.
18. Wackernagel, *Vorlesungen über Syntax*, 167.
19. Wackernagel, "Griechischen Perfektum," 4. Haspelmath offers examples of the German resultative (statal passive): "Ich bin gebogen (I am bent)," "Die Äpfel sind verfault (The apples are rotten)," or "Die Tür ist gescholossen (The door is closed)" (Haspelmath, "From Resultative to Perfect," 198, 216). See Stechow, "German *seit* 'since,'" 393–432; Nedjalkov and Jaxontov, "Resultative Construction," 39–41, 45.
20. Chantraine, *Parfait grec*, 7, 16, 18.
21. Chantraine, *Parfait grec*, 8–11.

3. State of the body: βέβριθα ("I am loaded"), ὄδωδα ("I exhale an odor")
4. Standing or lying: ἕστηκα, κέκλιμαι ("I am lying")
5. Rest: πέπηγα ("I am stuck"), δέδραγμαι ("I cling myself to")
6. Physical state: τέτηκα ("I am melted"), **σέσηπα** ("I am rotten"), ὄλωλα ("I am lost"), **τέθνηκα** ("I am dead")
7. Idea of becoming: **γέγονα**, ἔοικα
8. Movement: **βέβηκα**, εἴληλυθα, πέπευγα ("I have fled")
9. Noise: βέβρυχα ("I bellow out"), μέμυκα ("I moo"), **κέκληγα** ("I cry out")
10. Passive: **εἴρηται, κέκληται**, νένιπται ("It is washed")
11. Seeing: ὄρωρα ("I keep an eye on"), ὄπωπα ("I have seen")
12. Possession: λέλοιπα ("I have abandoned")

Chantraine observes that most of these categories denote a present state. For example, βέβρυχε(ν) ("it moos") expresses a cow's cry in the present time.[22] Many perfect forms in the list occur in the NT (οἶδα, ἕστηκα, γέγονα, σέσηπα, μέμνημαι, κέκληγα and ἔοικα).

The weakness of this list, however, is that Chantraine offers too many categories. It raises the question whether each category is meaningful and distinct. Even so, several categories are noteworthy, such as the perfect of mind, noise, becoming, or passive. It is remarkable that most of these verbs carry a present meaning. Chantraine concludes that the Homeric perfects express a present state resulting from a past event.[23]

Referring to Wackernagel and Chantraine, Fanning notes that the perfect in Homer was predominantly stative, usually with intransitive verbs. Fanning states that from Homer to the Hellenistic period the perfect forms seem to have gone through a change.[24] In line with Fanning's expectation, we now turn to focus on the semantic changes of the Greek perfect in order to solve the puzzling issue of the stative perfect.

---

22. Chantraine, *Parfait grec*, 18.
23. Chantraine, *Parfait grec*, 18–20, 70.
24. Fanning, *Verbal Aspect*, 105–6. Fanning says that during the Classical Greek era, the transitive verbs were employed to focus on the action more.

FIRST STAGE OF THE GREEK PERFECT

Studying the historical development of the Greek perfect provides hints to understand the "stative perfect." Haspelmath and Allan insightfully probe the historical development of the Greek perfect and present three distinct stages of the perfect: (1) PIE (Proto Indo-European) and Homeric Greek, (2) Classical Greek, and (3) Koine Greek and afterwards.[25] In the same vein, Haug and Bentein indicate two major semantic changes of the perfect: (a) from *resultative* to *anterior (current relevance)*;[26] and (b) from *anterior* to *simple past*.[27] Several other scholars have also noted the diachronic development of the Greek perfect.[28] The "stative perfect" is related to the first stage—PIE and Homeric Greek.

Resultative-Stative Perfect

Most of the Homeric perfects show a present state. Monro says that the meaning of the Homeric perfect is "a lasting condition or attitude," unlike the English "have-perfect" forms.[29] Gerö and Stechow state that in ancient Greek it was not possible to employ past-referring adverbs with the perfect tense, as seen from Chantraine's category above (δέδοικα ["I am afraid"], γέγηθα ["I am happy"], σέσηπα ["I am rotten"], etc.).[30] Even in the Classical Greek period, several verbs take the perfect form but express a present state, without any reference to past time. Haspelmath describes that these "stative" perfect forms as remnants from an earlier age. He states,

> In Homeric Greek, the present state meaning of the Perfect is the rule rather than exception. An aspectual category that combines with dynamic verbs and expresses a state is now generally called RESULTATIVE (Nedjalkov (ed.) 1983, 1988), so we will

---

25. Haspelmath, "From Resultative to Perfect," 185–224; Allan, "Tense and Aspect," 101.

26. The term "anterior" means the situation occurring prior to reference time, which "is relevant to the situation at reference time." The English perfect is a good example of anterior (Bybee et al., *Evolution of Grammar*, 54, 61).

27. Haug, "From Resultatives to Anteriors," 291–303; Bentein, *Verbal Periphrasis*, 114–16, 153–56; Bentein, "Perfect," 46–49.

28. Anderson, "Perfect," 227–64; Gerö and Stechow, "Tense in Time," 251–94; Duhoux, *Le verbe grec ancien*, 419–31.

29. Monro, *Homeric Dialect*, 31–32.

30. Gerö and Stechow, "Tense in Time," 272.

say that the Homeric Perfect was a resultative or at least that it expresses resultative function most of the time.[31]

Haspelmath states that the Homeric perfect conveys a present state as a result of some action, i.e., resultative.

Maslov explains this resultative perfect: It is "some state (or statal relation) caused by a preceding change, i.e., action proper."[32] "Resultative" is to be distinguished from stative. Nedjalkov differentiates them:

> The stative expresses a state of a thing without any implication of its origin, while the resultative expresses both a state and the preceding action it has resulted from.[33]

Despite these definitions, there is no sharp line to discriminate between them. According to Nedjalkov, it is not easy to distinguish them sharply because resultative and stative nuances are very closely related in ancient Greek.[34]

Many scholars maintain that the perfect in the Homeric era generally conveys a resultative notion.[35] At the same time, many others insist that the ancient perfect conveys pure stativity.[36] Since the endings of the PIE perfect are similar to those of the PIE stative, they assume that the former belongs to the category of the latter. Allan opposes this suggestion, averring that there was a distinct stative category in the PIE. Examples of these stative verbs are (1) *$h_1éh_1s$-oi ("he is seated" cf. ἧμαι); (2) *$kéi$-oi ("he lies"

---

31. Haspelmath, "From Resultative to Perfect," 191.

32. Maslov, "Resultative, Perfect, and Aspect," 63. Bybee et al. also define resultatives as a state resulted from a past event (Bybee et al., *Evolution of Grammar*, 54).

33. Nedjalkov and Jaxontov, "Resultative Construction," 6. Wackernagel and Chantraine assert that the Greek perfect denotes the state of the object, which they call as "resultative" perfect. In this book, I will follow Nedjalkov's definition of the term "resultative."

34. Nedjalkov, "Resultative Constructions," 928; Nedjalkov and Jaxontov, "Resultative Construction," 7; Perel'muter, "Stative, Resultative, Passive and Perfect," 280; Haspelmath, "From Resultative to Perfect," 207.

35. Haspelmath, "From Resultative to Perfect," 187–99; Allan, "Tense and Aspect," 102–5; Gerö and Stechow, "Tense in Time," 268; Ruijgh, "Les valeurs temporelles," 208; Haug, "From Resultatives to Anteriors," 296–98; Bentein, "Periphrastic Perfect," 171–211. Mandilaras states that the resultative perfect was already widespread in Attic (Mandilaras, *Non-Literary Papyri*, 224).

36. Porter, *Verbal Aspect*, 252; Sihler, *New Comparative Grammar*, 564; Drinka, "Development of the Perfect," 82–83; Willi, *Origins of the Greek Verb*, 225–44; Clackson, *Indo-European Linguistics*, 121. See Allan, "Stative Verbs," 316–18.

cf. κεῖμαι); and (3) *ṷés-toi ("he is wearing").[37] These pure-stative verbs do not contain an anterior implication.[38]

The perfect is different from the stative verbs,[39] according to Allan. The perfect has reduplication (and its ablaut) and the possible semantic connotation of a state resulting from a prior event.[40] Allan maintains that the PIE perfect is mainly resultative-stative rather than purely stative.[41] The next section will investigate the resultative-stative nuance of the ancient Greek perfect.

Οἶδα

The perfect οἶδα is a representative of a resultative-stative perfect. It indicates a state of knowing, occurring frequently in the NT. Οἶδα occupies 25 percent of perfect indicative usage in the Greek New Testament (210 out of 839).[42] It is impossible to cite here every use because the number is so large.[43]

---

37. Allan, "Tense and Aspect," 105; Allan, "Stative Verbs," 317–18. Allan offers more examples of PIE stative: the imperfect *déato* ("seemed," Homer, *Odyssey* 6.242) and *krémamai* ("hang [intransitive]," functioning as middle perfect to present *krímamai*). See Madariaga, "Development of Indo-European Middle-passive Verbs," 154.

38. Allan, "Tense and Aspect," 105; Allan, "Stative Verbs," 317.

39. In his thesis Aubrey notes atelic verbs of pure stative which do not have perfect forms: ἀγαλλιάω ("I am overjoyed"), ἀσθενέω ("I am sick"), γέμω ("I am full"), λάμπω ("I shine"), εὐδοκέω ("I am pleased"), καθέζομαι ("I sit [down]"), etc. (Aubrey, "Greek Perfect," 97–98, 104, 128).

40. For example, in Mark 9:42 (καλόν ἐστιν αὐτῷ μᾶλλον εἰ περίκειται μύλος ὀνικὸς περὶ τὸν τράχηλον αὐτοῦ καὶ βέβληται εἰς τὴν θάλασσαν "it would be better for him if a great millstone were hung around his neck and he *were thrown* into the sea), περίκειται is a purely stative present-tense verb, not having a perfect form. On the other hand, the perfect βέβληται is employed here to emphasize the event of being thrown into the sea. The last section of the chapter will handle this matter in detail.

41. Allan, "Stative Verbs," 317. Allan adds for ablaut, saying that "a stative verb had e-grade in the root (bearing the accent), while a perfect had o-grade in the singular and zero-grade in the plural.

42. In the Gospels, οἶδα occupies 34.6 percent of all perfect indicative forms in Matthew, 27.6 percent in Mark, 21.6 percent in Luke, and 29.6 percent in John (Campbell, *Indicative Mood*, 188). Similarly, in Plato the occurrence of οἶδα consists of almost 20 percent of the perfect forms (Trotter, "Perfect Tenses," 38). The perfect σύνοιδα almost has the same meaning (1 Cor 4:4, οὐδὲν γὰρ ἐμαυτῷ σύνοιδα, "For I am not aware of anything against myself") (Decker, *Temporal Deixis*, 109).

43. The perfect οἶδα occurs 64 times in Aeschylus, 203 times in Sophocles, 345 times in Euripides, 216 times in Aristophanes, 67 times in Thucydides, 119 times in Lysias, and 66 times in Xenophon (Sicking and Stork, *Two Studies*, 190, 197, 207, 218, 229, 237, 243).

Οἶδα is a very old Greek verb with an Indo-European stem *u̯oid- ("know").[44] Clackson states that *u̯oid- semantically delivers the present meaning (Sanskrit véda, Gothic wait, Greek οἶδα, and Old Church Slavonic vědě). In early Greek, the perfect *u̯oid- would have meant: "he has found out and consequently is now in a state of knowing."[45] The same root *u̯eid- appears in other "see" or "find" words in Indo-European languages.[46]

Many regard οἶδα as purely stative.[47] Allan disagrees and claims that οἶδα is resultative-stative. Allan suggests that the perfect *u̯oid-h₂e went through a change, "I have seen" into "know." The old perfect *u̯oid-h₂e (1st sg, "I have seen") with root *u̯eid- ("see") had been established into "know" in PIE.[48] In the same vein, Alwin Kloekhorst argues that *u̯eid- "in the state of having seen/found" developed into "know." The perfect *u̯oid ("know") is an old unreduplicated form, which is derived of *u̯eid- ("see").[49] Kloekhorst says,

> *uóid-e is generally seen as an original perfect that is derived from the verbal root *ueid- "to see, to find". Its original meaning would have been "to be in the state of having seen/found", which underwent a specific development into "to know." . . . Here the root *ueid- not only forms the unreduplicated formation *uóid-e "knows" (Skt. véda, Av. vaédā), but also the reduplicated perfect *ue-uóid-e "has seen/found" (Skt. vivénda, Av. vīnnuaēδa). . . . [I]t seems clear that the synchronically unpredictable form *uóid-e "knows" must be old, and the synchronically predictable form *ue-uóid-e is a newer, analogical creation. We therefore have to accept that at the pre-PIE time that the original perfect to *ueid- was created (which first meant "to be in the state of

---

44. Beekes, *Etymological Dictionary of Greek*, 1053.
45. Clackson, *Indo-European Linguistics*, 121.
46. Chantraine, *Parfait grec*, 25.
47. See footnote 2 in chapter 1.
48. Allan, "Tense and Aspect," 103.
49. Willi, *Origins of the Greek Verb*, 212. Οἶδα is the only perfect that does not have reduplication. Drinka says, "For example, Szemerényi (1996: 260) reconstructs reduplication as a productive marker of the perfect for Proto-Indo-European, insisting that even the most notoriously non-reduplicating perfect *woida, ("I have seen" > "I know") must have reduplicated (as *wewoida) in earlier times. This analysis undervalues an important fact: that only Indo-Iranian and Greek developed fully productive reduplicated perfects with o-grades, while most other Indo-European languages show only vestigial forms or have no perfect reduplication at all." Drinka says that *woida is not reduplicated anywhere (cf. Greek οἶδα, Sanskrit véda, Gothic wait, Aves. vaēdā, and Old Church Slavonic vědě, OPr. waissei) (Drinka, "Development of the Perfect," 78, 91).

having seen/found," but later developed into "to know"), reduplication was not yet obligatory for all perfects.⁵⁰

According to Kloekhorst, it would have been possible to form the reduplicated perfect form *ue-uóid-e* "has seen/found." However, it seems that the reduplication was not obligatory in pre-PIE time and the unreduplicated form *u̯oid* happened to remain. The perfect *u̯oid* ("know") is a development from the root *u̯eid-* "in the state of having seen/found."⁵¹

Allan states that the prototypical meaning of the perfect in this stage was to express a resulting state. The perfect represents a state of the subject resulting from an anterior event. For example,

[Homer, *Iliad* 15.90] Ἥρη τίπτε βέβηκας;
    Hera, why have you come?⁵²

[Plato, *Crito* 43a] τί τηνικάδε ἀφῖξαι, ὦ Κρίτων; ἢ οὐ πρῲ ἔτι ἐστίν;
    Why have you come at this time, Crito? Or isn't it still early?⁵³

The perfect βέβηκας signifies the persistent state in the present that came because of the implied past. The anterior action is hinted at, but it is

---

50. Kloekhorst, "Hittite *ḫi*-conjugation," 92–94. In order to solve the conundrum of the unreduplicated perfect οἶδα, as a starting point Jasanoff takes the perfect *ue-uóid-e* 'has seen/found' (Skt. *vivénda*, Av. *vīvaēδa*), the perfect middle *ue-uid-ór* 'is visible, is recognized' (Skt. *vividé*) and a 'stative-intransitive present' *uid-ór* 'is/becomes visible/recognizable' (not attested as such), which all three would be regularly formed form the root *ueid-* 'to see, to find.' Jasanoff argues that *uid-ór* goes through a semantic shift to "is known" (Skt. *vidé* "is known") from *ue-uid-ór* ("is visible, is recognized"). Likewise, Jasanoff conjectures that *ue-uóid-e* ("has seen/found") may have affected the form *uóid-e* ("knows"), so that the former would bring forth the latter (Jasanoff, *Hittite and the Indo-European*, 228–33). Kloekhorst opposes Jasanoff's assertion in that the form *uóid-e* ("knows") was possibly innovated from *ue-uóid-e* ("has seen/found") by a semantic shift. If so, says Kloekhorst, an innovated form *uóid-e* should mean "has known," instead of "knows" according to Jasanoff's methodology.

51. Kloekhorst notes that before Proto Indo-European era, the perfect may have had both reduplicated and unreduplicated forms. The unreduplicated perfect *uoid-* is clearly an archaic form because the reduplicated perfect is normally expected. Instead of the predictable form *ue-uóid-e*, it takes the unpredictable form *uoid-e* ("knows"). The latter is an unpredictable older form while the former is a newer predictable formation. Kloekhorst concludes that in pre-PIE time the original perfect *ueid-* was created, but reduplication was not mandatory for all perfects. Rather, the perfect originally had variants of reduplicated and unreduplicated forms (Kloekhorst, "Hittite *ḫi*-conjugation," 92–94, 103).

52. Homer, *Iliad*, 112–13.

53. Plato, *Crito*, 150–51.

not explicitly revealed.⁵⁴ Another case from Plato above is similar. A similar nuance of the perfect (from ἀφικνέομαι) is observed, "why are you here?"

Τέθνηκα

The perfect τέθνηκα is another example of the resultative-stative notion.⁵⁵ Examples of this verb include

> [Matt 2:20] ἐγερθεὶς παράλαβε τὸ παιδίον καὶ τὴν μητέρα αὐτοῦ καὶ πορεύου εἰς γῆν Ἰσραήλ· τεθνήκασιν γὰρ οἱ ζητοῦντες τὴν ψυχὴν τοῦ παιδίου.
>
> Rise, take the child and his mother and go to the land of Israel, for those who sought the child's life are dead.

> [Mark 15:44] ὁ δὲ Πιλᾶτος ἐθαύμασεν εἰ ἤδη τέθνηκεν καὶ προσκαλεσάμενος τὸν κεντυρίωνα ἐπηρώτησεν αὐτὸν εἰ πάλαι ἀπέθανεν.
>
> Pilate wondered if he was dead by this time, and summoning the centurion, he questioned him as to whether he was already dead.

> [Josephus, *Antiquities* 1.248] πατὴρ δέ μοι Βαθούηλος ἦν· ἀλλ' ὁ μὲν ἤδη τέθνηκε.
>
> My father was Bethuel, but he has died [is dead] already.⁵⁶

---

54. Chantraine, *Parfait grec*, 19, 70; Allan, "Tense and Aspect," 102–3. The example is from Chantraine and Allan. Sicking and Stork comment that Themis asks because Hera's arrival was so quick that they did not expect her presence (Sicking and Stork, *Two Studies*, 145).

55. Chantraine, *Parfait grec*, 71–73, 233; Gerö and Stechow, "Tense in Time," 281; Orriens, "Involving the Past in the Present," 226; Horrocks, *Greek*, 176; Willi, *Languages of Aristophanes*, 129; Rau, "Greek and Proto-Indo-European," 186; Aubrey, "Greek Perfect," 117, 126; Andrason and Locatell, "Perfect Wave," 51. Robertson also regards τέθνηκα (Luke 8:49) as purely durative notion (*Grammar*, 845, 895). This perfect occurs twenty-three times in Sophocles, forty-five times in Euripides, seven times in Aristophanes, seven times in Thucydides, and ten times in Lysias (Sicking and Stork, *Two Studies*, 195, 204, 214, 226, 235).

56. Josephus, *Antiquities*, 122–23. See *The Shepherd of Hermas* 98.2, οἱ τοιοῦτοι οὔτε ζῶσιν οὔτε τεθνήκασιν, "Such people are neither alive nor dead" (Holmes, *Apostolic Fathers*, 660–61). Cf. LXX 2 Chr 22:10, καὶ Γοθολια ἡ μήτηρ Οχοζια εἶδεν ὅτι τέθνηκεν αὐτῇ ὁ υἱός καὶ ἠγέρθη καὶ ἀπώλεσεν πᾶν τὸ σπέρμα τῆς βασιλείας ἐν οἴκῳ Ιουδα ("Now when Athaliah the mother of Ahaziah saw that her son was dead, she arose and destroyed all the royal family of the house of Judah").

[1 Tim 5:6] ἡ δὲ σπαταλῶσα ζῶσα τέθνηκεν.
But she who is self-indulgent is dead while she lives.

In Matthew 2:20, the perfect τεθνήκασιν emphasizes the present state of those who are dead, with the prior event of their death implied.[57] In the same vein, τέθνηκεν in 1 Timothy 5:6 focuses on the present dead state.[58] In Mark 15:44 and Josephus, Michael Aubrey notes that the usage of the adverb ἤδη bolsters the resultative nuance of τέθνηκεν.[59] The term "resultative-stative" seems to match well all this instances of τέθνηκεν.

Ἔστηκα

The perfect ἔστηκα is from an old Greek in PIE (root *steh2- [3rd sg.], Ved. *tastháu*, Lat. *stetī*).[60] Many regard ἔστηκα as conveying a present state.[61] This perfect verb occurs in Homer and remains for a long time until Koine.[62]

[Homer, *Iliad* 5.485] τύνη δ᾽ **ἕστηκας**, ἀτὰρ οὐδ᾽ ἄλλοισι κελεύεις λαοῖσιν μενέμεν καὶ ἀμυνέμεναι ὤρεσσι.
Whereas thou *standest* and does not even urge thy hosts to abide and defend their wives.[63]

[LXX Exod 3:5] μὴ ἐγγίσῃς ὧδε λῦσαι τὸ ὑπόδημα ἐκ τῶν ποδῶν σου ὁ γὰρ τόπος ἐν ᾧ σὺ **ἕστηκας** γῆ ἁγία ἐστίν.

---

57. Luke 8:49 is the same case: τέθνηκεν ἡ θυγάτηρ σου ("Your daughter is dead").

58. Crellin introduces Wulfia's Gothic translation of the New Testament, which renders the verse as a present tense, "is dead" (Crellin, "Gothic Eyes," 32).

59. Aubrey, "Greek Perfect," 94–95, 117.

60. Chantraine, *Parfait grec*, 197, 219; Willi, *Origins of the Greek Verb*, 234.

61. Robertson, *Grammar*, 895; Moulton, *Prolegomena*, 147; Wackernagel, "Griechischen Perfektum," 4; Chantraine, *Parfait grec*, 233; Porter, *Verbal Aspect*, 250; Fanning, *Verbal Aspect*, 299; Wallace, *Beyond the Basics*, 579; Andrason and Locatell, "Perfect Wave," 50; Kimball, "Greek κ-Perfect," 146. Kimball says that ἔστηκα is intransitive and stative, not resultative.

62. Chantraine, *Parfait grec*, 9, 37, 85, 108. More examples of **ἔστηκα** in the NT are: Matt 12:47 (and Luke 8:20), ἡ μήτηρ σου καὶ οἱ ἀδελφοί ἔξω ἑστήκασιν ("Your mother and your brothers *are standing* outside"); John 1:26, μέσος ὑμῶν ἕστηκεν ὃν ὑμεῖς οὐκ οἴδατε ("among you *stands* one you do not know"); Acts 1:11, ἄνδρες Γαλιλαῖοι, τί ἑστήκατε [ἐμ]βλέποντες εἰς τὸν οὐρανόν; ("Men of Galilee, why do you *stand* looking into heaven?"); Acts 26:6, 22, καὶ νῦν ἐπ᾽ ἐλπίδι τῆς εἰς τοὺς πατέρας ἡμῶν ἐπαγγελίας γενομένης ὑπὸ τοῦ θεοῦ ἕστηκα ... ἕστηκα μαρτυρόμενος μικρῷ τε καὶ μεγάλῳ ("And now I *am standing* here on trial because of my hope in the promise made by God ... and so I stand here testifying both to small and great"); and Rom 11:20, σὺ δὲ τῇ πίστει ἕστηκας ("but you stand by faith").

63. Homer, *Iliad*, 230–31.

Do not come near here; remove your sandals from your feet, for the place on which you *are standing* is holy ground.⁶⁴

[John 8:44] ἐκεῖνος ἀνθρωποκτόνος ἦν ἀπ' ἀρχῆς καὶ ἐν τῇ ἀληθείᾳ οὐκ **ἔστηκεν**, ὅτι οὐκ ἔστιν ἀλήθεια ἐν αὐτῷ.

He was a murderer from the beginning, and does not *stand* in truth, because there is no truth in him.

[Rom 5:2] δι' οὗ καὶ τὴν προσαγωγὴν ἐσχήκαμεν [τῇ πίστει] εἰς τὴν χάριν ταύτην ἐν ᾗ **ἑστήκαμεν**.

Through whom also we have obtained our introduction by faith into this grace in which we *stand*.⁶⁵

[1 Cor 7:37] ὃς δὲ **ἔστηκεν** ἐν τῇ καρδίᾳ αὐτοῦ ἑδραῖος μὴ ἔχων ἀνάγκην, ἐξουσίαν δὲ ἔχει περὶ τοῦ ἰδίου θελήματος.

But he who *stands* firm in his heart, being under no constraint, but has authority over his own will.

[Col 1:17] καὶ αὐτός ἐστιν πρὸ πάντων καὶ τὰ πάντα ἐν αὐτῷ **συνέστηκεν**.

And he is before all things, and in him all things *stand together*.⁶⁶

[2 Tim 2:19] ὁ μέντοι στερεὸς θεμέλιον τοῦ θεοῦ **ἔστηκεν**, ἔχων τὴν σφραγῖδα ταύτην· ἔγνω κύριος τοὺς ὄντας αὐτοῦ.

Nevertheless, the firm foundation of God *stands*, having this seal, "The Lord knows those who are his."

[Heb 10:11] Καὶ πᾶς μὲν ἱερεὺς **ἔστηκεν** καθ' ἡμέραν λειτουργῶν καὶ τὰς αὐτὰς πολλάκις προσφέρων θυσίας.

And every priest *stands* daily at his service and offering repeatedly the same sacrifices.

---

64. Similarly, Stephen's speech of Acts 7:33 is: ἐφ' ᾧ ἕστηκας γῆ ἁγία ἐστίν ("where you are standing is holy ground").

65. See 1 Cor 15:1, ἐν ᾧ καὶ ἑστήκατε ("in which also you stand"); and 2 Cor 1:24, τῇ γὰρ πίστει ἑστήκατε ("for you stand firm in your faith").

66. Hatina states that if the temporality is inherent in verbs, the present form would be more appropriate. The perfect, which denotes an ongoing action with anteriority, does not fit here. Hatina thus maintains that the perfect should mean a "continuous sustaining activity" (Hatina, "Perfect Tense-Form in Colossians," 232–33). With the consideration that ἕστηκα is from ancient Greek, however, there is no necessity that the category "stative perfect" should be applied to overall perfects because a lot of Greek perfects of a current relevance with anteriority exist.

[James 5:9] μὴ στενάζετε, ἀδελφοί, κατ' ἀλλήλων, ἵνα μὴ κριθῆτε· ἰδοὺ ὁ κριτὴς πρὸ τῶν θυρῶν **ἕστηκεν**.

Do not complain, brethren, against one another, that you yourselves may not be judged; behold, the judge *is standing* at the door.

[Rev 8:2] Καὶ εἶδον τοὺς ἑπτὰ ἀγγέλους οἳ ἐνώπιον τοῦ θεοῦ **ἑστήκασιν**.

Then I saw the seven angels who *stand* before God.[67]

In the NT ἕστηκα appears eighteen times (excluding compound forms).[68] It is also attested numerous times in Classical Greek.[69] As the passages above indicate, most usages of ἕστηκα denote a pure stative of "standing" rather than a result, "having stood."[70] It seems that the "stand" rendering for ἕστηκα fits better than "have stood."

Persistent Situation of the Perfect

The perfect ἕστηκα is a tricky case because "resultative-stative" does not satisfactorily explain its nuance. In order to solve this issue, Willi maintains that in Homeric Greek the perfect is intrinsically a state.[71] According to Willi, the stative or subject-resultative is predominant in Indo-Iranian and early Greek.[72] On the basis of Wackernagel's definition of "the perfect of persistent situation," Willi argues for the priority of the persistent situation over subject-resultative [i.e., nactostatic]. Comrie also introduces the category of

---

67. Dougherty regards three perfects (ἕστηκα [3:2], ἑστήκασιν [8:2], ἕστηκεν [12:4]) in Revelation as equivalent to the present tense (Dougherty, "Syntax of the Apocalypse," 401, 424). Mathewson rejects this idea because it "confuses the semantics of the tense forms and their temporal pragmatic manifestations" (Mathewson, *Verbal Aspect in Revelation*, 102).

68. The compound-forms occur in Acts 4:10, ἐν τούτῳ οὗτος παρέστηκεν ἐνώπιον ὑμῶν ὑγιής ("this man stands before you, healed"); Mark 4:29, ὅτι παρέστηκεν ὁ θερισμός ("because the harvest has come"); 2 Thess 2:2, ὡς ὅτι ἐνέστηκεν ἡ ἡμέρα τοῦ κυρίου ("to the effect that the day of the Lord has come"); and Col 1:17 above.

69. Chantraine, *Parfait grec*, 34, 80–81. The perfect ἕστηκα occurs ten times in Sophocles, twenty-eight times in Euripides, twenty times in Aristophanes, four times in Thucydides, two times in Lysias, and three times in Xenophon (Sicking and Stork, *Two Studies*, 196, 205, 215, 227, 235, 242).

70. Matt 20:6 is "exceptional," implying a prior event: τί ὧδε ἑστήκατε ὅλην τὴν ἡμέρον ἀργοί ("Why have you stood here all day long?"). So is Rev 12:4 (Καὶ ὁ δράκων ἕστηκεν ἐνωπίον τῆς γυναικὸς "And dragon stood before the woman").

71. Willi, *Origins of the Greek Verb*, 219.

72. Willi, *Origins of the Greek Verb*, 229.

"perfect of persistent situation," which is similar to English perfect, as in "I have lived here for ten years."[73]

Although the ancient Greek (Homeric) perfect has a tendency of being resultative, not all Homeric perfects convey a resultative nuance. As for τέθνηκα, Willi states,

> A "nactostatic" value is therefore automatically attached to τέθνηκα or . . . ὄπωπα: for the *quality* that characterises a "dier/ not-so-far-seer of an army of this sort and size" can only be predicated on someone who fulfils the necessary condition of having performed the activity. . . . In other words, a "nactostatic" value develops by semantic and pragmatic implicature from a purely "static/stative" one.[74]

Willi claims that the intrinsic stative quality of the perfect naturally brings forth a subjective resultative, i.e., nactostatic.[75] In other words, both τέθνηκα and ὄπωπα originally represent pure stative meanings "I am dead" and "I am a seer" respectively. This stative perfect has naturally come to express subject-result [nactostatic], ὄπωπα "I have seen," for example. Thus, Willi suggests that subject-resultative (nactostatic) is in fact "epiphenomenal" to a basic purely stative meaning.[76]

Willi's suggestion is in contrast to viewing the perfect in a traditional way on the basis of subject-resultative as a default. For example, οἶδα is resultative-stative, having been through a slight change of the meaning from "in the state of having seen/found" to "know." In 2 Timothy 3:15, οἶδα ("you *have been acquainted* with the Holy Scriptures") implies a resultative or anterior nuance.[77] Secondly, γέγραπται ("it has been written") may have become a customary form of "it is written" after its widespread frequent usages. Readers have no problem conceiving a notion of "resultative-stative"

---

73. Comrie, *Aspect*, 60.

74. Willi, *Origins of the Greek Verb*, 234; emphasis original.

75. Willi, *Origins of the Greek Verb*, 233. Willi quotes Kümmel who says, "*nactostatic* in analogy with *static*. In this function, the perfect syntactically corresponds to a present and may be used, like the latter, in a general/timeless or an actual manner. The past event, though factually implied, plays no essential role, its point in time is irrelevant" (Kümmel, *Das Perfekt*, 66, trans. by Willi).

76. Willi, *Origins of the Greek Verb*, 233–34. Willi explicates his argument by illustrating more, "John is a boar-hunter" which indicates that John has become a (professional) boar-hunter at some point and would have already hunted a boar. It implies the "permanent quality" while "John has hunted a boar/boars" indicates that he has hunted at least one time.

77. I am indebted to the conversation with a fellow PhD student, Nathaniel Erickson, and Dr. John Polhill in his seminar *General Epistles* in 2016 fall at the Southern Baptist Theological Seminary.

with perfects like οἶδα, ὄπωπα, γέγραπται or τέθνηκα. However, a problem arises with the perfect conveying a stative nuance. For instance, ἕστηκα does not seem to be in harmony with the resultative nuance.

Willi points out that *steh₂- (3rd sg. "stands") does not necessarily imply a resultative nuance.[78] Willi opines that it would be impossible for the resultative to produce a pure stative notion, such as "intensive" perfects of noise (βέβρυχα, μέμυκα), if the attribute of the PIE perfect is intrinsically resultative. The reverse would be possible, says Willi, that the stative present-perfect yielded the resultative epiphenomenally. Willi prefers the priority of "the perfect of persistent situation" to the traditional notion of subject-resultative.[79]

Summary

It is difficult to draw a firm line between the resultative-stative and pure stative.[80] It is observed that the ancient perfect not only conveys a resultative nuance, but also delivers a stative nuance. This section has proposed οἶδα and τέθνηκα as resultative-stative while considering ἕστηκα to deliver a purely stative nuance.

The ancient perfect evidently shows two characteristics—resultative and stative. Several scholars take both the resultative and the stative as main characteristics of the Perfect tense in ancient Greek. Andrason and Locatell state, "In accordance with the PIE origin, in Archaic Greek (700–500 BCE), the resultative proper and stative present values predominated."[81] Similarly,

---

78. Willi, *Origins of the Greek Verb*, 235.

79. Willi, *Origins of the Greek Verb*, 237–44. On the other hand, Allan maintains that even though ἕστηκα looks like a pure stative, it is actually a resultative-stative. He suggests that the perfect reduplication changes the PIE (unmarked) root aorists into the resulting state. Allan states, "Root aorists are morphologically unmarked in that they do not have an additional morpheme expressing aorist aspect. These morphologically *unmarked* aorist forms expressed a *change* of state (i.e., they had a telic lexical *Aktionsart*). . . . On the other hand, the perfect forms built from these roots *are* morphologically marked (reduplicated). The marked perfect expressed the state resulting from the change of state designated by the root. In other words, perfect morphology is used to turn the change of state meaning of the root into a resultative state." Examples include Aorist *(h₁e-)gʷeh₂-t ("made a step, went") » Perfect *gʷe-gʷoh₂-e ("has gone"); Aorist *(h₁e-)mn-to ("brought into mind") » Perfect *me-mon-e ("has in mind"); and Aorist *(h₁e-)steh₂-t ("stood up") » Perfect *se-stoh₂-e ("stands"). Allan notes that even though these perfects may look like purely stative, they are in fact resultative-stative. See Allan, "Tense and Aspect," 103–4.

80. Nedjalkov, "Resultative Constructions," 928.

81. Andrason and Locatell, "Perfect Wave," 79.

Bentein mentions both categories together, saying, "stative/resultative perfect (e.g., ὄλωλα (olōla) "I am destroyed", λέλυται (lelutai) "it is solved"), denoting the state in which the subject finds him/her/itself (whether or not as a result of a past event)."[82] Magni also notes that in Homeric Greek the stative meanings with reduplication "coexist with the resultative values of the perfect."[83]

In light of these observations, I will employ the term "resultative-stative." Some may prefer the term "stative-resultative," like Lucien van Beek in his characterization of the Homeric perfect.[84] The reason of selecting the term "resultative-stative" in this book is that in the NT, the majority of "stative perfects" are resultative-stative rather than "pure stative." In the corpus of the Greek New Testament, more than three quarters of 461 are resultative-stative. The cases for stative meaning (about sixty cases [13 percent]) are ἕστηκα (eighteen times; and the compound-verb forms παρέστηκα [two times], ἐνέστηκα, συνέστηκα), πέποιθα/πέπεισμαι (eleven times), ἔοικεν (two times), stative perfect middle/passive forms (sixteen cases), and about a dozen instances of the perfect with an intensive notion.[85]

ANCIENT INTRANSITIVE PERFECT

So far we have shown that the early Greek perfect was originally resultative-stative. The next notable point of the ancient Greek perfect is intransitivity.[86]

---

82. Bentein, "Ecological-Evolutionary Account," 205–6; Bentein, "Periphrastic," 183.

83. Magni, "Pluractionality and Perfect," 342. See Moser, "Tense and Aspect," in Runge and Fresch, *Greek Verb Revisited*, 550–51; Moser, "Perfect Periphrases," 226.

84. Beek, "Perfect in Homeric Greek"; Beek and Migliori, "Active versus Middle Perfect, 73.

85. Similarly, Gerö and Stechow say that the resultative was prevailing in the ancient Greek (Gerö and Stechow, "Tense in Time," 268).

86. Monro, *Homeric Dialect*, 32; Chantraine, *Parfait grec*, 20–46; Duhoux, *Le verbe grec ancien*, 426; Haug, "From Resultatives to Anteriors," 298–300; Gerö and Stechow, "Tense in Time," 253, 268; Buth, "Perfect Greek Morphology," 419; Haspelmath categorizes Homeric perfects into (1) subject (patient) of intransitive active verbs (subjective resultative); (2) direct object (patient) of transitive active verbs (objective resultative); and (3) subject (patient) of intransitive middle (Haspelmath, "From Resultative to Perfect," 194–201); Haug also categorizes them into: (1) intransitive active present–intransitive active perfect (βαίνω–βέβηκα); (2) transitive active present–active perfect (εἶδον–οἶδα); (3) middle-passive (deponent) present–active perfect (γίγνομαι–γέγονα); and (4) transitive active present and intransitive middle present–active perfect and middle perfect (ἵστημι/ἵσταμαι–ἕστηκα; λύω/λύομαι–λέλυται) (Haug, "From Resultatives to Anteriors," 297–98). Rijksbaron states that in Homer intransitive and passive perfects occur (Rijksbaron, *Syntax and Semantics*, 37). See Kulikov and Lavidas,

The perfect has an active form but its meaning is close to that of the middle voice. For instance, φθείρω (factitive/transitive "I ruin") has the perfect (compound) form διέφθορα conveying an intransitive sense, "I am ruined/destroyed."[87] Notably, the action affects the subject (patient), having the nuance of the middle voice with "subject-affectedness." For example,

> [Homer, *Iliad* 15.127] μαινόμενε φρένας ἠλὲ **διέφθορας**.
> Madman! Crazed of mind, you *are doomed!*[88]

> [LXX Num 17:27] καὶ εἶπαν οἱ υἱοὶ Ισραηλ πρὸς Μωυσῆν λέγοντες ἰδοὺ ἐξανηλώμεθα **ἀπολώλαμεν** παρανηλώμεθα
> And the people of Israel said to Moses, "Behold, we are undone, we *perish*, we are all dying!"[89]

In Homer, the perfect διέφθορας shows intransitivity with a resultative stative nuance. In Numbers 17:27, ἀπολώλαμεν behaves the same way. The present form ἀπόλλυμι is factitive ("I destroy"), but its perfect form shows a resultative-stative ("already perished") with subject-affectedness.

Perfect of Intransitive Verbs

The Homeric perfects survived through the Classical era up to Koine Greek. These active perfects with intransitivity appear in the Greek New Testament. We will look at intransitive perfects first.

Εἴωθα

This perfect is an old intransitive perfect of state (*$s\underset{\cdot}{u}eh_1d^h$- "be[come] accustomed").[90] In the NT pluperfect forms only occur to convey a state in the past with the sense "was accustomed to."

"Reconstructing passive," 117.

87. Chantraine, *Parfait grec*, 36, 61. Gerö and Stechow state that the Homeric Greek perfects are almost always intransitive, except in *Iliad* 2.272, ὢ πόποι, ἦ δὴ μυρί' Ὀδυσσεὺς ἐσθλὰ ἔοργε βουλάς τ' ἐξάρχων ἀγαθὰς πόλεμόν τε κορύσσων ("Out upon it! verily hath Odysseus ere now wrought good deeds without number as leader in good counsel and setting battle in array"); and in *Odyssey* 17.284, τολμήεις μοι θυμός, ἐπεὶ κακὰ πολλὰ πέπονθα κύμασι καὶ πολέμῳ ("Staunch in my heart, for much evil have I suffered amid the waves and in war") (Gerö and Stechow, "Tense in Time," 253).

88. This example is from Crellin, "Greek Perfect (2012)," 161.

89. This example is from Buth, "Perfect Greek Morphology," 427.

90. Monro, *Homeric Dialect*, 23; Willi, *Origins of the Greek Verb*, 214.

[Homer, *Odyssey* 17.394-95] Ἀντίνοος δ' εἴωθε κακῶς ἐρεθιζέμεν αἰεὶ μύθοισιν χαλεποῖσιν, ἐποτρύνει δὲ καὶ ἄλλους.

For Antinous is wont ever in evil wise to provoke to anger with harsh words, aye, and urges on the others too.[91]

[Matt 27:15] Κατὰ δὲ ἑορτὴν εἰώθει ὁ ἡγεμὼν ἀπολύειν ἕνα τῷ ὄχλῳ δέσμιον ὃν ἤθελον

Now at the feast the governor was accustomed to release a prisoner for the crowd

The perfect εἴωθα delivers a stative nuance, especially in the *Odyssey* with adverbs αἰεί ("always"). The perfect εἴωθα also occurs in Classical Greek with a stative sense (three times in Euripides, four times in Aristophanes, nineteen times in Thucydides, two times in Lysias, and two times in Xenophon).[92] It continues to exist until the Koine period as shown in Matthew 27:15.[93]

Ἔοικα

The perfect ἔοικα is from the early Greek (stem *(ϝ)έ(ϝ)οικ-).[94] This perfect conveys a stative nuance rather than resultative:

[James 1:6] αἰτείτω δὲ ἐν πίστει μηδὲν διακρινόμενος· ὁ γὰρ διακρινόμενος ἔοικεν κλύδωνι θαλάσσης ἀνεμιζομένῳ καὶ ῥιπιζομένῳ.

But let him ask in faith, with no doubting, for the one who doubts *is like* a wave of the sea that is driven and tossed by the wind.

[James 1:23] ὅτι εἴ τις ἀκροατὴς λόγου ἐστὶν καὶ οὐ ποιητής, οὗτος ἔοικεν ἀνδρὶ κατανοοῦντι τὸ πρόσωπον τῆς γενέσεως αὐτοῦ ἐν ἐσόπτρῳ.

For if anyone is a hearer of the word and not a doer, he *is like* a man who looks intently at his natural face in a mirror.

In Classical Greek, ἔοικα occurs many times: eighteen times in Aeschylus, nine times in Sophocles, forty-four times in Euripides, forty times

---

91. Homer, *Odyssey*, 180-81.
92. Sicking and Stork, *Two Studies*, 203, 213, 225, 234, 241.
93. Chantraine, *Parfait grec*, 218.
94. Willi, *Origins of the Greek Verb*, 212.

in Aristophanes, two times in Thucydides, one time in Lysias, and six times in Xenophon.⁹⁵ Not all these archaic perfects survived until Koine. In Attic, a great number of forms disappeared.⁹⁶

Perfect of Transitive Verbs

The second type of the perfect is intransitive, but its present tense is transitive, taking an object. This perfect, which does not take an object, is intransitive as well as patient-oriented.⁹⁷ These verbs are quite familiar because of their frequent occurrence in the NT.

Σέσηπα

This perfect delivers a resultative-stative nuance. It occurs in Homer, Classical Greek, and the Greek New Testament. The present form σήπω is a factitive ("to decay"), but its perfect form is active with an intransitive nuance ("it is rotten"), as a typical ancient-type perfect active. Examples are:⁹⁸

> [Homer, *Iliad* 2.135] καὶ δὴ δοῦρα σέσηπε νεῶν καὶ σπάρτα λέλυνται.
> And now our ships' timbers are rotted, and the tackling loosed.⁹⁹
>
> [Aristophanes, *Plutus* 1035] οὔκ, ἀλλὰ κατασέσηπας, ὥς γ' ἐμοὶ δοκεῖς.
> You are rotting away, it seems to me.¹⁰⁰
>
> [James 5:2] ὁ πλοῦτος ὑμῶν σέσηπεν καὶ τὰ ἱμάτια ὑμῶν σητόβρωτα γέγονεν
> Your riches have rotted and your garments are moth-eaten.

---

95. Sicking and Stork, *Two Studies*, 188, 190, 203, 213, 225, 235, 241. Chantraine notes that ἔοικα often occurs in Plato (Chantraine, *Parfait grec*, 146).

96. Chantraine, *Parfait grec*, 75. Chantraine says the disappearance of βέβουλα, δεδάηκα ("I am"), δέδηα ("I burn"), ἔολπα ("I hope"), ἐρήριπε, συνόχωκα, κεκόρηκα, ἔμμορε, ὄρωρα ("I watch"), τέτευχα, ἔφθορα, etc.

97. A patient is "an object that is *affected* by the event" (Allan, "Middle Voice," 7).

98. These examples are from: Chantraine, *Parfait grec*, 34, 80; Sicking and Stork, *Two Studies*, 209.

99. Homer, *Iliad*, 60–61.

100. Aristophanes, *Wealth*.

The usages of σέσηπα above denotes a resultative-stative. McKnight rightly states that "the author [James] depicts the act of rotting as complete and as having brought into being a state of affairs."[101] Some view σέσηπεν in James 5:2 as futuristic perfect,[102] but the future is different from the perfect. Especially the old perfect such as σέσηπα conveys resultative-stative connotation.[103]

Πέπονθα

This perfect (from πάσχω) is from early Greek. Chantraine states that πέπονθα frequently occurs in Homer.[104]

> [Homer, *Odyssey* 17.284] τολμήεις μοι θυμός, ἐπεὶ κακὰ πολλὰ πέπονθα κύμασι καὶ πολέμῳ.
> Staunch is my heart, for much evil have I suffered amid the waves and in war.[105]

In the text πέπονθα carries the sense of resultative-stative. Willi and Sicking and Stork state that πέπονθα denotes a present state rather than a past event.[106] The perfect πέπονθα appears in Classical Greek (Aeschylus, Thucydides, Sophocles, or Euripides).[107]

It is also attested in the Greek New Testament:

> [Heb 2:18] ἐν ᾧ γὰρ πέπονθεν αὐτὸς πειρασθείς, δύναται τοῖς πειραζομένοις βοηθῆσαι.
> For because he himself has suffered when tempted, he is able to help those who are being tempted.

---

101. McKnight, *Letters of James*, 386.

102. Porter, *Idioms*, 39–41; Robertson, *Grammar*, 898; Dibelius, *James*, 236.

103. Ropes, *Commentary on the Epistle of St. James*, 284–85; Moo, *Letter of James*, 213.

104. Chantraine, *Parfait grec*, 13, 72.

105. Homer, *Odyssey*, 172–73.

106. Sicking and Stork, *Two Studies*, 161; Willi, *Origins of the Greek Verb*, 229. Willi reads πέπονθα as "being a sufferer," saying that every Homeric perfect conveys a stative nuance.

107. Chantraine, *Parfait grec*, 72; Sicking and Stork, *Two Studies*, 190, 198, 208, 218, 229, 237. The perfect πέπονθα occurs two times in Aeschylus, eight times in Sophocles, twenty-nine times in Euripides, twenty-eight times in Aristophanes, eight times in Thucydides, and ten times in Lysias.

[Luke 13:2] δοκεῖτε ὅτι οἱ Γαλιλαῖοι οὗτοι ἁμαρτωλοὶ παρὰ πάντας τοὺς Γαλιλαίους ἐγένοντο, ὅτι ταῦτα πεπόνθασιν;
Do you think that these Galileans were worse sinners than all the other Galileans, because they suffered in this way?

Interestingly, the difficulty is that in each text πέπονθα indicates past experiences. Although the perfect is an archaic form, it seems that πέπονθα takes past meanings in accordance with the contexts.[108] Chapter 5 will handle this case in detail where the perfect expresses a past event.

Πέποιθα

The perfect πέποιθα ("I am persuaded") frequently appears in the NT. The present form (πείθω "I persuade") is factitive but the perfect conveys an intransitive sense with subject-affectedness.[109] Horrocks briefly explains how πέποιθα has carried from Homer to Koine.

> We might also take note of the semantically idiosyncratic Homeric and Ionic perfect πέποιθα [ˈpepotha] "I trust" (in paras. 19, 20 and 21: from πείθω [ˈpitho] "I persuade"), which is strongly disfavoured in classical Attic prose, but resurfaces here in the popular written Koine as another form with a continuous history in the (Ionicized) spoken vernacular.[110]

According to Horrocks, πέποιθα seems to have been disfavored in classical Attic prose, but it reappears in Koine. Πέποιθα frequently occurs in the NT (and Septuagint):

[Matt 27:43] πέποιθεν ἐπὶ τὸν θεόν, ῥυσάσθω νῦν εἰ θέλει αὐτόν· εἶπεν γὰρ ὅτι θεοῦ εἰμι υἱός.
He *trusts* in God; let God deliver him now, if he desires him; for he said, "I am the Son of God."

[Rom 2:19] πέποιθάς τε σεαυτὸν ὁδηγὸν εἶναι τυφλῶν, φῶς τῶν ἐν σκότει.
And you *are confident* that you yourself are a guide to the blind, a light to those who are in darkness.

---

108. Porter notes that πέπονθα "implicates past" (Porter, *Verbal Aspect*, 264). See Andrason and Locatell, "Perfect Wave," 45; Ng, "Greek Perfect in Hebrews," 18.

109. Chantraine, *Parfait grec*, 33. For example, 2 Cor 5:11, θεῷ δὲ πεφανερώμεθα ("but we are made manifest to God").

110. Horrocks, *Greek*, 108.

[Phil 2:24] πέποιθα δὲ ἐν κυρίῳ ὅτι καὶ αὐτὸς ταχέως ἐλεύσομαι.

And I *trust* in the Lord that I myself also shall be coming shortly.

[LXX 2 Kings 18:19-21] τίς ἡ πεποίθησις αὕτη ἣν πέποιθας ... νῦν ἰδοὺ πέποιθας σαυτῷ ἐπὶ τὴν ῥάβδον τὴν καλαμίνην τὴν τεθλασμένην ταύτην ἐπ' Αἴγυπτον.

What is this confidence that you *trust*? ... Now behold, you *rely on* the staff of this crushed reed, Egypt.[111]

[2 Thess 3:4] πεποίθαμεν δὲ ἐν κυρίῳ ἐφ' ὑμᾶς, ὅτι ἃ παραγγέλλομεν [καὶ] ποιεῖτε ποιήσετε.

We *have confidence* in the Lord about you, that you are doing and will continue to do what we command.

[2 Cor 10:7] Τὰ κατὰ πρόσωπον βλέπετε. εἴ τις πέποιθεν ἑαυτῷ Χριστοῦ εἶναι, τοῦτο λογιζέσθω πάλιν ἐφ' ἑαυτοῦ, ὅτι καθὼς αὐτὸς Χριστοῦ, οὕτως καὶ ἡμεῖς.

You are looking at things they are outwardly. If anyone *is confident* in himself that he is Christ's, let him consider this gain within himself, that just as he is Christ's, so also are we.

[Gal 5:10] ἐγὼ πέποιθα εἰς ὑμᾶς ἐν κυρίῳ ὅτι οὐδὲν ἄλλο φρονήσετε· ὁ δὲ ταράσσων ὑμᾶς βαστάσει τὸ κρίμα, ὅστις ἐὰν ᾖ.

I *have confidence* in you in the Lord, that you will adopt no other view; but the one who is disturbing you shall bear his judgment, whoever he is.

The perfect πέποιθα denotes a state as the passages above display. It is attested in Classical Greek: three times in Sophocles, twelve times in Aeschylus, nineteen times in Euripides, and five times in Aristophanes.[112]

---

111. See 2 Kgs 19:10, μὴ ἐπαιρέτω σε ὁ θεός σου ἐφ' ᾧ σὺ πέποιθας ἀπ' αὐτῷ λέγων οὐ μὴ παραδοθῇ Ιερουσαλημ εἰς χεῖρας βασιλέως Ἀσσυρίων ("Do not let your God in whom you *trust* deceive you by promising that Jerusalem will not be given into the hand of the king Assyria"); 2 Chr 14:11, κατίσχυσον ἡμᾶς κύριε ὁ θεὸς ὅτι ἐπὶ σοὶ πεποίθαμεν καὶ ἐπὶ τῷ ὀνόματί σου ἤλθαμεν ἐπὶ τὸ πλῆθος τὸ πολὺ τοῦτο ("Help us, O Lord our God, for we *trust* in Thee, and in Thy name have come against this multitude"); 2 Chr 32:10, ἐπὶ τίνι ὑμεῖς πεποίθατε καὶ κάθησθε ἐν τῇ περιοχῇ ἐν Ιερουσαλημ ("On what *are* you *trusting*, that you endure the siege in Jerusalem?"); Prov 28:25, ἀπλῆστος ἀνὴρ κρίνει εἰκῇ ὃς δὲ πέποιθεν ἐπὶ κύριον ἐν ἐπιμελείᾳ ἔσται ("A greedy man stirs up strife, but the one who *trusts* in the Lord will be enriched"); and Judith 7:10, ὁ γὰρ λαὸς οὗτος τῶν υἱῶν Ισραηλ οὐ πέποιθαν ἐπὶ τοῖς δόρασιν αὐτῶν ("for this people of sons of Israel do not *rely upon* their spears").

112. Sicking and Stork, *Two Studies*, 190, 198, 208, 218.

Interestingly, the perfect middle form πέπεισμαι also occurs with the same meaning. Πέπεισμαι appears in the Greek New Testament as well as Classical Greek (three times in Thucydides and once in Euripides):[113]

> [Rom 8:38] πέπεισμαι γὰρ ὅτι οὔτε θάνατος οὔτε ζωὴ οὔτε ἄγγελοι οὔτε ἀρχαὶ οὔτε ἐνεστῶτα οὔτε μέλλοντα οὔτε δυνάμεις.
>
> For I *am sure* that neither death nor life, nor angels nor rulers, nor things present nor things to come, nor powers.[114]

> [2 Tim 1:5] ὑπόμνησιν λαβὼν τῆς ἐν σοὶ ἀνυποκρίτου πίστεως, ἥτις ἐνῴκησεν πρῶτον ἐν τῇ μάμμῃ σου Λωΐδι καὶ τῇ μητρί σου Εὐνίκῃ, πέπεισμαι δὲ ὅτι καὶ ἐν σοί.
>
> I am reminded of your sincere faith, a faith that dwelt first in your grandmother Lois and your mother Eunice and now, I *am sure [persuaded]*, dwells in you as well.[115]

> [LXX Tobit 14:4] ἄπελθε εἰς τὴν Μηδίαν, τέκνον, ὅτι πέπεισμαι ὅσα ἐλάλησεν Ιωνας ὁ προφήτης περὶ Νινευη ὅτι καταστραφήσεται.
>
> Depart for Media, children, because I *am convinced* as much as the prophet Jonah spoke of Nineveh that it shall be overthrown.

The question is why the middle perfect πέπεισμαι appears and coexists with πέποιθα. The next section will investigate the middle perfect.[116]

---

113. Sicking and Stork, *Two Studies*, 208, 218. See Ignatius, *Trallians* 3.2, περὶ ὧν πέπεισμαι ὑμᾶς οὕτως ἔχειν ("I *am sure* that you agree with me regarding these matters"); *Polycarp* 2.3, τὸ θέμα ἀφθαρσία καὶ ζωὴ αἰώνιος, περὶ ἧς καὶ σὺ πέπεισαι ("the prize is incorruptibility and eternal life, about which you *are* already *convinced*") (Holmes, *Apostolic Fathers*, 216–17, 264–65).

114. Also see Rom 14:14, οἶδα καὶ πέπεισμαι ἐν κυρίῳ Ἰησοῦ ὅτι οὐδὲν κοινόν δι' ἑαυτοῦ ("I know and *am persuaded* in the Lord Jesus that nothing is unclean in itself"); and Rom 15:14, Πέπεισμαι δέ, ἀδελφοί μου, καὶ αὐτὸς ἐγὼ περὶ ὑμῶν ὅτι καὶ αὐτοὶ μεστοί ἐστε ἀγαθωσύνης ("And concerning you, my brethren, I myself also *am convinced* that you yourselves are full of goodness").

115. See 2 Tim 1:12, οἶδα γὰρ ᾧ πεπίστευκα καὶ πέπεισμαι ὅτι δυνατός ἐστιν τὴν παραθήκην μου φυλάξαι εἰς ἐκείνην τὴν ἡμέραν ("for I know whom I have believed, and I am convinced that he is able to guard until that day what has been entrusted to me").

116. Robertson does not regard πέπεισμαι in Romans 8:38 as intensive. The intensive nuance is not indispensable here for πέπεισμαι, which delivers a stative nuance. (Robertson, *Grammar*, 895).

Summary

In sum, the ancient-typed perfects survived for a long period and appeared in the Greek New Testament.[117] Forms such as εἴωθα, ἔοικα, σέσηπα, and πέποιθα occur in the NT. They deliver an intransitive nuance with subject-affectedness. A small number of perfects survived to the Classical epoch.[118] For instance, the perfects of ancient type occurring in Thucydides are (bold-font perfects occurring in the NT): **βέβηκα**, **ἔοικα**, δέδοικα, τέθνηκα, ἡμάρτηκα, κεκύφα, μεμένηκα, πέπτωκα, **εἴωθα**, **ἐλήλυθα**, πέπραγα, ἐπιλέλοιπα, among others.[119] However, not all these perfects survived until Koine but many of them faded away.[120]

ANCIENT PERFECT AND MIDDLE VOICE

The next notable point is the interrelation between the ancient perfect active and the middle form.[121] We have already observed that the early Greek perfects are subject-affected with intransitivity. Since the ancient active perfect has a trait of subject-affectedness, which is one of the main characteristics of the middle voice,[122] the active perfect and the middle perfect in Homer

---

117. Chantraine, *Parfait grec*, 37, 147.

118. Chantraine, *Parfait grec*, 78. They are **γέγονα**, δέδυκα, **ἔστηκα**, ὄλωλα, **σέσηπα**, **τέθνηκα**, **πέποιθα**, δέδοικα, πέφηνα, πέφυκα, etc. (bold-font perfects occurring in the NT). See Lavidas and Kulikov, "Voice, Transitivity and Tense/Aspect," 298.

119. Chantraine, *Parfait grec*, 71–73. Chantraine lists more from Thucydides: ἤνθηκα, ηὐτομόληκα, βεβλάστηκα, βεβοήθηκα, δεδράμηκα, τεθάρσηκα, κεκράτηκα, etc. Chantraine also illustrates the ancient-typed perfect forms from Demosthenes: βέβιωκα, **ἔοικα**, **εἴωθα**, εἰσπέπλευκα, πεπλούτηκα, προσπέπτωκα, **εἰσελήλυθα**, **ἀναβέβηκα**, **κέκραγα**, **τέθνηκα**, δέδοικα, **συμβέβηκα**, τετελεύτηκα, παρώρμηκα, πέπλευκα, πέφφικα, etc. See Moulton and Turner, *Syntax*, 82.

120. Chantraine states that a great number of perfect active forms disappeared: βέβουλα, δεδάηκα ("I grasp"), δέδηα ("I burn"), ἐρήριπε, ἔολπα, ἔφθορα, ἔμμορε, ὄρωρα ("I stir"), τέτευχα, τέτρηχα, and ἔφθορα (Chantraine, *Parfait grec*, 75).

121. Sicking and Stork argue that the perfect tense and middle voice have some semantic affinity with each other. Many ancient perfect-active forms are derived from the present middle-passive forms: ἔολπα–ἔλπομαι; γέγονα–γίγνομαι; ὄρωρα–ὄρνυμαι; πέποιθα–πείθομαι (Sicking and Stork, *Two Studies*, 130–31); Drinka, "Development of the Perfect," 86.

122. Allan, "Middle Voice," 13, 26, 32, 37–40; Clackson, *Indo-European Linguistics*, 143. Due to the difficulty of grasping the middle voice at once, Miller divides Greek middle voice into categories: (1) reciprocity; (2) reflexivity; (3) self-involvement; (4) self-interest; (5) receptivity; (6) passivity; and (7) state & condition (Miller, "Deponent Verbs," 427–29).

are hardly distinguishable so that they are indiscriminately employed.[123] For example, the nuance of the ancient-typed perfect ὄλωλα "I am destroyed" (from ὄλλυμι "I destroy something/someone") is almost equivalent to that of the present middle ὄλλυμαι "I perish."[124] In terms of meaning, the archaic perfects are not much different from the middle voice.

Drinka notes that both the perfect and the middle voice affect the subject rather than an object in Indo-European.

> Stang made the important observation that both the perfect and the middle voice refer to an action which concerns or affects the subject. In essence, both the stative perfect and the middle are capable of taking only one argument; neither can take an object.[125]

In short, the point is that both the ancient perfect and middle voice are related to the subject rather than an object. There is almost no difference in terms of nuance between the Homeric perfect-active and the middle/passive perfect.[126] Haug points out rightly that the perfect and the middle voice are close semantically, even though the perfect denotes a resultant state.[127]

The Innovation and Spread of the Perfect Middle

We will now take a chronological look of the perfect middle. In Homer, the perfect-middle forms occur as frequently as the active perfects.[128] The ancient active perfect and newly-innovated perfect middle are concurrent. It is known that the perfect middle form appeared later than the perfect active form.[129] Referring to Chantraine, Sicking and Stork summarize,

---

123. Monro, *Homeric Dialect*, 32; Chantraine, *Parfait grec*, 117; Haspelmath, "From Resultative to Perfect," 207–8; Sicking and Stork, *Two Studies*, 130.

124. Chantraine, *Parfait grec*, 32–33.

125. Drinka, "Development of the Perfect," 85.

126. Chantraine, *Parfait grec*, 52–54. Chantraine notes that Herodotus employs the perfect middle γεγένημαι next to γέγονα, which implies that there is not much difference in terms of nuance.

127. Haug, "From Resultatives to Anteriors," 298.

128. Willi, *Origins of the Greek Verb*, 215; Haspelmath, "From Resultative to Perfect," 208; Chantraine, *Parfait grec*, 54, 63–65, 117. Chantraine illustrates many perfect middle forms in Homer: κατήκισται (π 290), ἠσχυμμένος (Σ 180), ἀμφιδεδίνηται, κεκράανται, κεκορήμεθα (Θ 98, Ψ 350), μέμβλεται (Τ 343), ὀρώρεται (τ 377), τέτυγμαι (thirty-two examples); ἀλάλημαι(ἀλάομαι), ἤσκηται(ἀσκέω), δεδάκρυσαι(δακρύω), πεποίημαι(ποιέω), νενίπται(νίζω), τετελεσμένος(τέλεω), τετιμῆσθαι(τιμάω), κεχαρισμένος(χαρίζομαι), κέχρηται(χράομαι), etc.

129. Chantraine, *Parfait grec*, 68–70; Haspelmath, "From Resultative to Perfect,"

1) Originally, the Perfect characteristically had Active forms; 2) subsequently, Middle-Passive Perfect forms were introduced; 3) finally, a systematic opposition has been created of transitive Active Perfect forms versus Passive Perfect forms.[130]

Chantraine maintains that the middle endings penetrated into the verbal system through the pluperfect. The pluperfect form was built with secondary endings in order to differentiate it from the perfect's active endings. For example, (ϝ)έ(ϝ)οικε had a pluperfect form with a secondary ending, differentiating the pluperfect (ϝ)έ(ϝ)ικτο from the perfect. However, the active endings and the middle endings—two grammatical manners—were not able to subsist side by side for long. Hence, the pluperfect (ϝ)έ(ϝ)ικτο disappeared. Instead, the pluperfect (ϝ)ε(ϝ)ώκει with active endings fills its place.[131]

As another example, φθείρω (middle φθείρεμαι) had its archaic pluperfect ἔφθαρτο with a secondary ending in order to distinguish it from the perfect active ἔφθορα. According to Chantraine, middle endings infiltrated the system through the pluperfect.[132] Willi offers a good summary.

> Since the oldest pluperfects were as usually intransitive as the oldest perfects, the middle endings were preferred. Thus, next to pres. (δια)φθείρομαι "perish" and intr. perf. (δι)έφθορα "am

---

208; Sicking and Stork, *Two Studies*, 131; Jasanoff, *Hittite and the Indo-European Verb*, 233; Weiss, "Morphology," 117. Weiss says that "The perfect middle was perhaps not fully elaborated in PIE." See Beek, "Etymology of Greek of πέπᾱμαι," 430n25. Beek states, "the middle perfect itself is generally supposed to be a post-PIE innovation."

130. Sicking and Stork, *Two Studies*, 130.

131. Chantraine, *Parfait grec*, 56–62. Chantraine states that two grammatical manners can only exist side by side if they are opposed, just like the active and the middle in times of the present. The pluperfect form with the active ending (ϝ)ε(ϝ)ώκει occurs in Homer (α 411). Chantraine gives more examples to illustrate the pluperfects with secondary endings: (ϝ)έ(ϝ)οικε–(ϝ)έ(ϝ)ικτο; ἔμμορε–εἵμαρτο; ἔφθορε–ἔφθαρτο; ἐρήριπε–ἐρέριπτο. Different types of active pluperfects were innovated: ἐμέμηκον, ἐπέπληγον, or ἐπέφυκον were created. In Attic, pluperfect forms δεδήει, εἰληλούθει, ἐμεμύκει, ὀπώπει, ὀρώρει, ἐπεπόνθει, πεποίθει, or ἐπεπήγει appear, even though these forms did not survive. Chantraine states that the distribution of pluperfect with -ει is a clue that these pluperfects are newly created in Homer. The pluperfect forms with secondary endings are also found in Classical Greek (examples from Duhoux, *Le verbe grec ancien*, 438–39): διέφθαρτο (Lysias 13.20); ἐλέλυντο (Thucydides 4.47.1); διήρπαστο, ἐξεκέχυτο, κατεκέκαυτο (Xenophon, *Hellenica* 5.6.50). See Rau, "Greek and Proto-Indo-European," 184–86.

132. Chantraine, *Parfait grec*, 56–62, 70. Chantraine maintains that the middle endings entered into the system through the participle as well. However, Beek and Migliori criticize Chantraine's suggestion. See Beek and Migliori, "Active versus Middle Perfect," 71–106.

ruined" (cf. *Il.* 15.128 διέφθορας "you have lost your wits"), the plupf. (δι)εφθάρμην "was ruined" was built.[133]

The present-tense verb φθείρω had the perfect active form ἔφθορα whose meaning was "I am ruined." It also had the pluperfect middle ἐφθάρτο which facilitated the perfect middle ἔφθαρμαι.[134] Since the perfect middle ἔφθαρμαι was equivalent to the ancient perfect ἔφθορα in terms of subject-affectedness and resultative meaning, it replaced the archaic perfect active ἔφθορα. In the long run, the spread of the innovated perfect middle was successful.[135]

The archaic active perfects and the perfect middle forms coexisted for a time, but many of the archaic perfect forms were eliminated in Attic, with only a minority remaining until the Koine. Instead, a great number of middle perfect forms are observed in Classical Greek.[136] For example, perfect middle forms occur about 180 times in Herodotus[137] and approximately

---

133. Willi, *Origins of the Greek Verb*, 220.

134. Willi, *Origins of the Greek Verb*, 221; Haug, "From Resultatives to Anteriors," 299–302; Weiss, "Morphology," 117. The perfect πείθω also has the present middle form πείθομαι, along with a new perfect form πέπεισμαι. The middle perfect with an active pluperfect form does not seem to occur.

135. Willi, *Origins of the Greek Verb*, 220–21. For example, Sicking and Stork state that the middle-passive form σεσίγηται ("is silent") is found a lot more than the active forms. The perfect active forms σεσίγηκας (Aeschines, III. 218) and σεσίγηκεν are the only two occurrences before 300 BC (Leonidas, *Anth. Gr.* X.I. 3–4) (Sicking and Stork, *Two Studies*, 141).

136. Chantraine, *Parfait grec*, 117; Schwyzer, *Griechische Grammatik*, 779. Even in Homer, according to Chantraine, the middle perfect occurs more frequently than the perfect active (Chantraine, *Grammaire Homerique*, 431). Lavidas and Kulikov state, "The Perfect has a similar ratio of active and mediopassive in Homeric Greek, but the frequency of Perfect forms becomes higher for the mediopassive than active morphology in the following periods" (Lavidas and Kulikov, "Voice, Transitivity and Tense/Aspect," 306).

137. Chantraine lists the 180 perfect-middle forms in Herodotus (perfects occurring in the NT in bold): (ἀπ)ῆγμαι, ἀραίρημαι, ἀλήλεσμαι, (συν)ῆμμαι, (ὑπ)ῆργμαι, (ἀν)άρτημαι, ἠτίμωμαι, (περι)βέβλημαι, βέβαμμαι, βεβούλευμαι, **γεγένημαι**, (κατα)γέγραμμαι, δέδαρμαι, καταδέδεγμαι, δέδμημαι, **δέδεμαι**, δεδήλωμαι, δέδογμαι, **δεδούλωμαι, δέδομαι**, (κατ)είλιγμαι, ἐλήλαμαι, **εἴρημαι** (sixteen times), ἔργασμαι, ἔσσωμαι, ἔζευγμαι, (ἀπ)ῖγμαι, κεκάκωμαι, **κέκλημαι**, κατηγόρημαι, κέκλειμαι, **κέκριμαι, κέκρυμμαι**, ἔκτημαι, λέλεγμαι, λέλειμμαι, **μέμνημαι**, (δια)νένωμαι, οἴκημαι (ten times), οἰκοδόμημαι, ὤπλισμαι, ὄρμημαι (five times), **πέπαυμαι**, πεπείρημαι, πεπλάνημαι, πέπλεγμαι, **πεπλήρωμαι, πεποίημαι** (sixteen times), πεπόλισμαι (three times), πεπόρθημαι, σέσαγμαι, (παρ)εσκεύασμαι (twenty-two times), ἔσταλμαι (five times), ἐστέργημαι, ἐστράτευμαι, ἔστραμμαι, ἔστρωμαι, τέταγμαι (sixteen times), τέτραμμαι, τετύλωμαι, πεφύλαγμαι, κεχάραγμαι, κέχυμαι, κέχρησμαι, and κεχώρισμαι (Chantraine, *Parfait grec*, 87–88).

600 times in Thucydides (along with less than 400 perfect active forms).[138] The perfect middle forms were richly developed during the fifth century BC, according to Chantraine, as observed in Herodotus and Thucydides.[139] They frequently occur in Greek New Testament as well.

Last but not least, the innovation of the perfect middle is crucial. The widespread perfect-middle ἔφθαρμαι ("I am destroyed") triggered the transitive active meaning of ἔφθορα ("have destroyed"). This ancient form was later replaced with ἔφθαρκα ("have destroyed").[140] Willi points out,

> Moreover, the establishment of the middle perfect then allowed (a) the use of act. (δι)έφθορα in the transitive sense "have destroyed", corresponding to pres. (δια)φθείρω, (b) the production of perfect paradigms to denominal and other verbs previously lacking a perfect (e.g., τετίμημαι "am honored", to τιμάω; πεφόβημαι "am frightened" to φοβέομαι "be(come) scared"), and (c) the creation of secondary active pluperfects.[141]

Willi's point is that the opposition between the active and middle forms facilitated the employment of the perfect active in transitive contexts.

In conclusion, Sicking and Stork provide a good summary: "If we provisionally take it that Perfect verb forms basically *describe a present State*

---

138. Chantraine, *Parfait grec*, 89–90. From Thucydides, Chantraine illustrates the perfect-middle attested in Homer (perfects occurring in the NT in bold): ἧμμαι, **βέβλημαι, δέδεμαι,** δέδομαι, **εἴρημαι,** κεκάκωμαι, κέκλιμαι, **κέκριμαι, κέκρυμμαι,** ἔκτημαι, λέλειμμαι, **μέμνημαι, πέπαυμαι,** πεπείραμαι, **πεποίημαι,** πέπυσμαι, ἔστρωμαι, τετέλεσμαι, τετίμημαι, τέτραμμαι, and πεφόβημαι. Then, he lists the perfect-middle forms (from Thucydides) not attested in Homer: ἤγγελμαι, ἦγμαι, ἠδίκημαι, ἤρημαι, ἦρμαι, ἦσθημαι, ἤλλαγμαι, ἠλλοίωμαι, ἡμάρτημαι, ἡμάτωμαι, ἠμέλημαι, ἠνάγκασμαι, (ὑπ)ήργμαι, ἤρτημαι, ἤρτυμαι, ἠτοίμασμαι, (ἀπ)ήχθημαι, βεβούλευμαι, γέγευμαι, **γεγένημαι, ἔγνωσμαι,** δεδήλωμαι, δεδιήτημαι, δέδογμαι, **δεδούλωμαι,** δέδραμαι, ἐγήγερμαι, εἴθισμαι, εἴλκυσμαι, εἴργασμαι, ἠρέθισμαι, εὐτύχημαι, ἐζώγρημαι, ἥσσημαι, (ἐν)τεθύμημαι, τεθωράκισμαι, ἵδρυμαι, ἵερωμαι, (ἀφ)ῖγμαι, κέκαυμαι, κεκήρυγμαι, κεκοινολόγημαι, κεκόμισμαι, κεκόσμημαι, κεκύκλωμαι, κεκώλυμαι, εἴλημμαι, μεμάχημαι, μεμήνυμαι, μεμίασμαι, μεμόνωμαι, νεναυπήγημαι, νενέμημαι, νένημαι, **νενίκημαι,** νενόημαι, **ἀνέῳγμαι,** ᾤκημαι, ᾤκισμαι, ᾠκοδόμημαι, ὠνόμασμαι, ὥπλισμαι, ὤργημαι, ὥρμημαι, παραβέβαμαι, πεπαίδνισμαι, πέπεμμαι, πέπληγμαι, **πεπλήρωμαι,** πεπολέμημαι, πεπολιόρκημαι, πεπόρισμαι, πέπραγμαι, ἔρρωμαι, ἐσκέδασμαι, ἔσκεμμαι, (παρ)εσκεύασμαι, ἐσκήνημαι, ἔσπασμαι, ἔσπαρμαι, ἔσπεισμαι, ἔσπεισμαι, ἔσταλμαι, ἐστέρημαι, ἐστράτευμαι, ἐστρατοπέδευμαι, ἔστραμμαι, ἔσφαλμαι, τεταλαιπώρημαι, τετάραγμαι, τέταγμαι, τετείχισμαι, τετέλεσμαι, τετιμώρημαι, τετραυμάτισμαι, τέθραμμαι, ἔφθαρμαι, πέφρυγμαι, κέχωσμαι, ἐψήφισμαι, and (ἀπ)έωσμαι.

139. Chantraine, *Parfait grec*, 105. See Drinka, "Evolution of Grammar," 124.

140. Haug, "From Resultatives to Anteriors," 302. Chapter 3 will analyze this issue in more detail.

141. Willi, *Origins of the Greek Verb*, 221–22. Furthermore, Willi asserts that this transition would have triggered the innovation of the active pluperfect.

of the (referent of the) *subject* and if, when doing so, we realize that States characteristically *lack the feature 'control'*, this would explain the overlap of the semantic fields of Perfect and Middle."[142] Although the perfect shows more nuances in the NT, this statement seems to work for the ancient Greek perfect at least.

Perfect Middle/Passive in the Greek New Testament

Perfect middle forms denote almost the same meaning as the ancient perfect active, so that they became widespread by replacing the archaic perfects. Numerous occurrences of the middle perfect are found in Classical Greek literatures, such as in Herodotus and Thucydides. A large number of middle (passive) perfect forms also appear in the Greek New Testament.[143] Many of them show the same nuance as the middle perfects representing the resultative-stative in Homer and Classical Greek period. Chantraine states the middle perfect plays a very important role in the Greek New Testament, saying that perfect middle forms appear almost twice as often as the perfect active forms in Luke and 1 Corinthians, for example.[144]

In Matthew 8:6 (κύριε, ὁ παῖς μου βέβληται "Lord, my servant *is lying*"), for example, the perfect conveys a present state with the past event implied. More examples are as follows:

[Luke 13:12] ἰδὼν δὲ αὐτὴν ὁ Ἰησοῦς προσεφώνησεν καὶ εἶπεν αὐτῇ· γύναι, **ἀπολέλυσαι** τῆς ἀσθενείας σου,
When Jesus saw her, he called her over and said to her, "Woman, you *are freed* from your disability."[145]

---

142. Sicking and Stork, *Two Studies*, 137; emphasis original.

143. From Homeric era the perfect middle constitutes a passive meaning (Monro, *Homeric Dialect*, 9–10; Chantraine, *Parfait grec*, 60–70, 87–98, 129; Allan, "Middle Voice," 33, 41; Porter, *Verbal Aspect*, 274). I will follow Sicking and Stork who employ the term "Middle-Passive." This term represents either middle or passive in interpretation (Sicking and Stork, *Two Studies*, 130); Madariaga, "Development of Indo-European Middle-passive Verbs," 149–78.

144. Chantraine, *Parfait grec*, 218–22. Gospel of Luke includes eighty-seven perfect middle and fifty-five perfect active forms, and 1 Corinthians contains forty-four perfect middle and twenty perfect active forms (including non-indicative).

145. The English Bibles translate this verb as present: ESV, "you are freed from your disability"; NASB, "you are freed from your sickness"; NIV, "you are set free from your infirmity"; and KJV, "thou art loosed from thine infirmity."

[2 Cor 5:11] Εἰδότες οὖν τὸν φόβον τοῦ κυρίου ἀνθρώπους πείθομεν, θεῷ δὲ **πεφανερώμεθα**· ἐλπίζω δὲ καὶ ἐν ταῖς συνειδήσεσιν ὑμῶν πεφανερῶσθαι.

Therefore, knowing the fear of the Lord, we persuade me. We *are made manifest* to God; and I hope that we are manifest also in your consciences.[146]

The middle/passive perfects above deliver a resultative-stative nuance. Haspelmath also notes that these perfects show the states resulting from previous events.[147]

Πεπλήρωται

One of the plainest examples of perfect middle-passive with a resultative-stative sense in the NT is πεπλήρωται ("it has been fulfilled"). The verb πληρόω occurs many times in the NT especially in reference to the fulfillment of time or prophecies. The perfect middle-passive πεπλήρωται appears:[148]

[Mark 1:15] **πεπλήρωται** ὁ καιρὸς καὶ ἤγγικεν ἡ βασιλεία τοῦ θεοῦ.
The time is fulfilled, and the kingdom of God is at hand.

[John 7:8] ὅτι ὁ ἐμὸς καιρὸς οὔπω **πεπλήρωται**.
For my time has not yet been fulfilled.

[LXX Gen 29:21] ἀπόδος τὴν γυναῖκά μου **πεπλήρωται** γὰρ αἱ ἡμέραι μου.
Give me my wife, for my time is completed.

The nuance of πεπλήρωται is the present state with the implication of past events. There is not much difference in the Septuagint example from Genesis with respect to this nuance.

---

146. Similarly, see Heb 9:26, εἰς ἀθέτησιν [τῆς] ἁμαρτίας διὰ τῆς θυσίας αὐτοῦ πεφανέρωται ("He has been manifested to put away sin by the sacrifice of Himself"); and 1 Thess 2:4, ἀλλὰ καθὼς δεδοκιμάσμεθα ὑπὸ τοῦ θεοῦ ("but just as we have been approved by God").

147. Haspelmath, "From Resultative to Perfect," 207–8.

148. More passages are: John 3:29, αὕτη οὖν ἡ χαρὰ ἡ ἐμὴ πεπλήρωται ("joy of mine is now complete"); 2 Cor 7:4, πεπλήρωμαι τῇ παρακλήσει ("I am filled with comfort"); Gal 5:14, ὁ γὰρ πᾶς νόμος ἐν ἑνὶ λόγῳ πεπλήρωται ("For the whole law is fulfilled in one word"); Phil 4:18, πεπλήρωμαι δεξάμενος παρὰ Ἐπαφροδίτου τὰ παρ' ὑμῶν ("I am well supplied, having received from Epaphroditus the gifts you sent"); and LXX Gen 15:16, οὔπω γὰρ ἀναπεπλήρωνται αἱ ἁμαρτίαι τῶν Αμορραίων ἕως τοῦ νῦν ("for the iniquity of the Amorites is not yet complete").

Perfect middle/passive forms in the NT

Due to the numerous occurrences of the perfect middle-passive forms in the Greek New Testament, listing them is a helpful way to introduce these forms. Many perfect middle/passive forms in the NT express resultative-stative.[149]

[Mark 11:21] ῥαββί, ἴδε ἡ συκῆ ἣν κατηράσω **ἐξήρανται**.
Rabbi, behold, the fig tree which you cursed has withered.

[Mark 16:4] καὶ ἀναβλέψασαι θεωροῦσιν ὅτι **ἀποκεκύλισται** ὁ λίθος.
And looking up, they saw that the stone was [had been] rolled away.[150]

[Luke 4:6] ὅτι ἐμοὶ **παραδέδοται** καὶ ᾧ ἐὰν θέλω δίδωμι αὐτήν.
For it has been delivered to me [Satan] and I give it to whom I will.[151]

---

149. More passages are (perfects in bold): Mark 5:29, καὶ ἔγνω τῷ σώματι ὅτι **ἴαται** ἀπὸ τῆς μάστιγος ("and she felt in her body that she has been healed"); Mark 15:47, ἐθεώρουν ποῦ **τέθειται** ("[they] saw where he was [has been] laid"); John 7:47, **πεπλάνησθε**; ("Have you also been deceived?"); Acts 10:45, καὶ ἐξέστησαν οἱ ἐκ περιτομῆς πιστοὶ ὅσοι συνῆλθαν τῷ Πέτρῳ ὅτι καὶ ἐπὶ τὰ ἔθνη ἡ δωρεὰ τοῦ ἁγίου πνεύματος **ἐκκέχυται** ("And the believers among the circumcised who had come with Peter were amazed, because the gift of the Holy Spirit has been poured out"); Acts 21:24, καὶ γνώσονται πάντες ὅτι ὧν **κατήχηνται** περὶ σοῦ οὐδέν ἐστιν ("and all will know that there is nothing to the things which they have been told about you"); Rom 5:5, ἡ ἀγάπη τοῦ θεοῦ **ἐκκέχυται** ἐν ταῖς καρδίαις ἡμῶν ("God's love has been poured into our hearts"); Rom 6:7, ὁ γὰρ ἀποθανὼν **δεδικαίωται** ἀπὸ τῆς ἁμαρτίας ("For the one who died has been justified from sin"); 1 Cor 4:4, οὐδὲν γὰρ ἐμαυτῷ σύνοιδα, ἀλλ' οὐκ ἐν τούτῳ **δεδικαίωμαι**, ὁ δὲ ἀνακρίνων με κύριός ἐστιν ("For I am not aware of anything against myself, but I am not thereby acquitted. It is the Lord who judges me"); 1 Cor 7:27, **δέδεσαι** γυναικί, μὴ ζήτει λύσιν· **λέλυσαι** ἀπὸ γυναικός ("Are you bound to a wife? Do not seek to be free. Are you free from a wife?"); 2 Cor 9:2, Ἀχαΐα **παρασκεύασται** ἀπὸ πέρυσι ("Achaia has been ready since last year"); 2 Cor 9:7, ἕκαστος καθὼς **προῄρηται** τῇ καρδίᾳ ("Each one must give as he has decided in his heart"); Col 4:3, ἵνα ὁ θεὸς ἀνοίξῃ ἡμῖν θύραν τοῦ λόγου λαλῆσαι τὸ μυστήριον τοῦ Χριστοῦ, δι' ὃ καὶ **δέδεμαι** ("that God may open to us a door for the word, to declare the mystery of Christ, for which I have also been imprisoned"); 1 Thess 1:8, ἀφ' ὑμῶν γὰρ **ἐξήχηται** ὁ λόγος τοῦ κυρίου οὐ μόνον ἐν τῇ Μακεδονίᾳ καὶ ἐν τῇ Ἀχαΐᾳ, ἀλλ' ἐν παντὶ τόπῳ ἡ πίστις ὑμῶν ἡ πρὸς τὸν θεὸν ἐξελήλυθεν ("For the word of the Lord has sounded forth from you, not only in Macedonia and Achaia, but also in every place your faith toward God has gone forth"); 2 Pet 2:17, Jude 1:13, οἷς ὁ ζόφος τοῦ σκότους εἰς αἰῶνα **τετήρηται** ("for whom the gloom of utter darkness has been reserved forever"); and 1 John 2:29, 3:9, 4:7, 5:1 **γεγέννηται** ("has been born").

150. Cf. Luke 21:5, ὅτι λίθοις καλοῖς καὶ ἀναθήμασιν κεκόσμηται ("how it was adorned with noble stones").

151. More examples are: Matt 13:11, ὅτι ὑμῖν δέδοται γνῶναι τὰ μυστήρια τῆς

[John 8:4] διδάσκαλε, αὕτη ἡ γυνὴ **κατείληπται** ἐπ᾽ αὐτοφώρῳ μοιχευομένη.

Teacher, this woman has been caught in the act of adultery.

[John 11:11–12] Λάζαρος ὁ φίλος ἡμῶν **κεκοίμηται**· ἀλλὰ πορεύομαι ἵνα ἐξυπνίσω αὐτόν. εἶπαν οὖν οἱ μαθηταὶ αὐτῷ· κύριε, εἰ **κεκοίμηται** σωθήσεται.

"Our friend Lazarus has fallen asleep, but I go to awaken him." The disciples said to him, "Lord, if he has fallen asleep, he will recover."

[John 19:28, 30] Μετὰ τοῦτο εἰδὼς ὁ Ἰησοῦς ὅτι ἤδη πάντα **τετέλεσται**. . . . ὅτε οὖν ἔλαβεν τὸ ὄξος ὁ Ἰησοῦς εἶπεν· **τετέλεσται**,

After this, Jesus, knowing that it has been already finished. . . . When Jesus had received the sour wine, he said, "It is finished!"[152]

[Luke 12:7] ἀλλὰ καὶ αἱ τρίχες τῆς κεφαλῆς ὑμῶν πᾶσαι **ἠρίθμηνται**.

But even the hairs of your head are all numbered.

[Acts 22:10] κἀκεῖ σοι λαληθήσεται περὶ πάντων ὧν **τέτακταί** σοι ποιῆσαι.

And there you will be told all that is appointed for you to do.

βασιλείας τῶν οὐρανῶν, ἐκείνοις δὲ οὐ δέδοται ("To you it has been given to know the secrets of the kingdom of heaven, but to them it has not been given"); Matt 19:11, οὐ πάντες χωροῦσιν τὸν λόγον [τοῦτον] ἀλλ᾽ οἷς δέδοται ("Not everyone can receive this saying, but only those whom it is given"); Mark 4:11, ὑμῖν τὸ μυστήριον δέδοται τῆς βασιλείας του θεοῦ ("To you has been given the secret of the kingdom of God"); Luke 8:10, ὑμῖν δέδοται γνῶναι τὰ μυστήρια τῆς βασιλείας τοῦ θεοῦ ("To you it has been given to know the secrets of the kingdom of God"); and 1 Cor 11:15, ὅτι ἡ κόμη ἀντὶ περιβολαίου δέδοται [αὐτῇ] ("For her hair is given to her").

152. Similarly, 1 John 2:5, ὃς δ᾽ ἂν τηρῇ αὐτοῦ τὸν λόγον, ἀληθῶς ἐν τούτῳ ἡ ἀγάπη τοῦ θεοῦ τετελείωται ("but whoever keeps his word, in him truly the love of God is perfected"); 1 John 4:17–18, Ἐν τούτῳ τετελείωται ἡ ἀγάπη μεθ᾽ ἡμῶν, ἵνα παρρησίαν ἔχωμεν ἐν τῇ ἡμέρᾳ τῆς κρίσεως . . . ὁ δὲ φοβούμενος οὐ τετελείωται ἐν τῇ ἀγάπῃ ("By this, love is perfected with us, so that we may have confidence for the day of judgment . . . and whoever fears has not been perfected in love"); Phil 3:12, ἔλαβον ἢ ἤδη τετελείωμαι, διώκω δὲ ("Not that I have already obtained this or am already perfect, but I press on to make it my own"). See Ignatius, *Smyrnaeans* 7.2, προσέχειν δὲ τοῖς προφήταις, ἐξαιρέτως δὲ τῷ εὐαγγελίῳ, ἐν ᾧ τὸ πάθος ἡμῖν δεδήλωται καὶ ἡ ἀνάστασις τετελείωται ("Do pay attention, however, to the prophets and especially to the gospel, in which the passion has been made clear to us and the resurrection has been accomplished") (Holmes, *Apostolic Fathers*, 254–55).

[Luke 11:7] ἤδη ἡ θύρα **κέκλεισται** καὶ τὰ παιδία μου μετ᾽ ἐμοῦ εἰς τὴν κοίτην εἰσίν.

The door is already shut and my children are with me in bed.

[John 17:10] καὶ τὰ ἐμὰ πάντα σά ἐστιν καὶ τὰ σὰ ἐμά καὶ **δεδόξασμαι** ἐν αὐτοῖς.

All mine are yours, and yours are mine, and I am glorified in them.[153]

[Gal 2:7] ἀλλὰ τοὐναντίον ἰδόντες ὅτι **πεπίστευμαι** τὸ εὐαγγέλιον τῆς ἀκροβυστίας

But on the contrary, seeing that I am entrusted with the gospel to the uncircumcised[154]

[Gal 2:19] ἐγὼ γὰρ διὰ νόμου νόμῳ ἀπέθανον, ἵνα θεῷ ζήσω. Χριστῷ **συνεσταύρωμαι**.

For through the law I died to the law, so that I might live to God. I have been crucified with Christ.[155]

Surprisingly, the perfect middles above all show resultative-stative nuances. They pay attention to the present state while implying preceding events. Some of the perfect middle forms express a nuance almost like the present tense.

The perfect middle, representing a resulting state from a prior event, may overlap with a present tense verb in terms of delivering a nuance of a present state.[156] For example,

---

153. English Bibles show a variety of translations: ESV ("I am glorified"); NASB ("I have been glorified"); NIV ("And glory has come to me"); and KJV ("I am glorified"). Similarly, 2 Cor 3:10 says: οὐ δεδόξασται τὸ δεδοξασμένον ἐν τούτῳ τῷ μέρει ("what once had glory has come to have no glory at all").

154. Similarly, 1 Cor 9:17 says: εἰ γὰρ ἑκὼν τοῦτο πράσσω, μισθὸν ἔχω· εἰ δὲ ἄκων, οἰκονομίαν πεπίστευμαι ("For if I do this of my own will, I have a reward, but if not of my own will, I am still entrusted with a stewardship").

155. See Gal 6:14, δι᾽ οὗ ἐμοὶ κόσμος ἐσταύρωται ("the world has been crucified to me"); and Gal 5:11, ἄρα κατήργηται τὸ σκάνδαλον τοῦ σταυροῦ ("In that case the offense of the cross has been removed").

156. Sicking and Stork show a case where the present tense is possibly exchanged with the perfect-middle in Plato (Sicking and Stork, *Two Studies*, 127): *Cratylus* 403b, ὅτι τε γάρ, ἐπειδὰν ἅπαξ τις ἡμῶν ἀποθάνῃ, ἀεὶ ἐκεῖ ἐστιν, φοβοῦνται, καὶ ὅτι ἡ ψυχὴ γυμνὴ τοῦ σώματος παρ᾽ ἐκείνοι ἀπέρχεται, καὶ τοῦτο πεφόβηνται ("They are afraid because when we are once dead we remain in his realm for ever, and they are also terrified because the soul goes to him without the covering of the body"). In *Cratylus*, a present verb φοβέω occurs and then a perfect middle-passive form πεφόβηνται. Plato intentionally utilizes two verbal forms to express slightly different nuances.

[John 12:27] Νῦν ἡ ψυχή μου τετάρακται, καὶ τί εἴπω; πάτερ σῶσόν με ἐκ τῆς ὥρας ταύτης;
Now *is* my soul *troubled*; and what shall I say, "Father, save me from this hour?"

In this verse, the perfect middle/passive τετάρακται is similar to a present tense verb, appearing with the adverb νῦν indicating the present time.

In spite of this occasional overlap, the present and the perfect middle/passive are distinct.

[James 3:7] πᾶσα γὰρ φύσις θηρίων τε καὶ πετεινῶν, ἑρπετῶν τε καὶ ἐναλίων δαμάζεται καὶ **δεδάμασται** τῇ φύσει τῇ ἀνθρωπίνῃ,
For every species of beasts and birds, of reptiles and sea creatures, is tamed, and *has been tamed* by the human race.

The present tense describes a general statement while the perfect middle/passive denotes a custom that has been practiced from the past until now. Sicking and Stork differentiate the perfect from the present in that the former denotes an inalterable and permanent event while the latter a changeable state.[157] The next section will address this issue.

Also, the perfect middle/passive occurs with the aorist. The difficulty in Colossians 1:16 and 3:3 exists in that the aorist and the perfect are juxtaposed as shown below:

[Col 1:16] ὅτι ἐν αὐτῷ ἐκτίσθη τὰ πάντα ἐν τοῖς οὐρανοῖς καὶ ἐπὶ τῆς γῆς, τὰ ὁρατὰ καὶ τὰ ἀόρατα, εἴτε θρόνοι εἴτε κυριότητες εἴτε ἀρχαὶ εἴτε ἐξουσίαι· τὰ πάντα δι' αὐτοῦ καὶ εἰς αὐτὸν ἔκτισται.
For by him all things were created, in heaven and on earth, visible and invisible, whether thrones or dominions or rulers or authorities—all things *were created* through him and for him.

Fanning regards ἔκτισται as "perfect with accomplishments." Fanning defines the category "accomplishment" as the *result* of the verbal action rather than its activity.[158] Hatina raises the question why the author employs two different verbal forms, the aorist and the perfect, in order to express the same creation by God. Hatina argues that Paul utilizes one perfect form to

---

157. Sicking and Stork, *Two Studies*, 139–41.

158. Fanning, *Verbal Aspect*, 153–54. While agreeing with Fanning's description of the perfect as a state of affairs, Hatina doubts any temporal connotation that is grammatically inherent in Greek verbs (Hatina, "Perfect Tense-Form," 231).

highlight it as a frontground, instead of employing both aorist forms or both perfect forms.[159]

Clearly, the aorist ἐκτίσθη denotes a punctiliar creative work of God while the perfect middle/passive ἔκτισται seems to indicate a general result of the creation for God. Another example is,

> [Col 3:3] ἀπεθάνετε γὰρ καὶ ἡ ζωὴ ὑμῶν κέκρυπται σὺν τῷ Χριστῷ ἐν τῷ θεῷ.
> For you have died, and your life *is hidden* with Christ in God.

In Colossians 3:3, the different nuance between the aorist and the perfect is prominent. The aorist describes a punctiliar event that occurred once, "died." The perfect middle/passive κέκρυπται denotes a resultative-stative.

Γέγραπται

The perfect γέγραπται occurs frequently in the NT (sixty-five occurrences).[160] When the apostles or the writers quote from the OT, they often employ this expression of the perfect, "it is written . . ." Many regard γέγραπται as resultative-stative. Chantraine notes that the middle-passive perfect expresses a present state with γέγραπται, "the state of a thing written out."[161] Similarly, McKay states that γέγραπται denotes a state of affairs "it is written."[162] Bentein says that γέγραπται represents the resultative perfect which focuses more on the state rather than anteriority.[163]

Since its occurrences are numerous, every usage cannot be cited.

> [Matt 2:5] ἐν Βηθλέεμ τῆς Ἰουδαίας· οὕτως γὰρ γέγραπται διὰ τοῦ προφήτου.
> In Bethlehem of Judea, for so it is written by the prophet.

---

159. Hatina, "Perfect Tense-Form," 232.

160. The number excludes the compound verb ἐγγέγραπται (from ἐγγράφω, "your names are written in heaven") in Luke 10:20.

161. Chantraine, *Parfait grec*, 17, 87.

162. McKay, "Ancient Greek Perfect," 9.

163. Bentein notes that the term "resultative perfect" he employs is not the same as the "resultative perfect" of Wackernagel and Chantraine. While Wackernagel and Chantraine employ this term for stressing the state of the object, Bentein accepts the definition of "resultative" in cross-linguistics studies (Bentein, "Periphrastic Perfect," 177n14; Bentein, *Verbal Periphrasis*, 38n177; Bentein, "Perfect," 47).

> [LXX 2 Kings 23:21] ποιήσατε τὸ πασχα τῷ κυρίῳ θεῷ ἡμῶν καθὼς γέγραπται ἐπὶ βιβλίου τῆς διαθήκης ταύτης
> Keep the Passover to the Lord your God, as it is written in this book of the covenant.[164]
>
> [Thucydides, *Peloponnesian War* 5.24.2] ταῦτα δὲ τὰ δέκα ἔτη ὁ πρῶτος πόλεμος ξυνεχῶς γενόμενος γέγραπται.
> During these ten years the first war, of which the history has now been written, was waged continuously.[165]

Due to the widespread employment of γέγραπται ("has been written") its original resultative meaning may have become reduced to a present state in the end, like its usages in the NT.[166] In Thucydides, however, γέγραπται does not convey its typical nuance in the NT, "it is written" but preserves its resultative sense.

Some scholars see γέγραπται as intensive.[167] However, it is unlikely because it is difficult to argue that every quotation of the Scriptures contains an intensive notion.

Ἐγήγερται

The perfect ἐγήγερται is worthy to be examined. The perfect ἐγήγερται expresses a current result from the past.[168]

> [1 Cor 15:3–5] ὅτι Χριστὸς ἀπέθανεν ὑπὲρ τῶν ἁμαρτιῶν ἡμῶν κατὰ τὰς γραφὰς καὶ ὅτι ἐτάφη καὶ ὅτι **ἐγήγερται** τῇ ἡμέρᾳ τῇ τρίτῃ κατὰ τὰς γραφὰς καὶ ὅτι ὤφθη Κηφᾷ
> Christ died for our sins according to the Scriptures; and that he was buried, that he was raised on the third

---

164. Similar usages are found in 1 Kgs 8:53; 11:41; 20:11; 22:39; 2 Kgs 8:23; 14:6; etc.

165. This example is from Rijksbaron, *Syntax and Semantics*, 36–37.

166. See Allan, "Tense and Aspect," 103–11; contra Willi, *Origins of the Greek Verb*, 225–44.

167. Wallace, *Beyond the Basics*, 576; Köstenberger et al., *Going Deeper*, 298; Campbell, *Indicative Mood*, 208–9; Campbell notes that Luke's frequent use of γέγραπται indicates the vitality of the scripture quotation, i.e., heightened proximity. It is possible that some scripture citations are intensified, but it is unlikely that every case of its usage retains an intensive nuance. Similarly, not all of the 210 occurrences of οἶδα express an intensive nuance.

168. See Matt 11:11, οὐκ ἐγήγερται ἐν γεννητοῖς γυναικῶν μείζων Ἰωάννου τοῦ βαπτιστοῦ ("There has arisen no one greater than John the Baptist"); and Mark 6:14, Ἰωάννης ὁ βαπτίζων ἐγήγερται ἐκ νεκρῶν ("John the Baptist has been raised from the dead").

day in accordance with the Scriptures, and that he appeared to Cephas, then to the twelve.

Many commentators say that the perfect ἐγήγερται ("has been raised") indicates the present state of the risen Christ after he was raised.[169] Porter objects to the traditional interpretation, "Christ was raised and continues in result of being raised." Porter says that this interpretation might provide a good theology but not a healthy exegetical insight.[170] In 1 Corinthians 15 ἐγήγερται appears seven times, all of which indicate the continuing effect of the resurrection.[171]

Ἀνέῳγμαι

Chantraine notes that perhaps ἀνέῳγα is an ancient perfect form. In Attic, its perfect-middle form ἀνέῳγμαι occurs with a passive sense ("I am open").[172] This form occurs in the NT:

[1 Cor 16:9] θύρα γάρ μοι ἀνέῳγεν μεγάλη καὶ ἐνεργής, καὶ ἀντικείμενοι πολλοί.

For a wide door for effective work has opened to me, and there are many adversaries.

[2 Cor 6:11] Τὸ στόμα ἡμῶν ἀνέῳγεν πρὸς ὑμας, Κορίνθιοι, ἡ καρδία ἡμῶν πεπλάτυνται.

Our mouth is open to you, Corinthians, our heart is enlarged.

---

169. Grosheide, *First Epistle to the Corinthians*, 350; McKay, *New Syntax*, 32, 50; Fanning, *Verbal Aspect*, 301–2; Lockwood, *1 Corinthians*, 551; Schrage, *Brief an die Korinther*, 38; Garland, *1 Corinthians*, 686; Burton, *Syntax*, 41; Chantraine, *Parfait grec*, 234. Chantraine states that ἐγήγερται denotes a resultant state of the past event. Wallace considers ἐγήγερται as intensive perfect. However, this view is not inevitable (Wallace, *Beyond the Basics*, 576).

170. Porter, *Verbal Aspect*, 262. Porter maintains that the temporal deixis (τῇ ἡμέρᾳ τῇ τρίτῃ "on the third day") "specifically limits the temporal implicature to the state of raisedness that was in existence three days after the burial."

171. At the end of the Gospels, the aorist is employed (Matt 28:7, καὶ πορευθεῖσαι εἴπατε τοῖς μαθηταῖς αὐτοῦ ὅτι ἠγέρθη ἀπὸ τῶν νεκρῶν, "Then go quickly and tell his disciples that he has risen from the dead"; Mark 16:6, μὴ ἐκθαμβεῖσθε· Ἰησοῦν ζητεῖτε τὸν Ναζαρηνὸν τὸν ἐσταυρωμένον· ἠγέρθη, οὐκ ἔστιν ὧδε, "Do not be alarmed. You seek Jesus of Nazareth, who was crucified. He has risen; he is not here"; Luke 24:34, ὄντως ἠγέρθη ὁ κύριος καὶ ὤφθη Σίμωνι, "The Lord has risen indeed, and has appeared to Simon!").

172. Chantraine, *Parfait grec*, 38, 216.

The perfect ἀνέῳγμαι is an example of resultative-stative. In 2 Corinthians 6:11 especially, two perfects are employed to denote a resultative-stative nuance.

More examples from the NT

More examples of the perfect middle/passive in the NT are:

> [Heb 3:3] πλείονος γὰρ οὗτος δόξης παρὰ Μωϋσῆν **ἠξίωται**, καθ' ὅσον πλείονα τιμὴν ἔχει τοῦ οἴκου ὁ κατασκευάσας αὐτόν.
>
> For he [Jesus] has been counted worthy of more glory than Moses, by just so much as the builder of the house has more honor than the house.

> [2 Cor 7:13] διὰ τοῦτο **παρακεκλήμεθα**. Ἐπὶ δὲ τῇ παρακλήσει ἡμῶν περισσοτέρως μᾶλλον ἐχάρημεν ἐπὶ τῇ χαρᾷ Τίτου, ὅτι **ἀναπέπαυται** τὸ πνεῦμα αὐτοῦ ἀπὸ πάντων ὑμῶν.
>
> For this reason we are [have been] comforted. And besides our comfort, we rejoiced even much more for the joy of Titus, because his spirit has been refreshed by you all.[173]

> [Rom 3:21, 4:14] δικαιοσύνη θεοῦ **πεφανέρωται**. . . . **κεκένωται** ἡ πίστις καὶ **κατήργηται** ἡ ἐπαγγελία.
>
> But now the righteousness of God has been manifested. . . . faith is null and the promise is void.

> [John 3:18] ὁ δὲ μὴ πιστεύων ἤδη **κέκριται**, ὅτι μὴ **πεπίστευκεν** εἰς τὸ ὄνομα τοῦ μονογενοῦς υἱοῦ τοῦ θεοῦ.
>
> He who does not believe has been judged already, because he has not believed in the name of the only begotten Son of God.[174]

---

173. Similarly, Phlm 1:7 is: ὅτι τὰ σπλάγχνα τῶν ἁγίων ἀναπέπαυται διὰ σοῦ, ἀδελφέ ("because the hearts of the saints have been refreshed through you, brother"). Aubrey states that causative verb ἀναπαύω ("cause to rest") should take middle form in order to express a resultative nuance (Aubrey, "Greek Perfect," 125–26); 1 Pet 4:1, ὅτι ὁ παθὼν σαρκὶ πέπαυται ἁμαρτίας ("for whoever has suffered in the flesh has ceased from sin"). The perfect πέπαυμαι occurs two times in Aeschylus, three times in Sophocles, three times in Thucydides, and two times in Lysias (Sicking and Stork, *Two Studies*, 190, 198, 229, 237).

174. See John 16:11, ὅτι ὁ ἄρχων τοῦ κόσμου τούτου κέκριται ("because the ruler of this world has been judged"); and Rom 14:23, ὁ δὲ διακρινόμενος ἐὰν φάγῃ κατακέκριται ("But whoever has doubts is condemned if he eats").

[Titus 1:15] ἀλλὰ μεμίανται αὐτῶν καὶ ὁ νοῦς καὶ ἡ συνείδησις.
But both their minds and their consciences are defiled.

[James 5:3] ὁ χρυσὸς ὑμῶν καὶ ὁ ἄργυρος **κατίωται** καὶ ὁ ἰὸς αὐτῶν εἰς μαρτύριον ὑμῖν ἔσται.
Your gold and silver have corroded, and their corrosion will be evidence against you.

The middle/passive perfects above show resultative-stative. Notably, the usage of ἤδη ("already") in John 3:18 indicates the result, that the judgment has already occurred. In sum, the perfect middle/passive mainly occurs for a nuance of a present state with implied past.[175]

Γέγονα (γεγένημαι)

The old perfect γέγονα (root *ĝe-ĝonh₁-e) occurs forty-five times in the NT, meaning "exists, has come into being."[176] Chantraine points out that γέγονα, a debris of the ancient system, remains for a long time—until the Koine period.[177] The perfect middle form γεγένημαι is found in Attic, but the ancient form γέγονα still occurs very frequently. According to Chantraine, γέγονα occurs more frequently than γεγένημαι in Classical Greek literature (Herodotus, Xenophon, Aristophanes, Demosthenes, and Aeschines).[178]

---

175. In the Apostolic Fathers, the perfect middles express resultative-stative (perfects in bold). See Ignatius, *Magnesians* 12.1, Ὀναίμην ὑμῶν κατὰ πάντα, ἐάνπερ ἄξιος ὦ. εἰ γὰρ καὶ **δέδεμαι** ("May I have joy in you in every respect—if, that is, I am worthy. For even though I am in chains"); Ignatius, *Trallians* 5.2, καὶ γὰρ ἐγώ, οὐ καθότι **δέδεμαι** ("For myself, though I am in chains"); Ignatius, *Trallians* 10.1, ἐγὼ τί **δέδεμαι**; ("why am I in chains?"); Ignatius, *Romans* 5.1, ἐν δὲ τοῖς ἀδικήμασιν αὐτῶν μᾶλλον μαθητεύομαι· ἀλλ' οὐ παρὰ τοῦτο **δεδικαίωμαι** ("Yet because of their mistreatment I am becoming more of a disciple; nevertheless I am not thereby justified"); *The Shepherd of Hermas* 11.5, ἐπηρώτησα αὐτήν· Διοτί ὁ πύργος ἐπὶ ὑδάτων **ᾠκοδόμηται**, κυρία; Εἶπά σοι, φησίν, καὶ τὸ πρότερον, καὶ ἐκζητεῖς ἐπιμελῶς· ἐκζητῶν οὖν εὑρίσκεις τὴν ἀλήθειαν. διατί οὖν ἐπὶ ὑδάτων **ᾠκοδόμηται** ὁ πύργος, ἄκουε· ὅτι ἡ ζωὴ ὑμῶν διὰ ὕδατος ἐσώθη καὶ σωθήσεται. **τεθεμελίωται** δὲ ὁ πύργος τῷ ῥήματι τοῦ παντοκράτορος καὶ ἐνδόξου ὀνόματος ("I asked her, 'Why is the power built upon water, lady?' 'As I said to you before,' she said, 'you do seek diligently. By seeking, therefore, you are finding the truth. Hear, then, why the tower is built upon water: it is because your life was saved and will be saved through water. But the tower has been set on a foundation by the word of the almighty and glorious name'") (Holmes, *Apostolic Fathers*, 210–11, 218–21, 230–31, 476–77).

176. Moulton, *Prolegomena*, 146; Willi, *Origins of the Greek Verb*, 183.

177. Chantraine, *Parfait grec*, 85, 106, 110, 196.

178. Chantraine, *Parfait grec*, 79, 110–12, 195–97. Only in archaic prose of Thucydides γεγένημαι always appears (twenty-nine times), except one occurrence of γέγονα. Sicking and Stork provide the numbers of the occurrence: four times γέγονα and

Chantraine asserts that γέγονα tends to replace the verb "to be," even though Moulton doubts it.[179] In fact, γέγονα shows a variegated meaning from present time to a past event. For instance, in John 1:30 (ὀπίσω μου ἔρχεται ἀνὴρ ὃς ἔμπροσθέν μου γέγονεν, ὅτι πρῶτός μου ἦν, "After me comes a man who *ranks* before me, because he was before me"), English translations of γέγονα provide various renderings.[180] Moulton rightly observes that γέγονα is a perplexing perfect.[181] This chapter will concentrate on the usage of γέγονα with its preserved resultative-stative meaning from the ancient Greek. The following chapters will handle variant nuances of γέγονα in the NT.

[John 14:22] κύριε, τί **γέγονεν** ὅτι ἡμῖν μέλλεις ἐμφανίζειν σεαυτὸν καὶ οὐχὶ τῷ κόσμῳ;

Lord, how is it that you will manifest yourself to us and not to the world?

[Rom 2:25] Περιτομὴ μὲν γὰρ ὠφελεῖ ἐὰν νόμον πράσσῃς· ἐὰν δὲ παραβάτης νόμου ᾖς, ἡ περιτομή σου ἀκροβυστία **γέγονεν**.

For circumcision indeed is of value if you obey the law, but if you break the law, your circumcision becomes uncircumcision.

[1 Cor 13:1] Ἐὰν ταῖς γλώσσαις τῶν ἀνθρώπων λαλῶ καὶ τῶν ἀγγέλων, ἀγάπην δὲ μὴ ἔχω, **γέγονα** χαλκὸς ἠχῶν

If I speak in the tongues of men and angels, but have not love, I am [have become] a noisy gong[182]

---

two times γεγένημαι in Euripides; nine times γέγονα and twenty-four times γεγένημαι in Aristophanes; twenty-nine times γεγένημαι in Thucydides; twenty times γέγονα and forty-seven times γεγένημαι in Lysias; and four times γεγένημαι in Xenophon (Sicking and Stork, *Two Studies*, 174, 202, 212, 224, 233, 240).

179. Chantraine, *Parfait grec*, 79, 115. According to Moulton, Buresch says that γέγονα functions like εἰμί, but Moulton doubts it (Moulton, *Prolegomena*, 146).

180. English translations of John 1:30 are: ESV, "After me comes a man who *ranks* before me"; NASB, "After me comes a Man who *has* a higher rank than I"; NIV, "A man who comes after me *has surpassed* me"; and KJV, "After me cometh a man which *is preferred* before me." John 1:15 is the same: ὁ ὀπίσω μου ἐρχόμενος ἔμπροσθέν μου γέγονεν, ὅτι πρῶτός μου ἦν ("This was He of whom I said, 'He who comes after me *ranks* before me, because He existed before me'").

181. Moulton, *Prolegomena*, 145.

182. Main English-Bible translations are: ESV, "I am a noisy gong"; NASB, "I have become a noisy gong"; NIV, "I am only a resounding gong"; and KJV, "I am become *as* sounding brass" (emphasis original).

THE FIRST STAGE   65

[2 Cor 1:19] ὁ τοῦ θεοῦ γὰρ υἱὸς Ἰησοῦς Χριστὸς ὁ ἐν ὑμῖν δι' ἡμῶν κηρυχθείς, δι' ἐμοῦ καὶ Σιλουανοῦ καὶ Τιμοθέου, οὐκ ἐγένετο ναὶ καὶ οὒ ἀλλὰ ναὶ ἐν αὐτῷ **γέγονεν**.

For the Son of God, Jesus Christ, who is in you through our preaching, Silvanus and Timothy and I, was not yes and no, but is yes in him.

[James 2:10] ὅστις γὰρ ὅλον τὸν νόμον τηρήσῃ πταίσῃ δὲ ἐν ἑνί, **γέγονεν** πάντων ἔνοχος.

For whoever keeps the whole law but fails in one point has become accountable for all of it.[183]

[James 5:2] ὁ πλοῦτος ὑμῶν σέσηπεν καὶ τὰ ἱμάτια ὑμῶν σητόβρωτα **γέγονεν**,

Your riches have rotted and your garments are moth-eaten.

[2 Peter 2:20] εἰ γὰρ ἀποφυγόντες τὰ μιάσματα τοῦ κόσμου ἐν ἐπιγνώσει τοῦ κυρίου καὶ σωτῆρος Ἰησοῦ Χριστοῦ, τούτοις δὲ πάλιν ἐμπλακέντες ἡττῶνται, **γέγονεν** αὐτοῖς τὰ ἔσχατα χείρονα τῶν πρώτων.

For if after they have escaped the corruption of the world by knowing our Lord and Savior Jesus Christ and are again entangled in it and are overcome, the last state has become worse for them than the first.[184]

According to the texts above, γέγονα plays a role similar to εἰμί in many passages. It also carries a resultative-stative sense. In 1 Corinthians 13:1 and James 2:10 especially, γέγονα seems to convey a resultative-stative nuance, "have become." In 2 Peter 2:20, it may be a little difficult to decide whether γέγονα indicates "resultative-stative" or "a current relevance with anteriority," but the former fits well.

Perfects with Stative Nuance

Not only the resultative-stative perfects but also middle-passive perfects with a stative nuance occur. The perfect ἀφέωνται is notable in that it carries either a resultative-stative nuance or a stative nuance:

183. ESV, "has become accountable for all of it"; NASB, "he has become guilty of all"; NIV, "is guilty of breaking all of it"; and KJV, "he is guilty of all."

184. The English translations show variation: ESV, "the last state has become worse"; NASB, "the last state has become worse"; NIV, "they are worse off at the end"; and KJV, "the latter end is worse."

[Luke 5:20, 23] ἄνθρωπε, **ἀφέωνταί** σοι αἱ ἁμαρτίαι σου. . . . τί ἐστιν εὐκοπώτερον, εἰπεῖν· **ἀφέωνταί** σοι αἱ ἁμαρτίαι σου, ἢ εἰπεῖν· ἔγειρε καὶ περιπάτει;

Man, your sins are [have been] forgiven you. . . . Which is easier, to say, "Your sins have been forgiven you" or to say, "Rise and walk"?

[Luke 7:47–48] οὗ χάριν λέγω σοι, **ἀφέωνται** αἱ ἁμαρτίαι αὐτῆς αἱ πολλαί. . . . εἶπεν δὲ αὐτῇ· **ἀφέωνταί** σου αἱ ἁμαρτίαι.

Therefore I tell you, her sins, which are many, are forgiven. . . . And he said to her, "Your sins are forgiven."

[1 John 2:12] Γράφω ὑμῖν, τεκνία, ὅτι **ἀφέωνται** ὑμῖν αἱ ἁμαρτίαι διὰ τὸ ὄνομα αὐτοῦ.

I am writing to you, little children, because your sins are [have been] forgiven for his name's sake.

[John 20:23] ἄν τινων ἀφῆτε τὰς ἁμαρτίας **ἀφέωνται** αὐτοῖς, ἄν τινων κρατῆτε **κεκράτηνται**.

If you forgive the sins of any, they *are forgiven* them; if you withhold forgiveness from any, it *is withheld*.

Except John 20:23, ἀφέωνται shows resultative-stative. In Luke 5:20, Wallace takes ἀφέωνται as intensive.[185] However, the intensive notion is not indispensable in the text. Rather, the context tells the present situation as a result of the man's sins having been forgiven.

Notably, the perfect ἀφέωνται (and κεκράτηνται) in John 20:23 is peculiar because a resultative-stative nuance would be disruptive here. The text is more in harmony with a stative nuance. Not all perfect middle/passive forms represent the resultative-stative:

[Rom 7:2] ἡ γὰρ ὕπανδρος γυνὴ τῷ ζῶντι ἀνδρὶ **δέδεται** νόμῳ· ἐὰν δὲ ἀποθάνῃ ὁ ἀνήρ, **κατήργηται** ἀπὸ τοῦ νόμου τοῦ ἀνδρός.

For a married woman *is bound* by law to her husband while he lives, but if her husband dies, she *is released* from the law of marriage.[186]

---

185. Wallace, *Beyond the Basics*, 576.

186. More passages are: 1 Cor 7:39, Γυνὴ δέδεται ἐφ᾽ ὅσον χρόνον ζῇ ὁ ἀνὴρ αὐτῆς ("A wife *is bound* to her husband as long as he lives"); and 2 Tim 2:9, ἀλλὰ ὁ λόγος τοῦ θεοῦ οὐ δέδεται ("But the word of God *is not bound*"). Burton sees δέδεται as a Gnomic state (Burton, *Syntax*, 39).

[1 Cor 1:13] **μεμέρισται** ὁ Χριστός; μὴ Παῦλος ἐσταυρώθη ὑπὲρ ὑμῶν.
Is Christ *divided*? Was Paul crucified for you?[187]

[1 Cor 7:14] **ἡγίασται** γὰρ ὁ ἀνὴρ ὁ ἄπιστος ἐν τῇ γυναικὶ καὶ **ἡγίασται** ἡ γυνὴ ἡ ἄπιστος ἐν τῷ ἀδλεφῷ.
For the unbelieving husband *is made holy* because of his wife, and the unbelieving wife *is made holy* because of her husband.

[1 Cor 7:15] οὐ **δεδούλωται** ὁ ἀδελφὸς ἢ ἡ ἀδελφὴ ἐν τοῖς τοιούτοις· ἐν δὲ εἰρήνῃ κέκληκεν ὑμᾶς ὁ θεός.
In such cases the brother or the sister *is* not *enslaved*. God has called you to peace.

[1 Cor 15:27] πάντα γὰρ ὑπέταξεν ὑπὸ τοὺς πόδας αὐτοῦ. ὅταν δὲ εἴπῃ ὅτι πάντα **ὑποτέτακται**, δῆλον ὅτι ἐκτὸς τοῦ ὑποτάξαντος αὐτῷ τὰ πάντα.
For he has put all things in subjection under his feet. But when he says, "All things *are put in subjection*," it is evident that he is excepted who put all things in subjection to him.

[1 Tim 6:4] **τετύφωται**, μηδὲν ἐπιστάμενος.
He *is puffed up* and understands nothing.

[Titus 3:11] εἰδὼς ὅτι **ἐξέστραπται** ὁ τοιοῦτος καὶ ἁμαρτάνει ὢν αὐτοκατάκριτος.
Knowing that such a person *is warped* and sinful, being self-condemned.

[2 Pet 2:19] ἐλευθερίαν αὐτοῖς ἐπαγγελλόμενοι, αὐτοὶ δοῦλοι ὑπάρχοντες τῆς φθορᾶς· ᾧ γάρ τις **ἥττηται**, τούτῳ **δεδούλωται**.
They promise them freedom, but they themselves are slaves of corruption; for by what a man *is overcome*, by this he *is enslaved*.

A resultative-stative nuance does not fit these examples according to the contexts. In 2 Peter 2:19, two perfect middle forms seem to express a general state without implying preceding affairs. The perfect δεδούλωται in 1 Corinthians 7:15 also describes a present state, while the perfect active

---

187. ESV, "Is Christ divided?"; NASB, "Has Christ been divided?"; NIV, "Is Christ divided?"; and KJV, "Is Christ divided?" See 1 Cor 7:34 καὶ μεμέρισται ("and *his interests are divided*").

κέκληκεν shows the typical perfect meaning (anterior or current relevance). The question in 1 Corinthians 1:13 μεμέρισται might have a resultative-stative nuance, "Has Christ been divided?" but a simple present statement seems most natural.

In sum, most of the perfect middle/passive forms in the NT express a resultative-stative nuance while some of them show a stative meaning. In the next section the stative nuance will be handled in closer relation to the intensive perfect.

INTENSIVE PERFECT

So far we have examined a resultative-stative nuance in ancient perfect active and middle-passive forms as well as a pure stative nuance in perfect middle. The final issue is the existence of the perfect denoting an intensive state. Magni states,

> In particular, the investigation will focus on the perfect in Archaic Greek, a category usually marked by reduplication and with two different semantic values: the resultative, which denotes a state in the present resulting from an action in the past, and the intensive, which described action as ongoing processes and differs from the present only in the intensity with which the events are depicted.[188]

This kind of intensive perfect occurs approximately less than 3 percent of the time, about a dozen instances out of 461 resultative-stative in the NT. This section will handle the perfects containing an intensive nuance.

In his article "Valeurs temporelles," Ruijgh states that the ancient Greek perfect not only stands for the resulting state of the subject but also contains a reiterative notion. Ruijgh avers that the concept of iterativity of the perfect is found in Homer. He illustrates from Plato (*Ion* 541c): ὃν Ἀθηναῖοι πολλάκις ἑαυτῶν στρατηγὸν ᾕρηνται ("A man whom the Athenians have often chosen as their general, though a foreigner"). Ruijgh maintains that the employment of adverb πολλάκις ("many times") bolsters the iterative nuance of the perfect.[189] Another example is πέπονθα, which connotes "a series of suffering," according to Ruijgh. However, Sicking and

---

188. Magni, "Pluractionality."

189. Ruijgh, "Les valeurs temporelles," 208–10. In the same vein, Ruijgh states that the adverb (πολλά πέπονθα) signifies the iterative character.

Stork criticize Ruijgh in that πέπονθα does not necessarily imply a series of suffering.[190]

Allan notes, "Cross-linguistically, reduplicated forms overwhelmingly expressed iterativity (no doubt a case of form-function iconicity), or otherwise their history can be traced back to an older stage of iterativity." He states that reduplicated forms would possibly have conveyed this sense of iterativity cross-linguistically.[191] In a similar way, Regier claims that repetition is the central meaning of reduplication. He notes that reduplication often expresses intensity. Regier says that reduplication expresses repetition, plurality, incrementality, continuity, or completion in various languages.[192] According to Allan, the Homeric examples are βέβριθα ("be heavy"), ἔολπα ("hope"), and ὄδωδα ("smell"); and Classical Greek examples include ἥγημαι ("be firmly convinced"), πεφόβημαι ("be terrified"), σεσιώπηκα ("maintain complete silence"), and τεθαύμακα ("be surprised").[193]

Magni also supports the likelihood of the iterativity of the Homeric perfect in connection with the reduplication. She examines the noise verbs in Homer: βέβρυχα ("I bellow out"), λέληκα ("scream"), μέμηκα ("baa, bleat") and κέκληγα ("I cry out").[194] Magni notes that the event repetition is the key. Magni states that these actions of noise, such as bellowing, tend to be repetitive, and these verbs of noise take perfect forms. For example,

[Homer, *Odyssey* 5.411–12] ἀμφὶ δὲ κῦμα βέβρυχεν ῥόθιον
And around them the wave roars foaming.[195]

In the text βέβρυχεν depicts the sound of wave as all around and repetitive. To express the noise, the perfect is employed to stress that the action is being done repetitively. In this respect, she defends the notion of intensive perfect with verbs of noise.[196]

In the same vein, Drinka utters,

---

190. Sicking and Stork, *Two Studies*, 160–61.

191. Allan, "Tense and Aspect," 106–7. With reference to Drinka, Allan introduces the association of reduplication cross-linguistically with intensification (Drinka, "Development of the Perfect," 78). See Bybee et al., *Evolution of Grammar*, 172.

192. Regier, *Semantics of Reduplication*, 3–4, 9–10. Regier says that the intense action can lead to the completion of it (in Greek or Latin) just as working on project intensely will result in the completion of the entire project.

193. Allan, "Tense and Aspect," 107 (bold-font perfect occurring in the NT).

194. Magni, "Pluractionality and Perfect," 328–32. See Gerö and Stechow, "Tense in Time," 267; Moser, "Perfect Periphrases," 221.

195. Homer, *Odyssey*, 198–99.

196. Magni, "Pluractionality and Perfect," 330–32. Willi also refers to these verbs of noise as "intensive perfects" (Willi, *Origins of the Greek Verb*, 217).

> The Greek intensive perfect, confined almost exclusively to Homer, is formally noteworthy in its use of reduplication and a long vowel stem; semantically, it is purely stative, not resultative, and is connected to the present, but with intensive or iterative nuance. Only about twenty examples exist, mostly onomatopoeic, representing human shouts, animal sounds, or noises, as the following examples, all from Homer, illustrate: *bébrūkhe* "roars", *gégōne* "shouts to make himself heard", *lelēke* "screams, howls", *mémūke* "lows, bellows."[197]

To render these noise verbs as expressing a resulting state does not make sense of the text. A stative notion seems to fit better. Magni scrutinizes more verbs beyond the verbs of noise to show that intensity is relevant to the perfects: μέμονα ("be very eager"), δέδηα (from δαίω "burn"), ὄρωρα ("stir"), δέδορκα ("gaze"). Magni points out the occurrences of these verbs especially with emphatic adverbs, such as μέμονα with μάλιστα ("especially") and δέδορκα with σμερδαλέον ("terribly").[198]

Importantly, Magni notes that "with certain verbs, the transition from 'iteration' (e.g., repetitive sound) to 'iteration + intensification' (e.g., repetitive sound that grows progressively louder) has led to lexicalized forms in which plurality and degree effects co-occur. These are the *perfecta tantum* that, like the English pluractionals *stutter* or *knock*."[199] Allan concludes, "It is tempting to see the intensive perfect as a relic of an older stage in which the perfect expressed intensification."[200] Therefore, the existence of the ancient perfect with an intensive nuance cannot be ignored.

Intensive Perfect in the New Testament

We have so far explored how the repetitive notion of cross-linguistic reduplication related to the Homeric perfect. Similarly, some stative perfects in the Greek New Testament not only refuse to fit with the resultative-stative notion but also seem to contain an intensive connotation. These "intensive

---

197. Drinka, "Development of the Perfect," 91.

198. Magni, "Pluractionality and Perfect," 332–33. *Iliad* 22.95 says, σμεφδαλέον δὲ δέδορκεν ἐλισσόμενος περὶ χειῇ ("and terribly he glareth as he coileth him about within his lair") (Homer, *Iliad*, 460–61).

199. Magni, "Pluractionality and Perfect," 335. Magni states that pluractionality encompasses repetition, intensity, frequency, duration, habituality and even stativity (Magni, "Pluractionality and Perfect," 327).

200. Allan, "Tense and Aspect," 107. Gerö and Stechow note that the use of intensive perfect is scarce in Classical Greek: It was disappearing (Gerö and Stechow, "Tense in Time," 270).

perfects" occur about a dozen times in the Greek New Testament. The resultative-stative nuance is not suitable for them.

Ἥγημαι

It is likely that ἥγημαι delivers this intensive nuance.[201] Its occurrences are as follows:

> [Acts 26:2] Περὶ πάντων ὧν ἐγκαλοῦμαι ὑπὸ Ἰουδαίων, βασιλεῦ Ἀγρίππα, **ἥγημαι** ἐμαυτὸν μακάριον ἐπὶ σοῦ μέλλων σήμερον ἀπολογεῖσθαι.
> I *consider* myself fortunate that it is before you, King Agrippa, that I am about to make my defense against all the accusations of the Jews.

> [Phil 3:7] ['Ἀλλ'] ἅτινα ἦν μοι κέρδη, ταῦτα **ἥγημαι** διὰ τὸν Χριστὸν ζημίαν.
> But whatever things were gain to me, those things I [have] counted as loss for the sake of Christ.

The nuance of ἥγημαι from the texts above delivers a pure stative without reference to preceding events except Philippians 3:7. In Classical Greek, ἥγημαι denotes the same stative nuance.[202]

Campbell insists on the Greek perfect as the heightened proximity with intensity, rendering ἥγημαι in Acts 26:2 with emphasis, "King Agrippa, I *truly consider* myself…"[203] Interestingly, Campbell pays attention to Hatina's argument (same as Porter's) that the perfect form highlights the action

---

201. BDF §341; Moulton, *Prolegomena*, 147. Moulton sees ἥγημαι as *perfecta praesentia*.

202. See (perfects in bold) Herodotus, *Persian Wars* 1.126, καὶ ὑμέας **ἥγημαι** ἄνδρας Μήδων εἶναι οὐ φαυλοτέρους οὔτε τἆλλα οὔτε τὰ πολέμια ("and I deem you full as good men as the Medes in war and in all else") (Herodotus, *Persian Wars*, 166–67); Herodotus, *Persian Wars* 2.115, νῦν ὦν ἐπειδὴ περὶ πολλοῦ **ἥγημαι** μὴ ξεινοκτονέειν, γυναῖκα, μὲν ταύτην καὶ τὰ χρήματα οὔ τοι προήσω ἀπάγεσθαι ("Now, therefore, since I am careful to slay no stranger, I will not suffer you to take away this woman and these possessions") (Herodotus, *Persian Wars*, 404–5); Plato, *Timeo* 19e, τὸ δὲ τῶν σοφιστῶν γένος αὖ πολλῶν μὲν λόγων καὶ καλῶν ἄλλων μάλ' ἔμπειρον **ἥγημαι**, φοβοῦμαι δὲ μή πως, ἄτε πλανητὸν ὂν κατὰ πόλεις οἰκήσεις τε ἰδίας οὐδαμῇ διωκηκός ("Again, as to the class of Sophists, although I esteem them highly versed in many fine discourses of other kinds, yet I fear lest haply, seeing they are a class which roams from city to city and has no settled habitations of its own") (Plato, *Timaeus*, 24–25).

203. Campbell, *Indicative Mood*, 202. Campbell regards ἥγημαι as a lexically stative verb, following Rijksbaron, *Syntax and Semantics*, 36.

as a frontground.²⁰⁴ Despite the difference between himself and Hatina, Campbell agrees with Hatina in regard of the prominence of the perfect.²⁰⁵

To summarize, ἥγημαι shows stative and intensive nuance in the NT as well as in Classical examples.

Μέμνημαι

Like ἥγημαι, the perfect μέμνημαι expresses a pure stative.²⁰⁶ To read μέμνημαι as resultative-stative does not fit well.

> [1 Cor 11:2] Ἐπαινῶ δὲ ὑμᾶς ὅτι πάντα μου μέμνησθε, καί, καθὼς παρέδωκα ὑμῖν, τὰς παραδόσεις κατέχετε.
>
> Now I commend you because you *remember* me in everything and maintain the tradition, just as I delivered them to you.

This perfect appears not only in the NT but also in Homer and Classical Greek. Chantraine notes that μέμνημαι occurs thirty-five times in Homer.²⁰⁷

> [Homer, *Iliad* 5.818] ἀλλ' ἔτι σέων μέμνημαι ἐφετμέων
> But I still *remember* thy behest.²⁰⁸

> [Thucydides, *Peloponnesian War* 5.26.4] αἰεὶ γὰρ ἔγωγε μέμνημαι
> For always as I *remember*.

The perfect μέμνημαι here denotes a stative nuance without a resultative-stative connotation. The adverb ἔτι ("still") emphasizes the present meaning of the main verb in Homer. Likewise, the adverb αἰεί ("always") buttresses the stative meaning of μέμνημαι in Thucydides. Although this perfect may be overlapped with the category of stative perfect middle-passive, Robertson regards μέμνημαι as intensive perfect.²⁰⁹ This perfect may be best explained with an intensive connotation just like ἥγημαι.

---

204. See Hatina, "Perfect Tense-Form," 224–52; Hatina, "Galatians," 3–22.
205. Campbell, *Indicative Mood*, 206n105.
206. Robertson, *Grammar*, 881, 893; BDF §341.
207. Chantraine, *Parfait grec*, 65.
208. The example is from Perel'muter, "Stative, Resultative, Passive and Perfect," 285. The perfect μέμνημαι occurs twelve times in Aeschylus, six times in Sophocles, and twenty times in Aristophanes (Sicking and Stork, *Two Studies*, 190, 197, 217). See Smyth, *Greek Grammar*, 434.
209. Robertson, *Grammar*, 893.

῎Ηλπικα

This perfect is tricky. Blass and Debrunner regard ἤλπικα as a state, but "stronger than ἐλπίζω by virtue of the continuing character of the hope formed."[210] It is very difficult to decide whether ἤλπικα denotes a present state or implies a past reference.[211] It seems that John 5:45 can be rendered both ways: ἔστιν ὁ κατηγορῶν ὑμῶν Μωϋσῆς, εἰς ὃν ὑμεῖς ἠλπίκατε ("There is one who accuses you: Moses, on whom you [have] set your hope"). More illustrations are:

> [2 Cor 1:10] ὃς ἐκ τηλικούτου θανάτου ἐρρύσατο ἡμᾶς καὶ ῥύσεται, εἰς ὃν ἠλπίκαμεν [ὅτι] καὶ ἔτι ῥύσεται,
>
> He delivered us from such a deadly peril, and he will deliver us. On him we [have] set our hope that he will deliver us again.[212]

> [1 Tim 4:10] εἰς τοῦτο γὰρ κοπιῶμεν καὶ ἀγωνιζόμεθα, ὅτι ἠλπίκαμεν ἐπὶ θεῷ ζῶντι, ὅς ἐστιν σωτὴρ πάντων ἀνθρώπων μάλιστα πιστῶν.
>
> For to this end we toil and strive, because we have our hope set on the living God, who is the Savior of all people, especially of those who believe.

> [1 Tim 5:5] ἡ δὲ ὄντως χήρα καὶ μεμονωμένη ἤλπικεν ἐπὶ θεὸν καὶ προσμένει ταῖς δεήσεσιν καὶ ταῖς προσευχαῖς νυκτὸς καὶ ἡμέρας,
>
> She who is truly a widow, left all alone, has set her hope on God and continues in supplications and prayers night and day.

In the texts above, ἤλπικα can be translated as either conveying a past implication or a present state. In his epistles, Paul expresses the current state of hope implied from the past.

Crellin says that ἤλπικα does not occur before the Greek New Testament after searching through TLG. Therefore, it is unlikely that ἤλπικα is

---

210. BDF §341. Horrocks explains the Greek perfect with the verb of a state, for example, "hope" of which perfect would be "in the past I entered a state of hopefulness that now persists" (Horrocks, "Envoi," in Runge and Fresch, *Greek Verb Revisited*, 633).

211. Crellin, "Semantics of the Perfect," in Runge and Fresch, *Greek Verb Revisited*, 432. See Moulton and Turner, *Syntax*, 84. Porter renders ἤλπικα as "I am in a hopeful state" (Porter, *Idioms*, 39–40).

212. Several English translations render ἠλπίκαμεν as "have set a hope": ESV, "On him we have set our hope"; NASB, "He on whom we have set our hope"; NIV, "On him we have set our hope"; and KJV, "in whom we trust."

archaic. According to Crellin, it is striking that "three ancient manuscripts, namely the Vulgate, Gothic, and Old Syriac (Curetonian), all translate ἤλπικα without any explicit past reference." Nevertheless, he states that ἤλπικα of the three passages above is translated as a past tense in Gothic. Crellin concludes that ἤλπικα delivers "*both* pure state *and* resultant state."[213]

Ἀνθέστηκεν

It is difficult to know how to handle ἀνθέστηκεν in Romans 13:2. This perfect does not deliver a typical meaning of the perfect, that is, a current relevance with anteriority:

> [Rom 13:2] ὥστε ὁ ἀντιτασσόμενος τῇ ἐξουσίᾳ τῇ τοῦ θεοῦ διαταγῇ ἀνθέστηκεν, οἱ δὲ ἀνθεστηκότες ἑαυτοῖς κρίμα λήμψονται.
> Therefore whoever resists the authorities *resists* the ordinance of God, and those who resist will incur judgment.

The perfect ἀνθέστηκεν seems to express a stative nuance with possible intensity. In Hebrews 2:14, similarly it is not certain that κεκοινώνηκεν should signify an ongoing event from the past.

> [Heb 2:14] Ἐπεὶ οὖν τὰ παιδία κεκοινώνηκεν αἵματος καὶ σαρκός, καὶ αὐτὸς παραπλησίως μετέσχεν τῶν αὐτῶν
> Since therefore the children *share* in flesh and blood, he himself likewise partook of the same things

The perfect κεκοινώνηκεν describes characteristics of the children of God who have flesh and blood as human beings. A resultative-stative nuance does not fit here, but an emphatic nuance may be implied.

Permanent (Inalterable) State

Moreover, several perfects in the NT still seem to retain this intensive connotation as a relic. Interestingly, Sicking and Stork claim that the "state" of the Greek perfect is different from that of the present tense. Comparing the perfect to the present, they maintain that the former denotes an "unalterable or immutable" event while the latter a changeable situation.[214] Similarly,

---

213. Crellin, "Gothic Eyes," 33–38; Crellin, "Semantics of the Perfect," in Runge and Fresch, *Greek Verb Revisited*, 441n8.

214. Sicking and Stork, *Two Studies*, 139–41.

Monro claims, "we shall usually find that the Perfect denotes a permanent state."²¹⁵

The examples from the NT are:

[Luke 16:26] καὶ ἐν πᾶσιν τούτοις μεταξὺ ἡμῶν καὶ ὑμῶν χάσμα μέγα ἐστήρικται, ὅπως οἱ θέλοντες διαβῆναι ἔνθεν πρὸς ὑμᾶς μὴ δύνωνται, μηδὲ ἐκεῖθεν πρὸς ἡμᾶς διαπερῶσιν.

And besides all this, between us and you a great chasm *is fixed*, in order that those who would pass from here to you may not be able, and none may cross from there to us.

[Luke 17:2] λυσιτελεῖ αὐτῷ εἰ λίθος μυλικὸς περίκειται περὶ τὸν τράχηλον αὐτοῦ καὶ ἔρριπται εἰς τὴν θάλασσαν ἢ ἵνα σκανδαλίσῃ τῶν μικρῶν τούτων ἕνα.

It would better for him if a millstone were hung around his neck and he *were cast* into the sea than that he should cause one of these little ones to stumble.²¹⁶

The verses above employ perfect middle/passive forms. It is difficult to determine in Luke 16:26 whether the perfect is resultative-stative or pure stative. Both are possible, but the stative seems more likely. The chasm is great and eternal to the extent that it separates hell from heaven. The demarcation between heaven and hell is inalterable and unchangeable. In Luke 17:2, in the same vein, a resulting state does not fit in the context. The perfect middle/passive ἔρριπται denotes a pure state. The consequence of the action being thrown into the sea would be irreversible and permanent.²¹⁷

---

215. Monro, *Homeric Dialect*, 31; emphasis original. Monro says, "If we compare the meaning of any Perfect with that of the corresponding Aorist or Present, we shall usually find that the Perfect denotes a permanent *state*, the Aor. or Pres. an *action* which brings about or constitutes that state." Magni also mentions a similar term "a single permanent state" (Magni, "Pluractionality and Perfect," 339). Aubrey comments, "This does not definitively prove that intensification is expressed by the perfect, but the correlation is linguistically relevant, following the principle of linguistic redundancy (Aubrey, "Greek Perfect," 100).

216. It is almost the same construction in Mark 9:42, καλόν ἐστιν αὐτῷ μᾶλλον εἰ περίκειται μύλος ὀνικὸς περὶ τὸν τράχηλον αὐτοῦ καὶ βέβληται εἰς τὴν θάλασσαν ("it would be better for him if a great millstone were hung around his neck and he *were thrown* into the sea").

217. Sicking and Stork compare the present-tense verb with the perfect form πεφόβημαι in Sophocles (perfect in bold): *Ajax* 228, οἵαν ἐδήλωσας ἀνδρὸς αἴθονος ἀγγελίαν ἄτλατον οὐδὲ φευκτάν, τῶν μελέων Δαναῶν ὕπο κλῃζομέναν, τὰν ὁ μέγας μῦθος ἀέξει. ὤμοι, **φοβοῦμαι** τὸ προσέρπον ("What news regarding the valiant man have you revealed, not to be borne and not to be escaped, told by the miserable Danaans, a message which their loud rumour magnifies! Alas, I fear the future"); and *Ajax* 139–40,

The next example is πεπλούτηκα, which was introduced earlier. It is helpful to compare the perfect with the aorist.

[Rev 3:17] ὅτι λέγεις ὅτι πλούσιός εἰμι καὶ **πεπλούτηκα** καὶ οὐδὲν χρείαν ἔχω, καὶ οὐκ οἶδας ὅτι σὺ εἶ ὁ ταλαίπωρος καὶ ἐλεεινὸς καὶ πτωχὸς καὶ τυφλὸς καὶ γυμνός.

For you say, I am rich, and have prospered [prosper] and have no need, not realizing that you are wretched, pitiable, poor, blind, and naked.

[Rev 18:3] καὶ ἔμποροι τῆς γῆς ἐκ τῆς δυνάμεως τοῦ στρήνους αὐτῆς ἐπλούτησαν

And the merchants of the earth grew rich from her excessive luxuries[218]

Whether or not πεπλούτηκα represents a state or a current relevance with anteriority, it seems certain that the aorist ἐπλούτησαν indicates a prior event in the past. The perfect πεπλούτηκα is paralleled in 3:17 side by side with present tense verbs (εἰμί/ἔχω), so that its focus and nuance would rarely aim at the past event. This perfect seems to stress the present state of being rich.[219]

Sicking and Stork illustrate πεπλούτηκα from Aristophanes, comparing the perfect with the present.[220]

[Aristophanes, *Plutus* 335–36] τί ἂν οὖν τὸ πρᾶγυ' εἴη; πόθεν καὶ τίνι τρόπῳ Χρεμύλος **πεπλούτηκ'** ἐξαπίνης;

What can it mean? Old Chremylus grown wealthy! Then whence and how?

σὲ δ' ὅταν πληγὴ Διὸς ἢ ζαμενὴς λόγος ἐκ Δαναῶν κακόθρους ἐπιβῇ, μέγαν ὄκνον ἔχω καὶ **πεφόβημαι** πτηνῆς ὡς ὄμμα πελείας ("But when the stroke of Zeus assails you, or a quick-spreading rumour voiced by evil tongues comes from the Danaas, I am greatly anxious and *am fearful*, like the troubled glance of the winged dove") (Sophocles, *Ajax*, 46–47, 52–53). In *Ajax* 228, the present verb φοβοῦμαι describes a general fear for the future. In *Ajax* 140, on the other hand, the perfect form πεφόβημαι delivers a stronger nuance. The adverb μέγαν ("great") shows the intensity of the fear. Sicking and Stork describe this as "uncontrollable panic" (Sicking and Stork, *Two Studies*, 140).

218. Major English-Bible translations are: ESV, "and the merchants of the earth have grown rich"; NASB, "and the merchants of the earth have become rich"; NIV, "and the merchants of the earth grew rich from her excessive luxuries"; and KJV, "and the merchants of the earth are waxed rich."

219. Köstenberger et al., *Going Deeper*, 298.

220. Aristophanes, *Plutus*, 392–93; Sicking and Stork, *Two Studies*, 169. In Classical Greek, πεπλούτηκα occurs in Demosthenes as well (Chantraine, *Parfait grec*, 73).

[Aristophanes, *Plutus* 502–4] πολλοὶ μὲν γὰρ τῶν ἀνθρώπων ὄντες πλουτοῦσι πονηροί, ἀδίωκς αὐτὰ ξυλλεξάμενοι· πολλοὶ δ' ὄντες πάνυ χρηστοὶ πράττουσι κακῶς καὶ πεινῶσιν.

So often the best of the world is possessed by the most undeserving of men, who have gotten their pile of money by vile in justice.

The present-tense πλουτοῦσι speaks of a general situation that unjust men get rich. On the other hand, πεπλούτηκα shows a reaction of the speaker who is puzzled by the news that an old Chremylus has become a rich man. Sicking and Stork describe his richness as an "inalterable state." It seems that πεπλούτηκα denotes a stronger nuance in the text above.

Mathewson interestingly comments on πεπλούτηκα in Revelation 3:17, "Moreover, the incorrect self-evaluation of the Laodicean church is highlighted with the perfect πεπλούτηκα."[221] This assessment of the perfect is in accordance with the intensive nuance of the perfect, for which Allan, Magni, and Sicking and Stork argue.

CONCLUSION

It has been difficult to decipher so-called "stative" perfects in the Greek New Testament. The traditional definition of the Greek perfect has no choice but to allow the stative perfects as an exceptional category. Diachronic development of the Greek perfect aids in understanding this "abnormal" behavior of the perfect. Haspelmath and Allan insightfully analyze the three stages of the Greek perfect according to its development history. The first stage of the Greek perfect is the PIE and Homeric era. In this period, the perfect conveys a resultative-stative notion. The perfect οἶδα is representative.

Moreover, the characteristics of the ancient Greek perfect were different from the typical perfect notion. As shown from Homeric perfect examples, they are intransitive and subject-affected similar to the middle voice. Moreover, the perfect middle form was innovated in this period, and it spread widely. Since the perfect middle had the same resultative-stative meaning as the perfect active in Homer, it replaced the ancient perfect active forms. It is observed that a great number of perfect middle forms are attested in Classical Greek. Likewise, they frequently occur in the Greek New Testament. Many of them express a resultative-stative notion, but not all of them. Some are found with a stative nuance. Although further studies

---

221. Mathewson, *Verbal Aspect in Revelation*, 105.

are necessary, the broad conclusion of scholars is that the archaic perfect has two semantic features—resultative and stative.

Moreover, some perfects express an intensive nuance. The intensive nuance is likely from the repetitive notion of the reduplication, just as we see in many other languages. In Homeric Greek, for example, noise verbs are regarded as intensive because of the iterativity of the sound. About a dozen cases of intensive perfects seem to appear in the Greek New Testament. In relation to the intensive perfect, Sicking and Stork suggest the "permanent (inalterable) state" of the perfect, showing the difference between it and the present state.

Sicking and Stork rightly say, "The position of the Perfect in the Greek tense system is ambivalent."[222] Although the issue of how to understand the stative perfect in the NT is thorny, the explanations based upon the development of the Greek perfect are able to provide better elucidation of the labyrinth-like "abnormal stative perfect" of the Greek New Testament.

---

222. Sicking and Stork, *Two Studies*, 168.

3

STAGE TWO
FROM RESULTATIVE TO ANTERIOR

INTRODUCTION

THE PRECEDING CHAPTER ELUCIDATED how ancient Greek perfect forms like οἶδα, ἕστηκα, and πέποιθα (as well as perfect middle/passive forms) convey a resultative-stative connotation and survived up to the Koine period. This chapter will investigate the development of the perfect from resultative to anterior. The Greek New Testament shows a great number of verbs conveying the typical notion of the perfect—the anterior or current relevance perfect. This function of the perfect tense is one of its core essential concepts.[1] Horrocks says,

> This is the essence of the perfect aspect, which entails the notion of continuing relevance for the earlier event at the later viewing point.... In the case of the present perfect, there can be no present viewing point distinct from the time of utterance (the present is the present), and the event is simply earlier than "now."[2]

This use of the Greek perfect is very similar to the English perfect. They are dominant in Classical and Koine Greek. Gerö and Stechow state that the

---

1. Lindstedt, "Perfect–Aspectual," 368; Gerö and Stechow, "Tense in Time," 269–94; Haug, "From Resultatives to Anteriors," 285–305; Horrocks, *Greek*, 176; Andrason and Locatell, "Perfect Wave," 41.

2. Horrocks, *Greek*, 176.

perfects in Classical Greek generally are similar to the English perfect.³ For the terms "anterior perfect" and "current relevance perfect," scholars employ them almost identically.⁴

Moreover, the perfect went through a semantic change from resultative to anterior (current relevance) during the Classical era. Since the perfects like οἶδα, ἕστηκα, and πέποιθα convey a resultative-stative nuance, some scholars, such as Porter, reject the traditional definition of the Greek Perfect and regard it as stative. However, Crellin responds,

> Porter is certainly right that, if these present-state referring perfects are to be integrated into the semantics of the perfect, reference to a prior terminated or culminated event cannot be inherent to the semantics of the perfect itself. However, Porter's attempt to disregard efforts to explain those cases where the perfect does carry past time reference by integrating accounts of the perfect with lexical aspect may be misguided.⁵

As Crellin rightly points out, many Greek perfect indicatives undeniably occur with an anterior (current relevance) nuance. Similarly, Aubrey affirms, "The possibility that the Greek perfect is an anterior gram[matical morpheme]⁶ cannot be ruled out on the basis of these tests alone, since anteriors that develop from resultatives and completives may continue these usages, particularly in their early development."⁷

---

3. Gerö and Stechow, "Tense in Time," 270–75, 280–94.

4. See Slings, "Geschiedenis van het perfectum," 242; Lindstedt, "Perfect–Aspectual," 366; Allan, "Tense and Aspect," 108. Aubrey summarizes, "Anteriors denote a situation that takes place prior to a reference time, and is pragmatically relevant to the situation at the reference time" (Aubrey, "Greek Perfect," 57). Andrason and Locatell state, "In the majority of the perfectal uses, the nuance of current relevance—one of the most typical traits of perfects cross-linguistically—is easily identifiable" (Andrason and Locatell, "Perfect Wave," 41). Bentein says, "It should be kept in mind that 'current relevance' (i.e., the (subjective) relevance of (an) anterior event(s) to the current discourse situation) is characteristic for all the perfect functions" (Bentein, "Periphrastic Perfect," 178). Bentein states, "Within the transitivity-framework, it could be said that the shift from resultative to anterior (perfect of current relevance) is one of increasing transitivity ('transitivization')" (Bentein, *Verbal Periphrasis*, 139). Kavčič employs terms "anterior event with current relevance" or "anterior perfect that contains a current relevance" (Kavčič, "Decline of the Aorist Infinitive," 269, 287, 289). Lloyd B. Anderson analyzes the spectrum of the perfect: result-state, current relevance result, current relevance new situation, current relevance experience, current relevance anterior, anterior perfective, and perfective past (Anderson, "Perfect," 240).

5. Crellin, "Gothic Eyes," 10.

6. Aubrey abbreviates the term "grammatical morpheme" as "gram" in his thesis.

7. Aubrey, "Greek Perfect," 103.

It is crucial to elucidate the process how the anterior perfect sense developed from the core resultative idea. The important question is how and when the Greek Perfect takes on a current relevance (anterior) nuance. This development of the perfect is closely related to its transitivity. A great number of transitive active perfects occur all of a sudden in the fifth and fourth century BC. Before the rest of the chapter analyzes this issue in more detail, some examples from the NT can be briefly introduced to give a sample of this anterior perfect nuance:

[John 8:33] σπέρμα Ἀβραάμ ἐσμεν καὶ οὐδενὶ δεδουλεύκαμεν πώποτε.

We are offspring of Abraham and *have* not *been enslaved* ever to anyone.[8]

[John 2:10] σὺ τετήρηκας τὸν καλὸν οἶνον ἕως ἄρτι.

But you *have kept* the good wine until now.

[Acts 5:28] καὶ ἰδοὺ πεπληρώκατε τὴν Ἰερουσαλὴμ τῆς διδαχῆς ὑμῶν.

And behold, you *have filled* Jerusalem with your teaching.[9]

In John 8:33, the Jews maintain that they have never experienced slavery (δεδουλεύκαμεν) from the past up to this point. The adverb πώποτε functions to emphasize the content. In John 2:10, τετήρηκας is employed ("But you have kept the good wine") in the context of the master of the banquet recognizing that they have preserved the good wine throughout the feast until the last moment. In Acts 5:28, the disciples' precedent teaching eventually resulted in the current fullness of the city with the words of gospel.

---

8. See LXX Gen 30:26, ὧν δεδούλευκά σοι ἵνα ἀπέλθω σὺ γὰρ γίνωσκεις τὴν δουλείαν ἣν δεδούλευκά σοι ("for whom I have served, that I may go, for you know the service that I have rendered you"); Gen 30:29, ἃ δεδούλευκά σοι ("how I [Jacob] have served you").

9. In John 16:6, πεπλήρωκεν ("grief has filled your heart") delivers a typical perfect nuance like English perfect; Acts 13:33, ὅτι ταύτην ὁ θεὸς ἐκπεπλήρωκεν τοῖς τέκνοις [αὐτῶν] ἡμῖν ἀναστήσας Ἰησοῦν ("this he [God] has fulfilled to us their children by raising Jesus"); Rom 13:8, ὁ γὰρ ἀγαπῶν τὸν ἕτερον νόμον πεπλήρωκεν ("the one who loves another has fulfilled the law"). See Fanning, *Verbal Aspect*, 153–54. Wallace takes this perfect as "extensive perfect" (Wallace, *Beyond the Basics*, 572–82). See Polycarp, *Philippians* 3.3, ἐὰν γὰρ τις τούτων ἐντὸς ᾖ, πεπλήρωκεν ἐντολὴν δικαιοσύνης· ὁ γὰρ ἔχων ἀγάπην μακράν ἐστιν πάσης ἁμαρτίας ("For if anyone who is occupied with these has fulfilled the commandment of righteousness, for whoever has love is far from all sin"); *Martyrdom of Polycarp* 20.1, Ὑμεῖς μὲν οὖν ἠξιώσατε διὰ πλειόνων δηλωθῆναι ὑμῖν τὰ γενόμενα, ἡμεῖς δὲ κατὰ τὸ παρὸν ὡς ἐν κεφαλαίῳ μεμηνύκαμεν ("You did indeed request that the things that happened be reported to you in some detail, but for the present we have given a summary") (Holmes, *Apostolic Fathers*, 284–85, 328–29).

Andrason and Locatell correctly observe that πεπληρώκατε here denotes the current relevance of a past event, namely, the apostles' teaching.[10]

It is not very difficult to comprehend this notion of the Greek Perfect. It is a common and essential concept of the perfect from a linguistic perspective. It is crucial to scrutinize the process of how the transitive anterior perfect developed from the ancient resultative perfect.

THE SECOND STAGE: TRANSITIVE ANTERIOR PERFECT

The most prominent change of the perfect in Classical Greek was the evolution to the perfect conveying a present state resulting from a prior event. Many scholars maintain that the Greek perfect changed from resultative to anterior (current relevance) in the post-Homer era.[11] In Homeric Greek, subject-affected intransitive perfects were dominant. For instance, the present tense φθείρω had an intransitive perfect (δι)έφθορα ("I am ruined").[12] The innovation and spread of the perfect middle ἔφθαρμαι ("I am ruined") formed the opposition to the old form ἔφθορα that has the same meaning. This opposition facilitated the meaning change of ἔφθορα.

Interestingly, the archaic perfect ἔφθορα showed the changed meaning "I have destroyed" in the fifth century BC.[13]

> [Sophocles, *Electra* 306] μέλλων γὰρ ἀεὶ δρᾶν τι τὰς οὔσας τέ μου καὶ τὰς ἀπούσας ἐλπίδας διέφθορεν.
>
> For by always putting off his action he *has destroyed* the hopes I had not![14]

---

10. Andrason and Locatell, "Perfect Wave," 43. Andrason and Locatell state, "the disciples had filled Jerusalem with their teaching resulting in the fact that currently (at the reference time of uttering the words) the city was full of that teaching (at least from the speaker's perspective)."

11. Haspelmath, "From Resultative to Perfect," 209; Lindstedt, "Perfect–Aspectual," 368; Gerö and Stechow, "Tense in Time," 251–94; Haug, "From Resultatives to Anteriors," 291–303; Bentein, "Periphrastic Perfect," 189, 206; Bentein, "HAVE-Perfects," 152; Bentein, "Perfect," 46–49; Allan, "Tense and Aspect," 108; Kavčič, "Decline of the Aorist Infinitive," 287.

12. Willi, *Origins of the Greek Verb*, 227.

13. Veitch, *Greek Verbs*, 678; Monro, *Homeric Dialect*, 32; Haug, "From Resultatives to Anteriors," 302; Willi, *Origins of the Greek Verb*, 221–22. For more texts with (δι)έφθορα, see Kavčič, "Transitivity," 191–92.

14. Sophocles, *Electra*, 192–93.

It is surprising that this archaic perfect changed its meaning to become transitive because the early Greek perfects were intransitive and resultative. Furthermore, the old form ἔφθορα was later replaced by ἔφθαρκα with the same meaning, "I have destroyed."[15] Euripides uses ἔφθαρκα to convey the meaning "I have destroyed":

> [Euripides, Medea 225–6] ἐμοὶ δ' ἄελπτον πρᾶγμα προσπεσὸν τόδε ψυχὴν διέφθαρκ'.
> In my case, however, this sudden blow that has struck me *has destroyed* my life.[16]

Thus, in Classical Greek the perfect active ἔφθαρκα delivered a transitive anterior connotation.

We see then that the transition from the old perfect ἔφθορα ("I am ruined") to the transitive perfect-active with kappa ἔφθαρκα ("I have destroyed") occurred during the Classical period. Willi remarks, "And only when an opposition of active and middle perfects had thus arisen, facilitating the use of active perfects in transitive as well as intransitive contexts, the idea of an active pluperfect would also have sprung up."[17] It is vital to investigate how the transitive perfect emerged. The rise of the transitive perfect active in Classical period is very important because it was able to expand the verb's scope of expression with the addition of an explicit object.[18]

Resultative Perfect of Wackernagel and Chantraine

First of all, it is necessary to study the concept "resultative perfect" by Wackernagel and Chantraine in relation to transitivity of the perfect in Classical Greek. According to Wackernagel, the perfect after Homer denoted the state of the object, not that of the subject. Wackernagel names it the "resultative perfect."[19] Following Wackernagel, Chantraine claims that "the perfect still expresses a state; but it is the state of the object, no longer the state of the

---

15. Haug, "From Resultatives to Anteriors," 302; Willi, *Origins of the Greek Verb*, 227; Chantraine, *Parfait grec*, 253.

16. Euripides, *Medea*, 304–5. The example is from Sicking and Stork, *Two Studies*, 182. For more texts with (δι)έφθαρκα, see Kavčič, "Transitivity," 189–90.

17. Willi, *Origins of the Greek Verb*, 222.

18. Haug, "From Resultatives to Anteriors," 300–301.

19. Wackernagel, "Studien zum griechischen Perfektum," 4–9. Although I introduce this term of Wackernagel, I follow the definition of "resultative" by Nedjalkov, *Typology of Resultative Constructions*, 6.

subject" in the fifth century BC.[20] Pindar (c. 518–438 BC) and Plato provide examples.

> [Pindar, Isthmian 4.37] ἀλλ' Ὅμηρός τοι τετίμακεν δι' ἀνθρώπων.
> But Homer, to be sure, has made him [Ajax] honored among mankind.[21]

> [Plato, Ion 541c] ὃν Ἀθηναῖοι πολλάκις ἑαυτῶν στρατηγὸν ᾕρηνται ξένον ὄντα.
> A man whom Athens have often chosen as their general, though a foreigner.

Wackernagel and Chantraine assert that in Pindar τετίμακεν focuses on the state of the object [Ajax], not that of the subject [Homer].[22] Similarly, Chantraine maintains that ᾕρηνται in Plato expressed the state of the object.[23]

McKay contests their arguments for the "resultative perfect." In the first example of Pindar, the context emphasizes the importance of poets in general, like Homer, who made people famous (τετίμακεν).[24] It does not necessarily specify the object, Ajax. McKay argues thus that τετίμακεν here denotes the state of the subject. For the second example from Plato, McKay asserts that ᾕρηνται represents the state of the subject, not that of the object. In context, ᾕρηνται emphasizes the subjects, Ἀθηναῖοι, who select their general even though he is a foreigner.[25] Therefore, the argument that the perfect in Classical Greek represented the state of the object is not persuasive. Moreover, perfects in Classical Greek did not always convey the "state" of the object.[26] Many perfects in Classical literature communicate an anterior nuance.

---

20. Chantraine, *Parfait grec*, 122, 165.

21. Pindar, *Isthmian*, 166–67.

22. Wackernagel, "Studien zum griechischen Perfektum," 9; Chantraine, *Parfait grec*, 122.

23. Chantraine, *Parfait grec*, 165.

24. McKay, "Ancient Greek Perfect," 2. Others also disagree with this concept by Wackernagel and Chantraine's conception of a "resultative perfect": Duhoux, *Le verbe grec ancien*, 428; Rijksbaron, "Het Griekse perfectum," 403–19; Porter, *Verbal Aspect*, 276–81; Sicking and Stork, *Two Studies*, 146.

25. Chantraine, *Parfait grec*, 165; McKay, "Ancient Greek Perfect," 9–10.

26. McKay, "Ancient Greek Perfect," 9. McKay states, "I do not believe that γέγραφε ταῦτα has the same force as γέγραπται ταῦτα ὑπό. . . . The essence of the resultative perfect as expounded by Wackernagel and others is that an active transitive perfect expresses a state or condition which continues to affect the object."

Following McKay's criticism, many scholars have ignored the "resultative perfect" of Wackernagel and Chantraine.[27] Certainly, Wackernagel and Chantraine's perspective is skewed with respect to the essence of the change in the fifth century BC. Nevertheless, Wackernagel and Chantraine do pay attention to the crucial point that the perfect went through a major change.[28] This change was the transitivity of the perfect in the Classical era. Willi states,

> In the fifth century, the transitive perfect suddenly expands very quickly.... Although Wackernagel and Chantraine failed to explain clearly *what* was new, it is impossible to deny that there *was* something new about the perfect in the fifth-century Greek.[29]

Willi rightly points out that Wackernagel and Chantraine do find something meaningful. Bentein concurs with Willi's view: "In fact, the work of Wackernagel and Chantraine fits well with the findings of cross-linguistically oriented studies, where two main types of perfect are typically distinguished, called 'resultative' and 'anterior.'"[30]

Many note that the transitive perfect forms rapidly became widespread in the fifth century BC.[31] Willi provides approximate numbers of the "resultative perfect" in Attic drama and prose: Aeschylus (12–20), Sophocles (50), Euripides ("many more"), Aristophanes (200), Thucydides (35), and Plato (125).[32] Although Wackernagel and Chantraine misjudge the essence of the change, their studies reveal that a great number of transitive perfects appeared in the fifth and fourth century BC.[33] In spite of Wackernagel and

---

27. Porter, *Verbal Aspect*, 275, 280, 489; Rijksbaron, *Syntax and Semantics*, 35–36; Duhoux, *Le verbe grec ancien*, 428; Bentein, *Verbal Periphrasis*, 115.

28. Wackernagel, "Studien zum griechischen Perfektum" 3–24; Chantraine, *Parfait grec*, 122, 165; Bentein, *Verbal Periphrasis*, 114–15.

29. Willi, *Languages of Aristophanes*, 129–30.

30. Bentein cites Willi's comment above (Bentein, *Verbal Periphrasis*, 115). See Bentein, "Transitivity, Ecology, and the Emergence," 294n49.

31. Duhoux, *Le verbe grec ancien*, 427; Slings, "Geschiedenis van het perfectum," 243; Willi, *Languages of Aristophanes*, 129–30; Haug, "From Resultatives to Anteriors," 300–302; Allan, "Tense and Aspect," 108; Bentein, "Ecological-Evolutionary Account," 206; Bentein, "Periphrastic Perfect," 193.

32. Willi, *Languages of Aristophanes*, 130. Willi refers to Chantraine, *Parfait grec*, 123–38.

33. Chantraine, *Parfait grec*, 122, 129. Wackernagel pays attention to the outgrowing of the transitive active perfects in the fifth and fourth century BC, providing a list of them, most of which occur with the suffix kappa (bold-font perfect occurring in the NT): from Thucydides (δεδήλωκα), Aristophanes (βεβαλάνωκα, ἐκκεκώφωκα, ἐξήμβλωκα), Hyppocrates (ἀποκεκάρπωκε, ἐρρίζωκε, σεσυρίγγωκε, ἠραχνίωκε),

Chantraine's misstep, their works can stimulate the search for the change in the perfect from intransitivity to transitivity in Classical Greek.

Haspelmath points out that this change in the perfect was already foreshadowed even in Homer:[34]

> [Homer, *Iliad* 10.145] τοῖον γὰρ ἄχος **βεβίηκεν** Ἀχαιούς.
> For great sorrow hath overmastered the Achaeans.[35]

It is notable that βεβίηκεν is functionally transitive, carrying along an object. This case is very rare in Homer. In ancient Greek, most of the perfects were resultative and intransitive, but the transitive perfect did appear on a few occasions in Homer.[36] In Classical Greek, transitivity within perfects became prominent. For instance,

> [Thucydides, *Peloponnesian War* 5.26.1] **γέγραφε** δὲ καὶ ταῦτα ὁ αὐτὸς Θουκυδίδης.
> Thucydides himself *has written* this.[37]

In Thucydides γέγραφε obviously expresses active transitivity.

In spite of their shortcomings, therefore, Wackernagel and Chantraine's analysis of the perfect continues to be noteworthy. The rapid increase of transitivity of the perfect in Classical Greek provides a crucial clue with regard to the transition from resultative to anterior. Bentein rightly states, "Within the transitivity-framework, it could be said that the shift from resultative to anterior (perfect of current relevance) is one of increasing

---

Demosthenes (ἐζημίωκα, ἐστεφάνωκα, ἠλλοτρίωκα), Antiphanes (τεθόλωκα), Menander (καταδεδούλωκα), Sophocles (δέδρακα, βεβούλευκα, ἀνατέτροφα, διέφθορα, ἀπεστέρηκα, ἐκβέβληκα, ἠπάτηκα), and Euripides (ἠγώνισμαι, ἠδίκηκα, διέφθαρκα, ἐξήντληκα, ἐπῄρκα, ἐπέσταλκα, συμβέβληκα, **σέσωκα**, τέθηκα, ὑπηγκάλισμαι) (Wackernagel, "Studien zum griechischen Perfektum," 11–12).

34. Haspelmath, "From Resultative to Perfect," 209–10.

35. Homer, *Iliad*, 446–47.

36. McKay, "Ancient Greek Perfect," 1. McKay notes that in Homer fewer verbs have attested so-called "perfect meaning" than in Classical Greek. Gerö and Stechow provide the examples of the transitive perfect in Homer: *Iliad* 2.272, ὦ πόποι, ἦ δὴ μυρί' Ὀδυσσεὺς ἐσθλὰ ἔοργε βουλάς τ' ἐξάρχων ἀγαθὰς πόλεμόν τε κορύσσων ("Out upon it! verily hath Odysseus ere now wrought good deeds without number as leader in good counsel and setting battle in array"); and in *Odyssey* 17.284, τολήμεις μοι θυμός, ἐπεὶ κακὰ πολλὰ πέπονθα κύμασι καὶ πολέμῳ ("Staunch in my heart, for much evil have I suffered amid the waves and in war") (Gerö and Stechow, "Tense in Time," 253).

37. Haspelmath, "From Resultative to Perfect," 190. Aubrey notes that the perfect γέγραφα mostly overlaps with the English perfect (current relevance perfect or anterior) (Aubrey, "Greek Perfect," 113).

transitivity ('transitivization')."[38] The sudden appearance of many transitive perfects bolsters the semantic change of the perfect from resultative to anterior.

Semantic Change: From Resultative to Anterior

The perfect went through a semantic change from resultative to anterior in Classical Greek. As considered earlier, the intransitive middle-passive endings (ἔφθαρμαι) created an opposition, with the transitive perfect active ἔφθαρκα. Since the perfect middle-passive with an intransitive nuance spread successfully, the scope of the perfect active increased. The perfect active (ἔφθαρκα, "have destroyed") conveys the transitivity with an object.[39] In the fifth century, ἔφθαρκα is found first, and it occurred frequently beginning in the fourth century BC.[40] In Classical Greek, the anterior perfect with a kappa, such as ἔφθαρκα ("have destroyed"), became dominant.

Haspelmath points out that changed perfects were composed with the suffix κ (kappa) in the Classical period. While in Homer the perfect with a κ occurred only scantly,[41] a great number of transitive perfects were formed with κ during the Classical period.[42] Foreshadowing of this phenomenon already existed in the seventh and at the end of the fifth century. Allan notes,

> Already in the seventh and the beginning of the sixth century forms like δέδωκε "has given" (Tyrtaeus) and τέτιμακ(ε) "has honored" (Sappho) make their appearance. But in the second half of the fifth century and especially in the fourth century the frequency of these transitive perfects (often built with -κ-) rapidly increases.[43]

38. Bentein, *Verbal Periphrasis*, 139.

39. Haug, "From Resultatives to Anteriors," 302; Chantraine, *Parfait grec*, 140; Willi, *Origins of the Greek Verb*, 221. See Moser, "Perfect Periphrases," 220.

40. Haug, "From Resultatives to Anteriors," 300–302; Willi, *Origins of the Greek Verb*, 227; Kavčič, "Decline of the Aorist Infinitive," 298. See Lysias 1.16, ὃς οὐ μόνον τὴν σὴν γυναῖκα διέφθαρκεν ἀλλὰ καὶ ἄλλας πολλὰς "he has debauched not only your wife, but many others besides" (example from Bentein "Transitivity, Ecology, and the Emergence," 294–95).

41. Wackernagel, "Studien zum griechischen Perfektum," 5; Haspelmath, "From Resultative to Perfect," 213–15. They are ἕστηκα, βέβηκα, τέθνηκα, πέφυκα, τέτοκα, etc. (Monro, *Homeric Dialect*, 25).

42. Chantraine, *Parfait grec*, 139–41.

43. Allan, "Tense and Aspect," 108. Haspelmath notes that this phenomenon is already foreshadowed in Homer: ἦ δὴ μυρί' Ὀδυσσεὺς ἐσθλὰ ἔοργεν "Odysseus has done innumerable noble deeds," in *Iliad* 2.272 (Haspelmath, "From Resultative to Perfect," 210).

As Allan says, many scholars maintain that the major change of the perfect occurred in the fourth and fifth century BC. Slings maintains that the Greek perfect developed into the perfect of current relevance after 450 BC.[44] Andrason and Locatell note that the "perfect sense" was dominant during the Classical period.

> In Classical Greek (500–300 BCE), the perfectal sense predominated, the stative and present values were restricted to certain verbs, and the past function was very rare.[45]

In the same vein, Bentein agrees with this semantic shift.[46] Willi pays attention to the change of the perfect in this period with radically increasing transitive active forms.[47]

Since the ancient perfects were intransitive and resultative, according to Haspelmath, the scope of their expression was limited by verbal lexicality. The Homeric perfects suffered from the limitation of expressions outside the intransitive resultative notion. However, the perfects during the Classical period showed an expansion of the range of their expression. Unlike the Homeric perfects, they were no longer limited by lexical restrictions, so that they could express the transitive notion along with the object. Haspelmath states,

> It [the perfect] has now a partially unrestricted lexical generality.[48] They can now be derived easily from any verb, and there is even a new segmental marker that unambiguously signals the perfect (the suffix -κ, which in Homer appeared only sporadically).[49]

---

44. Slings, "Geschiedenis van het perfectum," 243.

45. Andrason and Locatell, "Perfect Wave," 79. Gerö and Stechow also maintain that unlike the intransitive resultative perfects in Homer, many perfects in Classical Greek are like English perfect (Gerö and Stechow, "Tense in Time," 270–80).

46. Bentein, "Ecological-Evolutionary Account," 206; Bentein, "Periphrastic Perfect," 193–94; Bentein, "Transitivity, Ecology, and the Emergence," 294–95.

47. Willi, *Languages of Aristophanes*, 130.

48. Lexical generality indicates how much semantic content a morpheme possesses. A highly specific morpheme has less generality than a non-specific morpheme. See Bybee, *Morphology*, 17.

49. Haspelmath, "From Resultative to Perfect," 213–14. Haspelmath says that Wackernagel also notes the new transitive perfect. Wackernagel says, "A past action whose value in the object persists in the present. We shall name it Resultative Perfect tentatively" (Wackernagel, "Studien zum griechischen Perfektum," 4). Haspelmath states that Wackernagel describes the most widespread characteristics of the perfect, "a past event with current relevance." However, Haspelmath points out that Wackernagel unfortunately refers it to transitive "resultative perfect" because it does not distinguish

In Classical Greek, the range of meaning that the perfect could express increased. In other words, the semantic capability that the perfect was able to convey was greatly broadened. While Homeric perfects were subject-affected intransitive, many perfects in Classical Greek were agentive transitive. As we noted earlier, Willi observed the rapidly increasing number of transitive perfects in the fifth century also supports this statement of Haspelmath. All these new transitive perfects were formed with the tense formative κ.[50]

It is impossible to cite all the perfect active forms of the Classical period. Hence, the selected texts below will show that the perfects are transitive and denote the current relevance of a past event. They are chosen from literature from between the fifth and fourth centuries BC (perfects in bold).[51]

[Herodotus, *Persian Wars* 5.56] Γέρεά τε δὴ τάδε τοῖσι βασιλεῦσι Σπαρτιῆται **δεδώκασι**.

These prerogatives, then, the Spartans *have given* to their kings.[52]

[Thucydides, *Peloponnesian War* 3.63.1] Ὡς δὲ ὑμεῖς μᾶλλόν τε **ἠδικήκατε** τοὺς Ἕλληνας καὶ ἀξιώτεροί ἐστε πάσης ζημίας, πειρασόμεθα ἀποφαίνειν.

We will now try to show that you Plataeans *have wronged* the Hellenes more than we and are more deserving of any punishment, however severe.[53]

---

between the Homeric and the Classical perfect. See Bentein, "Transitivity, Ecology, and the Emergence," 295.

50. Haspelmath, "From Resultative to Perfect," 214; Kimball, "Origin of Greek κ-Perfect, 145. She says, "the -κ- perfect is clearly a Greek innovation; no other Indo-European language has anything quite like it, and any explanation for it must be found within Greek itself." See Buth, "Perfect Greek Morphology," 379–429; Horrocks, *Greek*, 61; Weiss, "Morphology," 117. Weiss says, "In post-Homeric Greek the κ-perfect enjoyed great success." Chantraine argues that the kappa-perfect replaced the perfect middle forms because it made the form clearer: the perfect ἔσταλκα replaced the perfect middle ἔσταλμαι, and ἔφθαρκα replaces ἔφθαρμαι which supplanted ἔφθορα (Chantraine, *Parfait grec*, 140). Bentein importantly states that in the fifth century BC, "an active perfect form was not available for all verbs, and in this respect the construction of ἔχω with the aorist participle provided 'temporary relief'" (Bentein, *Verbal Periphrasis*, 116).

51. The examples are from Haspelmath "From Resultative to Perfect," 210–11; Sicking and Stork, *Two Studies*, 149, 157; and Gerö and Stechow, "Tense in Time."

52. Herodotus, *Persian Wars*, 200–201.

53. Thucydides, *Peloponnesian War*, 110–11. For more examples, see Sicking and Stork, *Two Studies in the Semantics*, 146–47.

[Herodotus, *Persian Wars* 1.112] **τέτοκα** γὰρ καὶ ἐγώ, **τέτοκα** δὲ τεθνεός.

Know that I too *have borne* a child, but it was dead.[54]

[Lysias, *Lysias* 30.24–26] τίς οὖν τῶν ἐν τῇ πόλει ἐπιτηδειότερος Νικομάχου δοῦναι δίκην; τίς ἐλάττω τὴν πόλιν ἀγαθὰ **πεποίηκεν** ἢ πλείω **ἠδίκηκεν**; ὃς καὶ τῶν ὁσίων καὶ τῶν ἱερῶν ἀναγραφεὺς γενόμενος εἰς ἀμφότερα ταῦτα **ἡμάρτηκεν**. . . . ἀλλὰ ὅτε ὑμεῖς ἐκινδυνεύετε ἐκπλέοντες, οὗτος αὐτοῦ μένων τοὺς Σόλωνος νόμους ἐλυμαίνετο. ἀλλ' ὅτι χρήματα **δεδαπάνηκε** καὶ πολλὰς εἰσφορὰς **εἰσενήνοχεν**;

And from whom amongst our citizens could it be more suitably exacted than from Nicomachus? Who *has rendered* less service or *done* more *wrong* to the city? Appointed to transcribe our code of duties, secular and sacred, he *has offended* against both. . . . But while you were facing danger on naval expeditions, this man stayed at home and corrupted the laws of Solon. Or because he *has disbursed* money and *contributed* to numerous levies?[55]

[Plato, *Symposium* 172c] οὐκ οἶσθ' ὅτι πολλῶν ἐτῶν Ἀγάθων ἐνθάδε οὐκ **ἐπιδεδήμηκεν**.

---

54. Herodotus, *Persian Wars*, 146–47; Wackernagel "Studien zum griechischen Perfektum," 19; cf. LXX Gen 22:20, τέτοκεν Μελχα καὶ αὐτὴ υἱοὺς ("Milcah also has borne children").

55. Lysias, *Lysias*, 626–67. These examples are from Sicking and Stork, 148. One more example is from *Lysias* (14.41–42) (perfects in bold): Σκέψασθαι δὲ χρή, ὦ ἄνδρες δικασταί, διὰ τί ἄν τις τοιούτων ἀνδρῶν φείσαιτο; πότερον ὡς πρὸς μὲν τὴν πόλιν **δεδυστυχήκασιν**, ἄλλως δὲ κόσμιοί εἰσι καὶ σωφρόνως **βεβιώκασιν**; οὐχ οἱ μὲν πολλοὶ αὐτῶν **ἠταιρήκασιν**, οἱ δ' ἀδελφαῖς συγγεγόνασι, τοῖς δ' ἐκ θυγατέρων παῖδες **γεγόνασιν**, οἱ δὲ μυστήρια **πεποιήκασι** καὶ τοὺς Ἑρμᾶς **περικεκόφασι** καὶ περὶ πάντας τοὺς θεοὺς **ἠσεβήκασι** καὶ εἰς ἅπασαν τὴν πόλιν **ἡμαρτήκασιν**, ἀδίκως καὶ παρανόμως καὶ πρὸς τοὺς ἄλλους πολιτευόμενοι καὶ πρὸς σφᾶς αὐτοὺς διακείμενοι, οὐδεμιᾶς τόλμης ἀπεχόμενοι, οὐδὲ ἔργου δεινοῦ ἄπειροι γεγενημένοι; ἀλλὰ καὶ **πεπόνθασιν** καὶ **πεποιήκασιν** ἅπαντα ("And you should ask yourselves, gentlemen, what reason you could have for sparing such men as these. Is it because, *unfortunate* though their public career *has been*, they are otherwise orderly persons, who *have lived* sober lives? *Have* not most of them *been whoring*, while some have lain with their sisters, and others *have had* children by their daughters; others again, *have performed* Mysteries, *mutilated* the Hermae, and *committed* profanity against all the gods and *offences* against the whole city, showing injustice and illegality alike in their public treatment of their fellow-men and in their behavior to each other, refraining from no audacity, and unversed in no outrageous practice? Indeed, there is nothing that they *have been spared*, or *have spared*") (*Lysias*, 360–61).

You must know it is many a year that Agathon *has been away* from home and country.⁵⁶

[Lysias, *Lysias* 12.100] παύσομαι κατηγορῶν, **ἀκηκόατε, ἑωράκατε, πεπόνθατε**, ἔχετε· δικάζετε.
I will here conclude my accusation. You *have heard*, you *have seen*, you *have suffered*; you have them: give judgment.⁵⁷

The perfects above express the current relevance from a prior event. They do not deliver the ancient resultative-stative nuance. In the *Symposium* of Plato, for instance, Gerö and Stechow consider ἐπιδεδήμηκεν ("have been home") similar to the English perfect (Extended-Now), "a time interval extending from the reference time to an indefinite past."⁵⁸ Bentein maintains that the current relevance perfect is widespread in the fourth century BC.⁵⁹ Haspelmath also states, "In Herodotus (5th century) the old resultative is still quite common, but the perfect [i.e., current relevance] meaning is already well attested."⁶⁰

Campbell criticizes the idea of a semantic shift of the perfect from resultative to anterior. He avers that the existence of this semantic shift is

---

56. Plato, *Symposium*, 82–83. More texts from Plato are (perfects in bold): *Apology* 37a, ὀλίγον γὰρ χρόνον ἀλλήλοις **διειλέγμεθα** ("for we *have conversed* with each other only a little while"); *Charmides* 163a 10–11, ἐγὼ γάρ που, ἦ δ' ὅς, τοῦθ' **ὡμολόγηκα**, ὡς οἱ τὰ τῶν ἄλλων πράττοντες σωφρονοῦσιν ("And *have I*, pray, he said, *admitted* that those who do others' business are temperate?"); *Apology* 39c, φημὶ γάρ, ὦ ἄνδρες, οἳ ἐμὲ **ἀπεκτόνατε** ("And I say to you, ye men who *have slain* me"); *Timeo* 47a, **δεδώρηται**, μετὰ τοῦτο ῥητέον. ὄψις δὴ κατὰ τὸν ἐμὸν λόγον αἰτία τῆς μεγίστης ὠφελίας **γέγονεν** ἡμῖν, ὅτι τῶν νῦν λόγων περὶ τοῦ παντὸς λεγομένων οὐδεὶς ἄν ποτε ἐρρήθη μήτε ἄστρα μήτε ἥλιον μήτε οὐρανὸν ἰδόντων. νῦν δ' ἡμέρα τε καὶ νὺξ ὀφθεῖσαι μῆνές τε καὶ ἐνιαυτῶν περίοδοι καὶ ἰσημερίαι καὶ τροπαὶ **μεμηχάνηνται** μὲν ἀριθμόν, χρόνου δὲ ἔννοιαν περί τε τῆς τοῦ παντὸς φύσεως ζήτησιν ἔδοσαν ("benefit effected by them, for the sake of which God *bestowed* them upon us. Vision, in my view, is the cause of the greatest benefit to us, inasmuch as none of the accounts now given concerning the Universe would ever *have been* given if men had not seen the stars or the sun or the heaven. But as it is, the vision of the day and night and of months and circling years *has created* the art of number and has given us not only the notion of Time but also means of research into the nature of the Universe"). The examples are from Gerö and Stechow, "Tense in Time," 274–75; Sicking and Stork, *Two Studies*, 149, 157; and Chantraine, *Parfait grec*, 96.

57. The example is from Sicking and Stork. For more examples of ἀκήκοα in Classical literatures, see Sicking and Stork, *Two Studies*, 162–66.

58. Gerö and Stechow, "Tense in Time," 281–82. For the notion of Extended-Now, see McCoard, *English Perfect*, 123–63. Gerö and Stechow maintain that in Classical Greek period the core meaning of the perfect is like English perfect (Gerö and Stechow, "Tense in Time," 270–80).

59. Bentein, "Periphrastic Perfect," 208.

60. Haspelmath, "From Resultative to Perfect," 210.

unfounded in Classical Greek.⁶¹ However, the examples above refute his assertion. The transitive active perfects in the texts demonstrate a difference from the intransitive resultative nuance in early Greek. As additional examples, the transitive anterior perfects πέπεικα ("I have persuaded"),⁶² ἀπολώλεκα ("I have destroyed"), and πέφαγκα ("I have shown") are all attested in Classical Greek.⁶³ They have developed from the old forms πέποιθα ("I am persuaded"), (ἀπ)όλωλα ("I perish"), and πέφηνα ("I am manifest"),⁶⁴ respectively. In the end, these archaic forms either disappear or continue to occur as exceptions.⁶⁵ Moreover, this semantic change of the perfect is not something unique. A semantic change of the perfect from resultative to anterior is also observed later in Romance and Germanic languages, even though their cases are not exactly the same as Greek.⁶⁶

IITSC (Invited Inferencing Theory of Semantic Change)

So far we have examined how the lexical generality was no longer limited to resultative and many transitive anterior perfects occurred in Classical Greek. In order to understand the semantic change of the perfect from resultative to anterior, Allan refers to IITSC—*the Invited Inferencing Theory of Semantic Change*. IITSC is introduced and applied by Traugott and Dasher for grammatical studies. According to Traugott, "The prime objective of IITSC is to account for the conventionalizing of pragmatic meanings and their reanalysis as semantic meanings."⁶⁷ She demonstrates that the mean-

---

61. Campbell, *Indicative Mood*, 165. See Sicking and Stork, *Two Studies*, 158.

62. The perfect πέπεικα occurs in Lysias XXVI, 7 (Moulton, *Prolegomena*, 147; Malden, "Perfect Tenses," 175; Sicking and Stork, *Two Studies*, 173, 175).

63. The examples are from Haspelmath, "From Resultative to Perfect," 215.

64. The ancient form πέφηνα still occurs in Classical Greek: for example, one time in Aeschylus, two times in Sophocles, five times in Euripides, etc. (Sicking and Stork, *Two Studies*, 192, 198, 210; Chantraine, *Parfait grec*, 148).

65. Chantraine illustrates the perfect forms from Demosthenes (bold-font perfects occurring in the NT): βέβιωκα, ἔοικα, εἴωθα, εἰσπέπλευκα, **πεπλούτηκα, προσπέπτωκα, εἰσελήλυθα, ἀναβέβηκα, κέκραγα, τέθνηκα**, δέδοικα, **συμβέβηκα, τετελεύτηκα, παρώρμηκα, πέπλευκα**, πέφφικα, etc. (*Parfait grec*, 72–73). While most of them are kappa-perfect forms, only a few ancient-type perfects appear.

66. Bybee et al., *Evolution of Grammar*, 68–69; Lindstedt, "Perfect–Aspectual," 366–67. Despite some similarity, Haug points out that the early Greek perfect has dissimilarities from Romance and Germanic languages. These languages (Spanish, French, Italian, English, Dutch, or German) construct the perfect forms with the auxiliary *have* (Haug, "From Resultatives to Anteriors," 286).

67. Traugott and Dasher, *Regularity in Semantic Change*, 35, 38. Traugott and Dasher continue, "The overall concept of IITSC is . . . the mechanism by which innovations

ing of words is subject to change and can be redefined by those who use the words. Traugott states,

> Speakers innovatively use old forms and constructions with new meanings, subject to semantic and pragmatic constraints. If these innovations spread to other speakers the resources available for the category at that point on the path are renewed.[68]

For example, the meaning of the English expression "am going to" has gone through a semantic change from *motion* to *time*.[69] The word "America" originally represented the entire continent, but English speakers employed it mainly for the area in which immigrants from England settled. Today the word *America* refers to the United States of America.[70] In language, we often encounter this kind of meaning change.

By employing IITSC, Allan maintains that the meaning change of the perfect started off when a number of individuals employ the changed perfect. Then it became conventionalized. Allan states,

> The process of semantic change starts off when an individual speaker uses a word or grammatical form ad hoc in a new context of use. In case of the perfect, a speaker experiments by creating a new perfect form of an agentive transitive verb. By using the perfect in a new context. . . . The speaker invites the hearer to interpret the subject's prior action as otherwise relevant to the current speech situation. By repeated use of this implicature by other speakers and with other verbs it eventually became a new conventional meaning of the perfect form: the *current relevance*

---

may arise in the individual and be affected by community acceptance of salience, etc. For an innovation in the linguistic system of an individual to constitute a change 'in the language,' the innovation must be spread or propagated through the community."

68. Traugott and Dasher, *Regularity in Semantic Change*, 86–87. Traugott and Dasher cite Sweetser, who showed how the "verbs of seeing and grasping can come cross-linguistically to be metaphorized as verbs of understanding," in Greek: *eidon* "see" and the perfect *oida* "know" (cf. English word *idea*) (Traugott and Dasher, *Regularity in Semantic Change*, 77).

69. Hopper and Traugott, *Grammaticalization*, 2–3, 88–97. The word "harass" is from French in the seventeenth century, defined as: to wear out, tire out, devastate, plunder, trouble or vex with repeated attacks, distress with annoying labour, etc. It had come to include contexts involving verbal events in the nineteenth century, and in the twentieth century its meaning extended to verbal conduct like "sexual harassment" (Traugott and Dasher, *Regularity in Semantic Change*, 4, 32, 61–65).

70. Haspelmath, "Against Markedness," 51. A Latin word *carrus* "four-wheeled wagon" becomes *car* today (Traugott and Dasher, *Regularity in Semantic Change*, 11).

perfect. The older resultative-stative meaning, however, did not disappear.[71]

In contrast to the Homeric perfects that suffered from lexical limitation, as Haspelmath points out, the scope of the perfect expression expands in Classical Greek. In relation to the rapid increase of the transitive perfect, it is possible that the transitive active perfect filled up the grammatical gap in the verbal system for speakers during the Classical period.[72] Based on the application of IITSC, the expanded range of the transitive perfect may have given room for speakers to express the new connotation of the perfect: transitive anterior.

Using the development of the transitive perfect active ἔφθαρκα ("I have destroyed") from the intransitive perfect ἔφθαρμαι ("I am ruined"), Haug also points out the difference in nuance between the former and the latter. He says,

> But the agent of the event of destroying is not at all a participant in the resultant state of this event; only the theme is. Therefore, the perfect *epʰtʰarka* cannot refer to a resultant state at all, but only to a more loosely defined state of current relevance.[73]

Haug rightly states that the transitive perfect ἔφθαρκα cannot convey a resultant nuance, because it represents the agent of the action, not a recipient of the result of events as the intransitive perfect ἔφθαρμαι did. Haug acknowledges the difference between the Homeric resultant state (ἔφθαρμαι

---

71. Allan, "Tense and Aspect," 109; emphasis original. Allan refers to Hopper and Traugott, *Grammaticalization*, 71–98. Allan continues, "The emergence of the current relevance meaning of the perfect can be described as a form of subjectification: the *objective* (event-oriented) mental or physical property of the subject has bleached away and is replaced by the *subjective* (speaker-oriented) feature of current relevance" (Allan, "Tense and Aspect," 110).

72. Haspelmath, "From Resultative to Perfect," 212–14. See Moser, "From Aktionsart to Aspect," 77. Moser says, "In Classical Greek, the picture has changed quite dramatically. Verbs now possess full paradigms, with instances of practically every form attested in the very large corpus of texts. These forms are used with considerably greater freedom in order to express the speaker's vantage point, i.e., grammatical aspect."

73. Haug, "From Resultatives to Anteriors," 300; Bentein, "Transitivity, Ecology, and the Emergence," 289n21. Bentein states, "As we have seen, resultative perfects are typically limited to telic content verbs, whose final ('result') state is predicated as a property of the subject (e.g., 'the car is washed', or alternatively 'I have the car washed'). Perfects of current relevance, on the other hand, also combine with atelic content verbs, which are typically not construed as producing a result (e.g., 'I have spoken to him')." Bentein provides the cases of the usages of the perfect participle with εἰμί in Classical Greek. Interestingly, the percentages of current relevance perfects are the highest in the fourth and fifth century BC (Bentein, *Verbal Periphrasis*, 138–40).

"I am ruined") and the anterior perfect (ἔφθαρκα "I have destroyed") in the fifth century BC. During the Classical period, notably, the number of transitive agentive perfects rapidly increases, and the newly formed perfects with κ deliver a transitive active meaning, not a resultant nuance anymore.[74]

The typical Homeric perfect was resultative, such as, "*y* has been ruined." A typical nuance of the anterior perfect is "*x* has destroyed." The new formation with the agentive transitive perfect is "*x* has destroyed *y*." During this transition from intransitivity to transitivity, the anterior nuance may have been introduced by speakers. For example, the middle-passive form κέκληται denotes a resultative-stative: κέκληται in Revelation 19:13 ("his name is called").[75] However, the perfect takes on the anterior sense when it becomes transitive with an object.

> [1 Cor 7:15–17] ἐν δὲ εἰρήνῃ κέκληκεν ὑμᾶς ὁ θεός. . . . Εἰ μὴ ἑκάστῳ ὡς ἐμέρισεν ὁ κύριος, ἕκαστον ὡς κέκληκεν ὁ θεός.
> God *has called* you to peace. . . . Only let each person lead the life that the Lord has assigned to him, and to which God *has called* him.[76]

> [LXX 2 Kings 8:1] ὅτι κέκληκεν κύριος λιμὸν ἐπὶ τὴν γῆν καὶ γε ἦλθεν ἐπὶ τὴν γῆν ἑπτὰ ἔτη
> For the Lord *has called* a famine, and it shall even come on the land for seven years[77]

> [Thucydides, *Peloponnesian War* 5.26.1] γέγραφε δὲ καὶ ταῦτα ὁ αὐτὸς Θουκυδίδης.
> Thucydides himself *has written* this.

These transitive perfects express the current relevance of a prior event: God called them in the past and the calling affects the present moment. The difference between intransitive resultative perfect-middle and transitive anterior perfect-active can be observed. It is the same as γέγραπται

---

74. See footnote 50 of this chapter. Bentein notes that in the fifth century BC, perfect active forms were not available for all verbs (Bentein, *Verbal Periphrasis*, 116–17).

75. See Acts 15:17, καὶ πάντα τὰ ἔθνη ἐφ' οὓς ἐπικέκληται τὸ ὄνομά μου ("and all the Gentiles who are called by my name"); LXX 2 Chr 6:33, καὶ τοῦ γνῶναι ὅτι ἐπικέκληται τὸ ὄνομά σου ἐπὶ τὸν οἶκον τοῦτον ὃν ᾠκοδόμησα ("and they may know that this house that I have built is called by your name"). Also, see 2 Chr 7:14.

76. In Cor 7:15–17, Porter regards κέκληκεν as present tense ("He calls"), but it is not persuasive (Porter, *Verbal Aspect*, 278).

77. LXX 2 Kgs 3:10, ὦ ὅτι κέκληκεν κύριος τοὺς τρεῖς βασιλεῖς παρεχομένους δοῦναι αὐτοὺς ἐν χειρὶ Μωαβ ("Alas! The Lord has called these three kings to give them into the hands of Moab").

(Thucydides, *Peloponnesian War* 5.24.2 / 2.1), "it is written," which expresses a resultative-stative idea.[78] In Thucydides, *Peloponnesian War* 5.26.1, in contrast, the transitive perfect active γέγραφε denotes an anterior nuance, "he has written."[79]

The semantic change did not eradicate old meanings immediately.[80] In the Classical era, the perfect still often conveys a resultative nuance.[81] Although further study is necessary for elucidating the transition from resultative to anterior, the explanations so far provide some hint for the semantic change of the perfect that occurred in Classical Greek.

Summary

It is likely that the semantic change of the perfect occurred in the Classical Greek period, with the rise of the transitive perfect. In contrast to the limitation of the perfect to intransitive forms and a resultative-stative in Homer, the anterior perfect is attested well in the Classical era. Bentein rightly states,

> So that the fact that in fifth-century Classical Greek the perfect of current relevance is already attested need not necessarily be problematic. . . . Clearly, the "new" anterior meaning is becoming conventionalised.[82]

The consequences of the semantic change of the perfect are easily observed in the anterior perfects in Classical literatures. IITSC also supports the possibility of this meaning change of the perfect. Moreover, the anterior

---

78. See chapter 2 above.

79. Bentein, "Periphrastic Perfect," 176. A middle-passive form ἔγνωσται (1 Cor 8:3 "he is known by God") is resultative-stative (ESV, "But if anyone loves God, he is known by God"; NASB, "but if anyone loves God, he is known by him"; NIV, "But whoever loves God is known by God"; KJV, "But if any man loves God, the same is known by him"). In Acts 27:25, λελάληται is resultative-stative, but its transitive form λελάληκα denotes anterior (current relevance). See the section for λελάληκα in this chapter.

80. Hopper and Traugott, *Grammaticalization*, 97. Hopper and Traugott note, "Persistence of old meanings is a common phenomenon."

81. Haspelmath, "From Resultative to Perfect," 214–15; Gerö and Stechow, "Tense in Time," 251–54; Bentein, "Perfect," 48. See Bentein, "Periphrastic Perfect," 199. See footnote 60 of this chapter. Also see footnotes 43 and 119 in chapter 2. Smyth provides an example: Aeschylus 2.4, ἐφοβήθην, καὶ ἔτι καὶ νῦν τεθορύβημαι ("I was struck with fear, and even at the present moment am still in a state of agitation") (Smyth, *Greek Grammar*, 434).

82. Bentein, "Periphrastic Perfect," 194, 199, 208. Bentein provides the usages of the perfect periphrastic in the fourth and fifth century BC. Interestingly, many of them denotes a current relevance nuance. See Bentein, *Verbal Periphrasis*, 139; Duhoux, *Le verbe grec ancien*, 427.

transitive perfects with κ continue to appear not only in the Classical period but also up to the Hellenistic time and the era of Caesar.[83]

ANTERIOR PERFECT IN THE GREEK NEW TESTAMENT

Just as a great number of transitive active perfects with κ appear in Classical Greek, many transitive anterior perfects also occur in the Greek New Testament. These perfect forms express the current relevance of a past event. This section will investigate this kind of usage of the perfect in the NT. The Greek New Testament, as well as the Septuagint, is full of uses of the anterior perfect.[84] Several examples are:

> [Matt 22:4] πάλιν ἀπέστειλεν ἄλλους δούλους λέγων· εἴπατε τοῖς κεκλημένοις· ἰδοὺ τὸ ἄριστόν μου ἡτοίμακα.
> Again he sent other servants, saying, "Tell those who are invited, 'See, I *have prepared* my dinner.'"[85]

> [John 3:13] καὶ οὐδεὶς ἀναβέβηκεν εἰς τὸν οὐρανὸν εἰ μὴ ὁ ἐκ τοῦ οὐρανοῦ καταβάς, ὁ υἱὸς τοῦ ἀνθρώπου.
> No one *has ascended* into heaven except he who descended from heaven, the Son of Man.[86]

---

83. Many perfect active forms with kappa continue to appear up to Hellenistic time and Caesar era. Wackernagel lists ἠχρείωκα, κεκύκλωκα (Polybius), ἠλάττωκα (Diodorus), ἠμαύρωκα (Strabo), ἠτίμωκα (Plutarch), κεκένωκα (Appian), etc. (Wackernagel, "Studien zum griechischen Perfektum," 12).

84. The chapter will offer selective passages from the Septuagint.

85. The middle-passive form in Mark 10:40 denotes a resultative, ἀλλ' οἷς ἡτοίμασται ("but it is for those for whom it has been prepared"); Matt 20:23, οἷς ἡτοίμασται ὑπὸ τοῦ πατρός μου ("for whom it has been [is] prepared by my Father"); LXX 1 Chr 29:16, κύριε ὁ θεὸς ἡμῶν πᾶν τὸ πλῆθος τοῦτο ὃ ἡτοίμακα οἰκοδομηθῆναι οἶκον τῷ ὀνόματι τῷ ἁγίῳ σου ἐκ χειρός σού ἐστιν καὶ σοὶ τὰ πάντα ("O Lord our God, all this abundance that we have provided for building you a house for your holy name comes from your hand and is all your own").

86. Related examples are: John 20:17, οὔπω γὰρ ἀναβέβηκα πρὸς τὸν πάρερα ("for I have not yet ascended to the Father"); John 6:38, ὅτι καταβέβηκα ἀπὸ τοῦ οὐρανοῦ ("For I have come down from heaven"); 2 Pet 2:22, συμβέβηκεν αὐτοῖς τὸ τῆς ἀληθοῦς παροιμίας ("What the true proverb says has happened to them"); 1 John 3:14, ἡμεῖς οἴδαμεν ὅτι μεταβεβήκαμεν ἐκ τοῦ θανάτου εἰς τὴν ζωήν ("We know that we have passed out of death into life"). Horrocks regards this kind of perfect forms as "true perfects": ἐπιβέβηκα "I have gone" (Horrocks, *Greek*, 176). Andrason and Locatell state that in John 5:24 ("whoever hears my word and believes him who sent me has eternal life. He does not come into judgment, but has passed from death to life"), μεταβέβηκεν may convey a gnomic sense (Andrason and Locatell, "Perfect Wave," 37).

[John 15:18] Εἰ ὁ κόσμος ὑμᾶς μισεῖ, γινώσκετε ὅτι πρῶτον ἐμε ὑμῶν μεμίσηκεν.

If the world hates you, know that it *has hated* me before [it hated] you.

The perfects above denote current states connected with past events. Matthew 22:4 indicates the completion of preparing the dinner that the Master has been preparing from a preceding time. In John 3:13, ἀναβέβηκεν implies that in history no one except Jesus Christ has ever experienced having ascended into heaven. Similarly, John 15:18 describes the world as having hated Jesus Christ from the past until the present moment when he is speaking to the disciples.

Selected Texts from the Book of Revelation

The book of Revelation possesses many notable perfects, including some surprising usages, like the juxtaposition of the perfect with the aorist. Shifting tenses are often found in Revelation, baffling scholars in their search for an explanation.[87] The next chapter will handle the issue of shifting tenses. This section will only focus on the transitive anterior perfects in Revelation.

Revelation 2:3–5

This text contains current-relevance transitive perfects.

[Rev 2:3–5] καὶ ὑπομονὴν ἔχεις καὶ ἐβάστασας διὰ τὸ ὄνομά μου καὶ οὐ **κεκοπίακες**. ἀλλὰ ἔχω κατὰ σοῦ ὅτι τὴν ἀγάπην σου τὴν πρώτην ἀφῆκες. μνημόνευε οὖν πόθεν **πέπτωκας** καὶ μετανόησον καὶ τὰ πρῶτα ἔργα ποίησον.

I know you are enduring patiently and have endured for my name's sake, and you *have* not *grown weary*. But I have against you, that you have abandoned the love you had at first. Remember therefore from where you *have fallen*; repent, and do the works you did at first.

The text is interesting because the present, aorist and perfect are all juxtaposed. In verse 3, the resurrected Christ acknowledges the endeavor that the Ephesian believers have made from the past to the present. According to Porter's verbal aspect theory, the perfect κεκοπίακες does not

---

87. Mathewson, *Verbal Aspect in Revelation*, 117–23.

necessitate the anterior nuance of "having become weary," as in the traditional interpretation. Rather it denotes a general state of affairs: "in a state of being weary." In the text, however, κεκοπίακες implies the current state of being weary of the Ephesian Christians who have been working hard for some period of prior time. Moreover, the aorist connoting the past events appear side by side with these perfects. The aorists ἐβάστασας and ἀφῆκες both indicate previous events (perfective aspect). Porter's definition of the perfect as "a general state of affairs" does not fit well here. In Galatians 4:11 (φοβοῦμαι ὑμᾶς μή πως εἰκῇ κεκοπίακα εἰς ὑμᾶς "I fear for you, that perhaps I *have labored* for you in vain"), κεκοπίακα similarly describes the apostle Paul's endeavor toward the Galatian Christians from the past up to the present time.[88] Paul is afraid that what he has done for the Galatian churches may turn out to have been in vain.

The abstruseness of Revelation 2:3–5 lies in the way that the risen Lord *now* rebukes the Church of Ephesus for *having forsaken* their first love. Jesus Christ exhorts them to restore the relationship with him from which they have fallen. This designates the milieu as their having been apart from the Lord during some period of previous time. The current state of falling (πέπτωκας) results from the desertion of their first love for Christ at some point in the past. The fallen status continues from the past up to the present moment, when Christ is warning of removal. Strikingly, Mathewson disallows the temporal distinction between perfects and aorists in the text. He asserts that the aorist summarizes the event (ἐβάστασας "you bear up") and the perfect (κεκοπίακα) highlights the action of not being weary.[89]

Following Porter's markedness theory, Mathewson maintains that πέπτωκας highlights the need for repentance.[90] However, the mere use of πέπτωκας as an emphasis for "repentance" does not necessarily support Porter's stative perfect. Before they ever repent, the preceding event of "having fallen" (πέπτωκας) must exist. In order to highlight the need for repentance, as Mathewson argues, the implied prior event πέπτωκας is required.

---

88. Aubrey states that the perfect κεκοπίακα denotes the action which has been done by Paul beginning in the past (Aubrey, "Greek Perfect," 107). Similarly, in John 4:38 three perfects (κεκοπιάκατε, κεκοπιάκασιν, and εἰσεληλύθατε; "that for which you have not labored. Others have labored, and you have entered into their labor") also describe events from the past with current relevance.

89. Mathewson, *Verbal Aspect in Revelation*, 97. Fanning regards Revelation 2:5 as one of the examples of the traditional understanding of the perfect (Fanning, *Verbal Aspect*, 162). Aune states that the three tenses are employed for rhetorical purpose. The present tense shows their current state ("having endurance"), along with the aorist indicating the past behavior secondly, and then thirdly, the perfect tense denotes the labor the church of Ephesus has done up to the present (Aune, *Revelation 1–5*, 146).

90. Mathewson, *Verbal Aspect in Revelation*, 105.

Therefore, Mathewson's "highlighting perfect for the need of repentance" buttresses the preceding action of the perfect πέπτωκας ("having fallen") rather than a mere stative sense.

Revelation 3:2–3

The next notable anterior perfect is from Revelation 3.

> [Rev 3:2–3] οὐ γὰρ **εὕρηκά** σου τὰ ἔργα πεπληρωμένα ἐνώπιον τοῦ θεοῦ μου. μνημόνευε οὖν πῶς εἴληφας καὶ ἤκουσας καὶ τήρει καὶ μετανόησον.
>
> For I *have* not *found* your works complete in the sight of my God. Remember therefore what you have received and heard; and keep it and repent.

In this text, the resurrected Christ urges the church in Sardis to remember what they have taken and heard, for the sake of repentance. The notable perfect is εὕρηκα. The context of Revelation 3:2–3 is that Jesus Christ has been trying to find the completion of the works of the believers in Sardis.[91] Despite searching for some preceding period of time, the Lord is not able to find their complete work. Finally, the Son of God is *now* saying that *for a period of time* he has not found the completed work of the Christians in Sardis, from the past until now. Therefore, the description of the church in Sardis does not merely indicate the current state but connotes a period of time that includes past moments. Similarly, in John 1:41 and 45 ("we [have] found the Messiah ... who Moses wrote about in the Law"), Philip informs Nathanael that Jesus is the Messiah using the word εὑρήκαμεν.[92] With the background of the Jews having been waiting for the Messiah for thousands of years, Philip has now found the Messiah moments ago and the state of his being found remains, so that Philip can joyfully share the news with his comrade Nathanael.

On the other hand, the aorist ἤκουσας in Revelation 3:3 represents a prior action, the hearing of the Christians in Sardis at some point in the past. Then, the present form τήρει describes their ongoing endeavor to keep

---

91. Similarly, see 2 John 1:4, Ἐχάρην λίαν ὅτι εὕρηκα ἐκ τῶν τέκνων σου περιπατοῦντας ἐν ἀληθείᾳ ("I rejoiced greatly that I have found some of your children walking in the truth").

92. ESV, "We have found the Messiah (which means Christ)"; NASB, "We have found the Messiah (which translated means Christ)"; NIV, "We have found the Messiah (that is, the Christ)"; and KJV, "We have found the Messias, which is, being interpreted, the Christ."

the truth they received and heard.⁹³ These two verbs are distinguished from the perfect εὕρηκα of current relevance.

Πεπίστευκα

Another common example of the anterior perfect is πεπίστευκα. For example:

> [John 6:69] καί ἡμεῖς πεπιστεύκαμεν καὶ ἐγνώκαμεν ὅτι σὺ εἶ ὁ ἅγιος τοῦ θεοῦ.
> And we *have believed* and have come to know that you are the Holy One of God.⁹⁴
>
> [John 16:27] αὐτὸς γὰρ ὁ πατὴρ φιλεῖ ὑμᾶς, ὅτι ὑμεῖς ἐμὲ πεφιλήκατε καὶ πεπιστεύκατε ὅτι ἐγὼ παρὰ [τοῦ] θεοῦ ἐξῆλθον.
> For the Father himself loves you, because you [disciples] have loved me and *have believed* that I came from God.
>
> [John 20:29] λέγει αὐτῷ ὁ Ἰησοῦς· ὅτι ἑώρακάς με πεπίστευκας; μακάριοι οἱ μὴ ἰδόντες καὶ πιστεύσαντες.
> Jesus said to him, "Because you have seen me, *have you believed*? Blessed are they who did not see, and yet believed."⁹⁵

First, in John 6:69, the disciples have believed from the beginning of Jesus' ministry and have come to know that he is the Christ. Campbell asserts that πεπιστεύκαμεν and ἐγνώκαμεν are intensive perfects. He argues that they can be rendered, "we truly believe and know that you are the Holy

---

93. Interestingly, Robertson states that it would be easier if ἤκουσας had been ἀκήκοας in that if so, the latter would emphasize the permanence of the obligation: "It is as easy as to say that ἤκουσας = a perfect as that εἴληφας = an aorist" (Robertson, *Grammar*, 901).

94. In John 11:27 (ναὶ κύριε, ἐγὼ πεπίστευκα ὅτι σὺ εἶ ὁ χριστὸς ὁ υἱὸς τοῦ θεοῦ ὁ εἰς κόσμον ἐρχόμενος. "Yes, Lord; I *have believed* that you are the Christ, the Son of God, who is coming into the world"), Martha has believed from the past time up to now that Jesus is the Christ, the Son of God. The context confirms it when Martha confesses that she believes in the resurrection. Similarly, see 1 John 4:16, καὶ ἡμεῖς ἐγνώκαμεν καὶ πεπιστεύκαμεν τὴν ἀγάπην ἣν ἔχει ὁ θεὸς ἐν ἡμῖν ("And we have come to know and *have believed* the love which God has for us").

95. See 2 Tim 1:12, οἶδα γὰρ ᾧ πεπίστευκα καὶ πέπεισμαι ("for I know I *have believed*, and I am convinced").

One of God."⁹⁶ The disciples's confession happens in the middle of Jesus Christ's ministry, presupposing that the disciples already believed in Jesus as the Messiah and followed him at the beginning of his ministry. Whether or not these perfects denote an intensive notion here, the temporal connection in the text between now and the past cannot be ignored.

In John 16:27 a different nuance between the perfect and the aorist is observed. The perfects (πεφιλήκατε πεπιστεύκατε) denote the current relevance of the disciples' loving and believing Jesus Christ beginning in the past. In contrast, the aorist ἐξῆλθον expresses the past event of the incarnation of the Son of God. Similarly, the perfects ἑώρακας and πεπίστευκας in John 20:29 convey the anterior nuance—"having seen" and "having believed."

Ἀκήκοα

The perfect ἀκήκοα is a representative of the anterior perfect. For instance, in John 4:42 the Samaritans respond after hearing the words of Jesus Christ: ἀκηκόαμεν καὶ οἴδαμεν ὅτι οὗτός ἐστιν ἀληθῶς ὁ σωτὴρ τοῦ κόσμου ("for we *have heard* for ourselves and know that this is indeed the Savior of the world"). For two days they heard, and are now confessing their faith in the present moment. More texts containing ἀκήκοα are:

> [John 5:37] καὶ ὁ πέμψας με πατὴρ ἐκεῖνος μεμαρτύρηκεν περὶ ἐμοῦ. οὔτε φωνὴν αὐτοῦ πώποτε ἀκηκόατε οὔτε εἶδος αὐτοῦ ἑωράκατε.
>
> And the Father who sent me has himself borne witness about me. His voice you *have* never *heard*, his form you have never seen.

> [Acts 6:11, 14] ὅτι ἀκηκόαμεν αὐτοῦ λαλοῦντος ῥήματα βλάσφημα εἰς Μωϋσῆν καὶ τὸν θεόν . . . ἀκηκόαμεν γὰρ αὐτοῦ λέγοντος ὅτι Ἰησοῦς ὁ Ναζωραῖος οὗτος καταλύσει τὸν τόπον τοῦτον καὶ ἀλλάξει τὰ ἔθη ἃ παρέδωκεν ἡμῖν Μωϋσῆς.
>
> We *have heard* him speak blasphemous words against Moses and God . . . for we *have heard* him say that this Jesus of Nazareth will destroy this place and will change the customs that Moses delivered to us.

> [Rom 15:21] ἀλλὰ καθὼς γέγραπται· οἷς οὐκ ἀνηγγέλη περὶ αὐτοῦ ὄψονται, καὶ οἳ οὐκ ἀκηκόασιν συνήσουσιν.

---

96. Campbell, *Indicative Mood*, 202.

But as it is written, "They who had no news of him shall see, and they who *have* never *heard* shall understand."

[1 John 1:5] Καὶ ἔστιν αὕτη ἡ ἀγγελία ἣν ἀκηκόαμεν ἀπ' αὐτοῦ καὶ ἀναγγέλλομεν ὑμῖν, ὅτι ὁ θεὸς φῶς ἐστιν καὶ σκοτία ἐν αὐτῷ οὐκ ἔστιν οὐδεμία.

And this is the message we *have heard* from him and announce to you, that God is light, and in him there is no darkness at all.[97]

[LXX Gen 42:2] ἰδοὺ ἀκήκοα ὅτι ἔστιν σῖτος ἐν Αἰγύπτῳ· κατάβητε ἐκεῖ καὶ πρίασθε ἡμῖν μικρὰ βρώματα, ἵνα ζῶμεν καὶ μὴ ἀποθάνωμεν.

Behold, I [Jacob] *have heard* that there is grain in Egypt; go down there and buy grain for us there, that we may live and not die.

All the perfects denote a current relevance. In John 5:37, Jesus Christ points out that the Jews have not experienced a moment of hearing the voice of the Father. In Acts 6:11–14, the Jews are speaking of their experience of their *having heard* Stephen's blasphemous words against God which continually affects the present moment with regard to prosecuting him. Andrason and Locatell rightly evaluate ἀκηκόαμεν as showing relevance to the present state from a past experience.[98]

Not only in the NT, but also in the Septuagint ἀκήκοα shows an anterior nuance. In Genesis 42:2, ἀκήκοα indicates the current state of Jacob having heard the news about the grain in Egypt. Jacob experiences this news between now and the past. This anterior nuance of ἀκήκοα as experiential perfect also appears in Classical literatures.[99]

---

97. It is the same in 1 John 4:3, ὃ ἀκηκόατε ὅτι ἔρχεται ("of which you have heard that it is coming"). Andrason and Locatell consider ἀκηκόαμεν in 1 John 1:5 as past time (Andrason and Locatell, "Perfect Wave," 52). The next chapter will examine the perfect with a simple past nuance.

98. Andrason and Locatell, "Perfect Wave," 44–45.

99. The Classical texts are: Plato, *Apology* 17c, ὦ ἄνδρες, τῇδε τῇ ἡλικίᾳ ὥσπερ μειρακίῳ πλάττοντι λόγους εἰς ὑμᾶς εἰσιέναι. καὶ μέντοι καὶ πάνυ, ὦ ἄνδρες Ἀθηναῖοι, τοῦτο ὑμῶν δέομαι καὶ παρίεμαι· ἐὰν διὰ τῶν αὐτῶν λόγων ἀκούητέ μου ἀπολογουμένου, δι' ὧνπερ εἴωθα λέγειν καὶ ἐν ἀγορᾷ ἐπὶ τῶν τραπεζῶν, ἵνα ὑμῶν πολλοὶ ἀκηκόασι, καὶ ἄλλοθι ("And, men of Athens, I urgently beg and beseech you if you hear me making my defence with the same words with which I have been accustomed where many of you *have heard* me, and elsewhere") (Plato, *Apology*, 70–71); Lysias, *Lysias* 12.100, παύσομαι κατηγορῶν, ἀκηκόατε, ἑωράκατε, πεπόνθατε, ἔχετε· δικάζετε ("I will here conclude my accusation. You *have heard*, you have seen, you have suffered; you have them: give judgment"). Gerö and Stechow regard ἀκήκοα as an experiential perfect (Gerö and Stechow,

Texts with Anterior Perfects in the New Testament

Since a great number of anterior perfects occur in the Greek New Testament, listing them is an efficient way to illustrate these perfects.[100]

[Mark 10:28] Ἤρξατο λέγειν ὁ Πέτρος αὐτῷ· ἰδοὺ ἡμεῖς ἀφήκαμεν πάντα καὶ **ἠκολουθήκαμέν** σοι.

Peter began to say to him, "See, we have left everything and *have followed* you."[101]

[Luke 7:50] εἶπεν δὲ πρὸς τὴν γυναῖκα· ἡ πίστις σου **σέσωκέν** σε· πορεύου εἰς εἰρήνην.

And he said to the woman, "Your faith *has saved* you; go in peace."

[John 12:40] **τετύφλωκεν** αὐτῶν τοὺς ὀφθαλμοὺς καὶ ἐπώρωσεν αὐτῶν τὴν καρδίαν, ἵνα μὴ ἴδωσιν τοῖς ὀφθαλμοῖς καὶ νοήσωσιν τῇ καρδίᾳ καὶ στραφῶσιν, καὶ ἰάσομαι αὐτούς.

He *has blinded* their eyes and hardened their heart, lest they see with their eyes, and understand with their heart, and turn, and I would heal them.

[Acts 16:15] ὡς δὲ ἐβαπτίσθη καὶ ὁ οἶκος αὐτῆς, παρεκάλεσεν λέγουσα· εἰ **κεκρίκατέ** με πιστὴν τῷ κυρίῳ εἶναι, εἰσελθόντες εἰς τὸν οἶκόν μου μένετε· καὶ παρεβιάσατο ἡμᾶς.

And after she was baptized, and her household as well, she urged us, saying "If you *have judged* me to be faithful to the Lord, come to my house and stay." And she prevailed upon us.[102]

"Tense in Time," 272–73). Sicking and Stork offer more Classical examples (Sicking and Stork, *Two Studies*, 162–66). Sicking and Stork describe ἀκήκοα as a present state that he has heard something.

100. More examples are: Luke 24:29, κέκλικεν ἤδη ἡ ἡμέρα ("the day has been already spent"); 2 Cor 2:5, Εἰ δέ τις λελύπηκεν, οὐκ ἐμὲ λελύπηκεν ("Now if anyone has caused pain, he has caused it not to me"); 2 Cor 11:21, κατὰ ἀτιμίαν λέγω, ὡς ὅτι ἡμεῖς ἠσθενήκαμεν ("To my shame I must say that I have been weak"); Phil 4:12, ἐν παντὶ καὶ ἐν πᾶσιν μεμύημαι, καὶ χορτάζεσθαι καὶ πεινᾶν καὶ περισσεύειν καὶ ὑστερεῖσθαι ("In any and every circumstance, I have learned the secret of facing plenty and hunger, abundance and need").

101. The same expression occurs in 1 Tim 4:6, ἐντρεφόμενος τοῖς λόγοις τῆς πίστεως καὶ τῆς καλῆς διδασκαλίας ᾗ παρηκολούθηκας ("being trained in the words of the faith and of the good doctrine that you have followed").

102. See 1 Cor 5:3, ἤδη κέκρικα ὡς παρὼν τὸν οὕτως τοῦτο κατεργασάμενον ("I have already pronounced judgment on the one who did such a thing"); 1 Cor 7:37, καὶ τοῦτο

> [Acts 25:11] εἰ μὲν οὖν ἀδικῶ καὶ ἄξιον θανάτου **πέπραχά** τι, οὐ παραιτοῦμαι τὸ ἀποθανεῖν· εἰ δὲ οὐδέν ἐστιν ὧν οὗτοι κατηγοροῦσίν μου, οὐδείς με δύναται αὐτοῖς χαρίσασθαι· Καίσαρα ἐπικαλοῦμαι.
>
> For if I be an offender, or *have committed* any thing worthy of death, I do not refuse to die; but if there is nothing to their charges against me, no one can give me up to them. I appeal to Caesar.[103]

The perfects above express the anterior (current relevance) nuance. In Mark 10:28, ἠκολουθήκαμεν describes the disciples' continuing action of following Jesus Christ from a past moment, in contrast with the aorist ἀφήκαμεν indicating a punctiliar action that occurred once in the past. The use of τετύφλωκεν in John 12:40 also indicates the ongoing effect of being blind from a completed action. In Acts 16:15 where Lydia is speaking to Paul after hearing his sermon, κεκρίκατε conveys Paul's judgment of whether or not Lydia is now faithful looking from the past to the current time. The perfect σέσωκεν in Luke 7:50 also presents a current relevance.[104]

More illustrative passages include:

> [Rom 9:6] Οὐχ οἷον δὲ ὅτι **ἐκπέπτωκεν** ὁ λόγος τοῦ θεοῦ.
> But it is not as though the word of God *has failed*.

> [Heb 12:2] ἀφορῶντες εἰς τὸν τῆς πίστεως ἀρχηγὸν καὶ τελειωτὴν Ἰησοῦν, ὃς ἀντὶ τῆς προκειμένης αὐτῷ χαρᾶς ὑπέμεινεν σταυρὸν αἰσχύνης καταφρονήσας ἐν δεξιᾷ τε τοῦ θρόνου τοῦ θεοῦ **κεκάθικεν**.
> Looking to Jesus, the founder and perfecter of our faith, who for the joy that was set before him endured

---

κέκρικεν ἐν τῇ ἰδίᾳ καρδίᾳ ("and has decided this in his own heart"); and Titus 3:12, ἐκεῖ γὰρ κέκρικα παραχειμάσαι ("I have decided to spend the winter here").

103. In Acts 21:28 (ἔτι τε καὶ Ἕλληνας εἰσήγαγεν εἰς τὸ ἱερὸν καὶ κεκοίνωκεν τὸν ἅγιον τόπον τοῦτον "Moreover, he even brought Greeks into the temple and has defiled this holy place"), McKay says that the perfect refers to the stativity of the subject with responsibility, "he has defiled (is guilty of defiling) this holy place" (McKay, *New Syntax*, 32).

104. Andrason and Locatell, "Perfect Wave," 43. In the Gospels σέσωκεν denotes the same nuance: Matt 9:22, θάρσει, θύγατερ· ἡ πίστις σου σέσωκέν σε ("Take heart, daughter; your faith has made you well"); Mark 5:34, θύγατερ· ἡ πίστις σου σέσωκέν σε ("daughter, your faith has made you well"); Mark 10:52, ὕπαγε, ἡ πίστις σου σέσωκέν σε ("Go your way; your faith has made you well"); Luke 17:19, ἀναστὰς πορεύου· ἡ πίστις σου σέσωκέν σε ("Rise and go your way; your faith has made you well"); and Luke 18:42, ἀνάβλεψον· ἡ πίστις σου σέσωκέν σε ("Recover your sight; your faith has made you well"). Illustrating σέσωκεν, Runge states that the perfect provides the relevant information of what precedes (Runge, "Discourse Function," 480).

the cross, despising the shame, and *has sat down* at the right hand of the throne of God.[105]

[1 John 4:10] ἐν τούτῳ ἐστὶν ἡ ἀγάπη, οὐχ ὅτι ἡμεῖς **ἠγαπήκαμεν** τὸν θεόν, ἀλλ' ὅτι αὐτὸς ἠγάπησεν ἡμᾶς καὶ ἀπέστειλεν τὸν υἱὸν αὐτοῦ ἱλασμὸν περὶ τῶν ἁμαρτιῶν ἡμῶν.

In this is love, not that we *have loved* God but he loved us and sent his Son to be the propitiation for our sins.

[1 John 5:15] καὶ ἐὰν οἴδαμεν ὅτι ἀκούει ἡμῶν ὃ ἐὰν αἰτώμεθα, οἴδαμεν ὅτι ἔχομεν τὰ αἰτήματα ἃ **ᾐτήκαμεν** ἀπ' αὐτοῦ.

And if we know that he hears us in whatever we ask, we know that we have the requests that we *have asked* of him.

[Rev 14:8] ἐκ τοῦ οἴνου τοῦ θυμοῦ τῆς πορνείας αὐτῆς **πεπότικεν** πάντα τὰ ἔθνη.

From the wine of her immoral passion she *has made* all the nations *drink*.[106]

In Romans 9:6, Paul considers that the word of God has not failed from the past until the present time. Not only have the words of God been fulfilled from the OT but this is also a part of God's plan even though the Jews are still stubborn. The difference is notable between the perfect and the aorist in 1 John 4:10. While the aorist ἠγάπησεν points out the prior love of God the Father and the Son, the perfect ἠγαπήκαμεν indicates the believers' current state of not having loved God from the past until now.

The anterior perfects also occur in Septuagint. A couple of examples are:

[Gen 33:8] καὶ εἶπεν τί ταῦτά σοί ἐστιν πᾶσαι αἱ παρεμβολαὶ αὗται αἷς **ἀπήντηκα**;

And he [Esau] said, "What do you mean by all this company which I *have met*?"[107]

---

105. See Heb 10:14, μιᾷ γὰρ προσφορᾷ τετελείωκεν εἰς τὸ διηνεκὲς τοὺς ἁγιαζομένους ("For by a single offering he has perfected for all time those who are being sanctified").

106. Similarly, Rev 18:3, ὅτι ἐκ τοῦ οἴνου τοῦ θυμοῦ τῆς πορνείας αὐτῆς πέπωκαν πάντα τὰ ἔθνη ("For all nations have drunk of the wine of the wrath of her fornication"); Acts 13:47, οὕτως γὰρ ἐντέταλται ἡμῖν ὁ κύριος· τέθεικά σε εἰς φῶς ἐθνῶν ("For so the Lord has commanded us, saying 'I have made you a light for Gentiles'"); Rom 4:17, πατέρα πολλῶν ἐθνῶν τέθεικά σε ("I have made you the father of many nations"). A notable perfect πεπότικεν is causative. Aubrey states that causative verbs such as ἀναπαύω ("cause to rest") should take middle form in order to express a resultative nuance (Aubrey, "Greek Perfect," 125–26).

107. More passages are: Gen 24:21, 27, εἰ εὐόδωκεν κύριος τὴν ὁδὸν αὐτοῦ ἢ οὔ

[Exod 32:31] ὑπέστρεψεν δὲ Μωυσῆς πρὸς κύριος καὶ εἶπεν Δέομαι, κύριε· **ἡμάρτηκεν** ὁ λαὸς οὗτος ἁμαρτίαν μεγάλην καὶ ἐποίησαν ἑαυτοῖς θεοὺς χρυσοῦς.
So Moses returned to the Lord and said, "Alas, this people *have sinned* a great sin. They have made for themselves gods of gold."[108]

In Genesis 33:8, Esau has been meeting several herds that Jacob sent him as presents, up until he meets Jacob and asks him about them. Esau has an experience of meeting several herds for a period of time from the past up to the speaking moment. The scene of Exodus 32:31 is that the Israelites are in a present state of sin because of having sinned in the past.

Ἔγνωκα

Another notable perfect is ἔγνωκα. This perfect presents a current relevance (anterior) nuance.

[John 8:55] καὶ οὐκ ἐγνώκατε αὐτόν, ἐγὼ δὲ οἶδα αὐτόν.
But you *have* not *known* him, but I know him.

In John 8:55, Jesus Christ points out that from the past until now the Jews have not been in a state of knowing God.[109] In contrast, the disciples are now in a state of knowing about the Father since a certain period of moment in the past. The current relevance ἔγνωκα appears many times in the Greek New Testament.[110]

("whether the Lord has prospered his journey or not"); Gen 38:24, ἐκπεπόρνευκεν Θαμαρ ἡ νύμφη σου καὶ ἰδοὺ ἐν γαστρὶ ἔχει ἐκ πορνείας ("Tamar your daughter-in-law has played the harlot. Moreover, she is pregnant by harlotry").

108. The verb is the same as in 1 John 1:10, ἐὰν εἴπωμεν ὅτι οὐχ ἡμαρτήκαμεν, ψεύστην ποιοῦμεν αὐτόν ("If we say we have not sinned, we make him a liar").

109. John 14:7, 9, εἰ ἐγνώκατέ με, καὶ τὸν πατέρα μου γνώσεσθε. . . . τοσούτῳ χρόνῳ μεθ᾽ ὑμῶν εἰμι καὶ οὐκ ἐγνωκάς με, Φίλιππε; ("If you had known me, you would have known my Father also. . . . Have I been with so long, and you still do not know me, Philip?").

110. John 5:42, ἀλλὰ ἔγνωκα ὑμᾶς ὅτι τὴν ἀγάπην τοῦ θεοῦ οὐκ ἔχετε ἐν ἑαυτοῖς ("But I have known you that you do not have the love of God in you"); John 8:52, νῦν ἐγνώκαμεν ὅτι δαιμόνιον ἔχεις ("now we know that you have a demon!"); John 17:7, νῦν ἔγνωκαν ὅτι πάντα ὅσα δέδωκάς μοι παρὰ σοῦ εἰσιν ("Now they [have come to] know that everything that you have given me is from you"); 1 Cor 2:8, ἣν οὐδεὶς τῶν ἀρχόντων τοῦ αἰῶνος τούτου ἔγνωκεν ("None of the rulers of this age [has] understood"); 2 Cor 5:16 is the same, εἰ καὶ ἐγνώκαμεν κατὰ σάρκα Χριστόν ("Even though we have known Christ according to the flesh; 1 John 2:3–4, Καὶ ἐν τούτῳ γινώσκομεν ὅτι ἐγνώκαμεν αὐτόν, ἐὰν τὰς ἐντολὰς αὐτοῦ τηρῶμεν. ὁ λεγων ὅτι ἔγνωκα αὐτὸν καὶ τὰς ἐντολὰς αὐτοῦ μὴ τηρῶν,

1 John 2:13–14 needs to be examined:

[1 John 2:13–14] γράφω ὑμῖν, πατέρες, ὅτι ἐγνώκατε τὸν ἀπ' ἀρχῆς. γράφω ὑμῖν, νεανίστκοι, ὅτι **νενικήκατε** τὸν πονηρόν. ἔγραψα ὑμῖν, παιδία, ὅτι **ἐγνώκατε** τὸν πατέρα. ἔγραψα ὑμῖν, πατέρες, ὅτι **ἐγνώκατε** τὸν ἀπ' ἀρχῆς. ἔγραψα ὑμῖν, νεανίσκοι, ὅτι ἰσχυροί ἐστε καὶ ὁ λόγος τοῦ θεοῦ ἐν ὑμῖν μένει καὶ **νενικήκατε** τὸν πονηρόν.

I am writing to you, fathers, because you know [have known] him who is from the beginning. I am writing to you, young men, because you have overcome the evil one. I write to you, children, because you know [have known] the Father. I write to you, fathers, because you know him who is from the beginning. I write to you, young men, because you are strong, and the word of God abides in you, and you have overcome the evil one.[111]

The perfects ἐγνώκατε and νενικήκατε occur in the text. With respect to translating ἐγνώκατε, English-Bible translations are not in agreement. The ESV, NASB, and NIV translations render it as "know," while KJV and NET as "have known." The adverbial phrase ἀπ' ἀρχῆς ("from the beginning") contains a hint: ἐγνώκατε denotes the current relevance of a past event. With regard to νενικήκατε, on the other hand, Andrason and Locatell consider it to have a current relevant nuance, saying,

> Even though "the evil one" has already been overcome, it remains currently relevant as its results persist to the present. That is, from the general context, it is clear that the evil one still remains defeated.[112]

The perfect νενικήκατε describes a current state of resulting from the past of having conquered something or someone. It also conveys a current relevance nuance.[113]

ψεύστης ἐστίν ("And by this we know that we have come to know him, if we keep his commandments. Whoever says, 'I know him' but does not keep his commandments is a liar").

111. Similarly, see 1 John 3:6, πᾶς ὁ ἁμαρτάνων οὐχ ἑώρακεν αὐτὸν οὐδὲ ἔγνωκεν αὐτόν ("no one who keeps on sinning has either seen him or known him"); and 1 John 3:16, ἐν τούτῳ ἐγνώκαμεν τὴν ἀγάπην ("We know love by this").

112. Andrason and Locatell, "Perfect Wave," 42.

113. Andrason and Locatell, "Perfect Wave," 42. See John 16:33, Ταῦτα λελάληκα ὑμῖν ἵνα ἐν ἐμοὶ εἰρήνην ἔχητε. ἐν τῷ κόσμῳ θλῖψιν ἔχετε· ἀλλὰ θαρσεῖτε, ἐγὼ νενίκηκα τὸν κόσμον ("I have said these things to you, that in me you may have peace. In the world you will have tribulation. But take heart; I have overcome the world"); and 1 John 4:4,

Ἐλήλυθα

The perfect ἐλήλυθα is Homeric, but it does not belong to the oldest layer of epic.[114] Gerö and Stechow say that ἐλήλυθα presents a resultant state in Homer.[115] This perfect occurs in Classical Greek literatures, for example, Thucydides and Demosthenes.[116] In the NT ἐλήλυθα delivers a current relevance nuance many times.[117]

ὑμεῖς ἐκ τοῦ θεοῦ ἐστε, τεκνία, καὶ νενικήκατε αὐτούς, ὅτι μείζων ἐστὶν ὁ ἐν ὑμῖν ἢ ὁ ἐν τῷ κόσμῳ ("Little children, you are from God and have overcome them, for he who is in you is greater than he who is in the world").

114. Wackernagel, "Studien zum griechischen Perfektum," 17.

115. Gerö and Stechow, "Tense in Time," 268; *Iliad* 21.81, ἠὼς δέ μοί ἐστιν ἥδε δυωδεκάτη, ὅτ' ἐς Ἴλιον εἰλήλουθα ("it is now twelfth morning of my being in [lit. having come to] Troy"). Similarly, Buth expresses ἐλήλυθα as "in a state of having arrived" (Buth, "Perfect Greek Morphology," 427).

116. Chantraine, *Parfait grec*, 71–73. Sicking and Stork note that ἐλήλυθα occurs one time in Aeschylus, nine times in Sophocles, eleven times in Euripides, eleven times in Aristophanes, and two times in Lysias (Sicking and Stork, *Two Studies*, 188, 195, 204, 214, 235).

117. More usages are as follows (perfects in bold): Luke 5:32, οὐκ **ἐλήλυθα** καλέσαι δικαίους ἀλλὰ ἁμαρτωλοὺς εἰς μετάνοιαν ("I have not come to call the righteous but sinners"); Luke 7:33–34, **ἐλήλυθεν** γὰρ Ἰωάννης ὁ βαπτιστὴς μὴ ἐσθίων ἄρτον μήτε πίνων οἶνον. . . . **ἐλήλυθεν** ὁ υἱὸς τοῦ ἀνθρώπου ἐσθίων καὶ πίνων ("John the Baptist has come eating no bread and drinking no wine. . . . The Son of Man has come eating and drinking"); John 3:19, αὕτη δέ ἐστιν ἡ κρίσις ὅτι τὸ φῶς **ἐλήλυθεν** εἰς τὸν κόσμον καὶ ἠγάπησαν οἱ ἄνθρωποι μᾶλλον τὸ σκότος ("And this is the judgment: the light has come into the world, and people loved the darkness"); John 5:43, ἐγὼ **ἐλήλυθα** ἐν τῷ ὀνόματι τοῦ πατρός μου, καὶ οὐ λαμβάνετέ με ("I have come in my Father's name, and you do not receive me"); John 7:28, κἀμὲ οἴδατε καὶ οἴδατε πόθεν εἰμί· καὶ ἀπ' ἐμαυτοῦ οὐκ **ἐλήλυθα** ("You know me, and you know where I come from? But I have not come of my own accord"); John 8:42, εἰ ὁ θεὸς πατὴρ ὑμῶν ἦν ἠγαπᾶτε ἂν ἐμέ, ἐγὼ γὰρ ἐκ τοῦ θεοῦ ἐξῆλθον καὶ ἥκω· οὐδὲ γὰρ ἀπ' ἐμαυτοῦ **ἐλήλυθα**, ἀλλ' ἐκεῖνός με ἀπέστειλεν ("If God were your Father, you would love me; for I proceeded forth and have come from God, for I have not come on my own initiative, but he sent me"); John 12:46, ἐγὼ φῶς εἰς τὸν κόσμον **ἐλήλυθα**, ἵνα πᾶς ὁ πιστεύων εἰς ἐμὲ ἐν τῇ σκοτίᾳ μὴ μείνῃ ("I have come into the world as light, that everyone who believes in me may not remain in darkness"); John 16:28, ἐξῆλθον παρὰ τοῦ πατρὸς καὶ **ἐλήλυθα** εἰς τὸν κόσμον· πάλιν ἀφίημι τὸν κόσμον καὶ πορεύομαι πρὸς τὸν πατέρα ("I came forth from the Father, and I have come into the world; I am leaving the world again, and going to the Father"); John 18:37, σὺ λέγεις ὅτι βασιλεύς εἰμι. ἐγὼ εἰς τοῦτο γεγέννημαι καὶ εἰς τοῦτο **ἐλήλυθα** εἰς τὸν κόσμον, ἵνα μαρτυρήσω τῇ ἀληθείᾳ ("You say correctly that I am a king. For this I have been born, and for this I have come to the world, to bear witness to the truth"); Heb 12:18, 22, Οὐ γὰρ **προσεληλύθατε** ψηλαφωμένῳ καὶ κεκαυμένῳ πυρὶ καὶ γνόφῳ καὶ ζόφῳ καὶ θυέλλῃ. . . . ἀλλὰ **προσεληλύθατε** Σιὼν ὄρει καὶ πόλει θεοῦ ζῶντος ("For you have not come to what may be touched, a blazing fire and darkness and gloom and a tempest. . . . But you have come to Mount Zion and to the city of the living God").

[Mark 7:29] καὶ εἶπεν αὐτῇ· διὰ τοῦτον τὸν λόγον ὕπαγε, ἐξελήλυθεν ἐκ τῆς θυγατρός σου τὸ δαιμόνιον.

And he said to her, "For this statement you may go your way; demon *has left* your daughter."

[Mark 9:13] ἀλλὰ λέγω ὑμῖν ὅτι καὶ Ἠλίας ἐλήλυθεν, καὶ ἐποίησαν αὐτῷ ὅσα ἤθελον, καθὼς γέγραπται ἐπ' αὐτόν.

But I tell you that Elijah *has come*, and they did to him whatever they pleased, as it is written of him.

[John 12:23] Ὁ δὲ Ἰησοῦς ἀποκρίνεται αὐτοῖς λέγων· ἐλήλυθεν ἡ ὥρα ἵνα δοξασθῇ ὁ υἱὸς τοῦ ἀνθρώπου.

And Jesus answered them, "The hour *has come* for the Son of Man to be glorified."[118]

[Acts 21:22] τί οὖν ἐστιν; πάντως ἀκούσονται ὅτι ἐλήλυθας.

What then is to be done? They will certainly hear that you *have come*.

[Phil 1:12] Γινώσκειν δὲ ὑμᾶς βούλομαι, ἀδελφοί, ὅτι τὰ κατ' ἐμὲ μᾶλλον εἰς προκοπὴν τοῦ εὐαγγελίου ἐλήλυθεν.

I want you to know, brothers, that my circumstances *have turned out* for the greater progress of the gospel.

All the cases above show current relevance. For instance, Andrason and Locatell describe ἐλήλυθεν in Mark 9:13 as denoting a typical perfect meaning.[119] In Mark 7:29, the compound forms also deliver the same anterior nuance.[120]

Aubrey states that it is difficult to decide whether ἐλήλυθεν conveys completive ("*has certainly come*") or resultative ("*is certainly here*"), even though the Greek perfect originally denotes a result.[121] Some scholars ar-

---

118. The texts that express "The hour has come" are as follows: John 12:23, 17:1, ἐλήλυθεν ἡ ὥρα ("the hour has come"); 16:32, ἰδοὺ ἔρχεται ὥρα καὶ ἐλήλυθα ("Behold, the hour is coming, indeed it has come").

119. Andrason and Locatell, "Perfect Wave," 41–42.

120. See James 5:4, αἱ βοαὶ τῶν θερισάντων εἰς τὰ ὦτα κυρίου σαβαὼθ εἰσεληλύθασιν ("the cries of the harvesters have reached the ears of the Lord of hosts"); and 1 John 4:1, ὅτι πολλοὶ ψευδοπροφῆται ἐξεληλύθασιν εἰς τὸν κόσμον ("for many false prophets have gone out into the world").

121. Aubrey, "Greek Perfect," 112, 119. Aubrey adds, "However, considering that the category of completive was essentially an unknown option when these grammatical descriptions were written, we may not want to be too hasty in assuming one direction of change over the other. I am not confident that there is a definitive means of deciding which option should be preferred."

gue that ἐλήλυθα is used as perfective past (preterite).[122] As the texts show above, however, ἐλήλυθα shows the current effect of the anterior event of coming. Seemingly the best way to regard ἐλήλυθα in the NT is a current relevance perfect.[123]

Ἤγγικεν

Finally, the perfect ἤγγικεν is a little peculiar. The perfect generally conveys a continuing state of a completed action. Robertson says that the "punctiliar-durative perfect" is common and frequent (•———). Interestingly, Robertson analyzes ἤγγικεν as a backward look (———•), saying, "This act may be durative-punctiliar."[124] The main texts with ἤγγικεν are:

> [Matt 3:2] μετανοεῖτε· ἤγγικεν γὰρ ἡ βασιλεία τῶν οὐρανῶν.
> Repent, for the kingdom of heaven has come near.

> [Luke 21:8, 20] ὁ δὲ εἶπεν· βλέπετε μὴ πλανηθῆτε· πολλοὶ γὰρ ἐλεύσονται ἐπὶ τῷ ὀνόματί μου λέγοντες· ἐγώ εἰμι, καί· ὁ καιρὸς ἤγγικεν. μὴ πορευθῆτε ὀπίσω αὐτῶν. . . .Ὅταν δὲ ἴδητε κυκλουμένην ὑπὸ στρατοπέδων Ἰερουσαλήμ, τότε γνῶτε ὅτι ἤγγικεν ἡ ἐρήμωσις αὐτῆς.
> And he said, "See that you are not led astray. For many will come in my name, saying 'I am he!' and, 'The time is at hand!' Do not go after them. . . . But when you see

---

122. Campbell, *Basics of Verbal Aspect*, 108; Decker, *Temporal Deixis*, 109; Crellin, "Gothic Eyes," 32. Crellin states that the Gothic translation of the passage renders ἐλήλυθα as past tense.

123. The perfect ἥκασιν contains a similar nuance: Mark 8:3, καί τινες αὐτῶν ἀπὸ μακρόθεν ἥκασιν ("some of them have come from a distance"); LXX Gen 45:16, ἥκασιν οἱ ἀδελφοὶ Ιωσηφ ("Joseph's brothers have come"); Gen 42:9, κατάσκοποί ἐστε κατανοῆσαι τὰ ἴχνη τῆς χώρας ἥκατε ("You are spies; you have come to see the nakedness of the land"); Gen 37:17, ἀπήρκασιν ("They have gone away"); οἱ ἀδελφοί καὶ ὁ οἶκος τοῦ πατρός μου . . . ἥκασιν πρός με ("My brothers and my father's household . . . have come to me"); also, see Gen 47:4, 5.

124. Robertson, *Grammar*, 895. Similar passages are numerous: Matt 3:2; 4:7, 17, μετανοεῖτε· ἤγγικεν γὰρ ἡ βασιλεία τῶν οὐρανῶν ("Repent, for the kingdom of heaven has come near"); Matt 10:7, ἤγγικεν γὰρ ἡ βασιλεία τῶν οὐρανῶν ("The kingdom of heaven is at hand"); Mark 1:15, πεπλήρωται ὁ καιρὸς καὶ ἤγγικεν ἡ βασιλεία τοῦ θεοῦ ("The time is fulfilled, and the kingdom of God is at hand"); Mark 14:42, ἰδοὺ ὁ παραδιδούς ἤγγικεν ("behold, the one who betrays me has come near"); Luke 10:9, 11, ἤγγικεν ἐφ' ὑμᾶς ἡ βασιλεία τοῦ θεοῦ. . . . πλὴν τοῦτο γινώσκετε ὅτι ἤγγικεν ἡ βασιλεία τοῦ θεοῦ ("The kingdom of God has come near to you. . . . Nevertheless know this, that the kingdom of God has come near"); Rom 13:12, ἡ δὲ ἡμέρα ἤγγικεν ("the day is at hand [has come near]"). Dana and Mantey see ἐγγίζω as consummative perfect (Dana and Mantey, *Manual Grammar*, 203).

[James 5:8] μακροθυμήσατε καὶ ὑμεῖς, στηρίξατε τὰς καρδίας ὑμῶν, ὅτι ἡ παρουσία τοῦ κυρίου ἤγγικεν.
You also, be patient. Establish your hearts, for the coming of the Lord is at hand.[126]

All the usages of ἤγγικεν above present a near completion of the arrival of something. Trotter criticizes Robertson's view of this perfect as durative-punctiliar. He claims that ἤγγικεν delivers "a state of being near," not a completed act.[127] Regardless of this debate, the sense of ἤγγικεν is not far away from a current relevance nuance: "something" has been coming from the past, and it almost arrives in a present time.

If ἤγγικεν is compared to a present-tense verb, its distinct nuance is put in relief. For instance, John 16:25 has a present-tense verb delivering similar content: ἔρχεται ὥρα ὅτε ("The hour is coming when I will no longer speak to you"). While the present form ἔρχεται delivers an ongoing state, ἤγγικεν conveys the current relevance of the event in relation to the past.[128]

Anterior Perfects Having a Simple Past Nuance Occasionally

This section will introduce the perfects in the NT that mainly express current relevance denoting a past event only a few times. The next chapter will provide full details for cases of the perfects expressing a past connotation.

---

125. Similar expressions occur in Matt 26:45, 46, ἤγγικεν ἡ ὥρα. . . . ἤγγικεν ὁ παραδιδούς με ("the hour has come. . . . my betrayer is at hand"); Mark 14:42, ἐγείρεσθε ἄγωμεν· ἰδοὺ ὁ παραδιδούς με ἤγγικεν ("Rise, let us be going; see, my betrayer is at hand"); Rom 13:12, ἡ νὺξ προέκοψεν, ἡ δὲ ἡμέρα ἤγγικεν ("The night is far gone; the day is at hand").

126. 1 Pet 4:7, Πάντων δὲ τὸ τέλος ἤγγικεν. σωφρονήσατε οὖν καὶ νήψατε εἰς προσευχάς ("The end of all things is at hand; therefore be self-controlled and sober-minded for the sake of your prayers").

127. Trotter, "Perfect Tenses," 70–71.

128. A similar nuance is also found with other perfects in the NT: 1 Cor 10:11, ταῦτα δὲ τυπικῶς συνέβαινεν ἐκείνοις, ἐγράφη δὲ πρὸς νουθεσίαν ἡμῶν, εἰς οὓς τὰ τέλη τῶν αἰώνων κατήντηκεν ("Now these things happened to them as an example, and they were written for our instruction, upon whom the ends of the ages have come"); 2 Tim 4:6, Ἐγὼ γὰρ ἤδη σπένδομαι, καὶ ὁ καιρὸς τῆς ἀναλύσεώς μου ἐφέστηκεν ("For I am already being poured out as a drink offering, and the time of my departure has come"). These two perfects are not that different from ἤγγικεν in terms of nuance. They express a current relevance but as a backward look.

Λελάληκα

Most occurrences of λελάληκα convey a current relevance. The examples are as follows:[129]

[John 8:40] νῦν δὲ ζητεῖτέ με ἀποκτεῖναι ἄνθρωπον ὃς τὴν ἀλήθειαν ὑμῖν λελάληκα ἣν ἤκουσα παρὰ τοῦ θεοῦ.

But now you are seeking to kill me, a man who *has told* you the truth that I heard from God.

[John 15:3] ἤδη ὑμεῖς καθαροί ἐστε διὰ τὸν λόγον ὃν λελάληκα ὑμῖν.

Already you are clean because of the word that I *have spoken* to you.

[John 18:20] ἐγὼ παρρησίᾳ λελάληκα τῷ κόσμῳ, ἐγὼ πάντοτε ἐδίδαξα ἐν συναγωγῇ καὶ ἐν τῷ ἱερῷ, ὅπου πάντες οἱ Ἰουδαῖοι συνέρχονται, καὶ ἐν κρυπτῷ ἐλάλησα οὐδέν.

I *have spoken* openly to the world. I have always taught in synagogue and in the temple, where all Jews come together. I have said nothing in secret.

[LXX Judith 2:12] τὸ κράτος τῆς βασιλείας μοῦ, λελάληκα καὶ ποιήσω ταῦτα ἐν χειρί μου.

For as I live, and on the power of my kingdom, I *have spoken* and I will accomplish these things with my hand.[130]

Each employment of λελάληκα above indicates a current state relevant to past events. In John 8:40, Jesus has taught the Jews from the past, but they seek to kill him. Similarly, John 18:20 implies that Jesus Christ has been speaking openly to the world from the past up to this moment, testifying before the high priests. The perfect λελάληκα is different from the aorist

---

129. Chantraine, *Parfait grec*, 231. More passages are: John 6:63, τὰ ῥήματα ἃ ἐγὼ λελάληκα ὑμῖν πνεῦμά ἐστιν καὶ ζωή ἐστιν ("The words that I have spoken to you are spirit and life"); John 12:29, ἄλλοι ἔλεγον· ἄγγελος αὐτῷ λελάληκεν ("Others said, 'the angel has spoken to him'"); John 14:25, Ταῦτα λελάληκα ὑμῖν παρ' ὑμῖν μένων ("These things I have spoken to you while I am still with you"); John 15:3, τὸν λόγον ὃν λελάληκα ὑμῖν ("the word which I have spoken to you"); John 15:11; 16:1, 4, 6, 25, 33, Ταῦτα λελάληκα ὑμῖν ("I have said these things to you"); John 18:20, ἐγὼ παρρησίᾳ λελάληκα τῷ κόσμῳ, ἐγὼ πάντοτε ἐδίδαξα ἐν συναγωγῇ καὶ τῷ ἱερῷ, ὅπου πάντες οἱ Ἰουδαῖοι συνέρχονται ("I have spoken openly to the world. I have always taught in synagogues and in the temple, where all Jews come together").

130. The selected text of Judith is from Graham's dissertation, "Discourse Function of Koine Greek Verb Forms."

ἐλάλησα. In Luke 24:44, for example, ἐλάλησα denotes a punctiliar action that once occurred in the past: οὗτοι οἱ λόγοι μου οὓς ἐλάλησα πρὸς ὑμᾶς ἔτι ὢν σὺν ὑμῖν ("These are my words that I spoke to you while I was still with you").[131] Unlike ἐλάλησα, the perfect λελάληκα delivers the current state resulting from a prior event.

A difficult case of λελάληκα is:

> [John 9:29] ἡμεῖς οἴδαμεν ὅτι Μωϋσεῖ λελάληκεν ὁ θεός, τοῦτον δὲ οὐκ οἴδαμεν πόθεν ἐστίν.
>
> We know that God has spoken to Moses, but as for this man, we do not know where he comes from.[132]

In this passage, λελάληκεν points out a past event that occurred in the Old Testament. It is not a current relevance nuance, but the past event that God spoke to Moses in the bush of wilderness. In order to explain this tough case of the perfect, Robertson introduces a category of "historic vivid present perfect." Nevertheless, λελάληκεν here denotes a past event of God's speaking to Moses thousand years ago.[133] The next chapter will scrutinize the characteristics of this kind of perfects.

Πεποίηκα

Most of the usages of πεποίηκα present the anterior (current relevance) nuance:[134]

---

131. See John 17:1, Ταῦτα ἐλάλησεν' Ἰησοῦς καὶ ἐπάρας τοὺς ὀφθαλμοὺς αὐτοῦ εἰς τὸν οὐρανὸν εἶπεν· πάτερ, ἐλήλυθεν ἡ ὥρα ("These things Jesus spoke; and lifting up his eyes to heaven, and said, 'Father, the hour has come'").

132. ESV, "God has spoken to Moses"; NASB, "God has spoken to Moses"; NIV, "God spoke to Moses"; and KJV, "God spake unto Moses."

133. LXX Gen 42:30, λελάληκεν ὁ ἄνθρωπος ὁ κύριος τῆς γῆς πρὸς ἡμᾶς σκληρὰ καὶ ἔθετο ἡμᾶς ἐν φυλακῇ ("The man, the lord of the land, spoke roughly to us and put us in prison"); 1 Kgs 13:18, κἀγὼ προφήτης εἰμὶ καθὼς σὺ καὶ ἄγγελος λελάληκεν πρός με ἐν ῥήματι κυρίου ("I also am a prophet as you are, and an angel spoke to me by the word of the Lord").

134. Mark 7:37, καλῶς πάντα πεποίηκεν ("He has done all things well"); Luke 1:25, ὅτι οὕτως μοι πεποίηκα κύριος ("Thus the Lord has done for me"); 1 John 5:10, ὁ πιστεύων εἰς τὸν υἱὸν τοῦ θεοῦ ἔχει τὴν μαρτυρίαν ἐν ἑαυτῷ, ὁ μὴ πιστεύων τῷ θεῷ ψεύστην πεποίηκεν αὐτόν, ὅτι οὐ πεπίστευκεν εἰς τὴν μαρτυρίαν ἣν μεμαρτύρηκεν ὁ θεὸς περὶ τοῦ υἱοῦ αὐτοῦ ("The one who believes in the Son of God has the witness in himself; the one who does not believe God has made him a liar, because he has not believed in the witness that God has borne concerning his Son"). See *The Shepherd of Hermas* 88.8, εἶτα παρῆν ὁ ποιμήν, καὶ λέγει ταῖς παρθένοις· Μή τινα αὐτῷ ὕβριν πεποιήκατε; "Then the shepherd came and said to the virgins, 'Have you done him any harm?'" (Holmes, *Apostolic Fathers*, 642–43).

[Mark 5:19] καὶ οὐκ ἀφῆκεν αὐτόν, ἀλλὰ λέγει αὐτῷ· ὕπαγε εἰς τὸν οἶκόν σου πρὸς τοὺς σοὺς καὶ ἀπάγγειλον αὐτοῖς ὅσα ὁ κύριός σοι πεποίηκεν καὶ ἠλέησέν σε.

And he did not permit him but said to him, "Go home to your friends and tell them how much the Lord *has done* for you, and how he has had mercy on you."

[Mark 11:17] ὁ οἶκός μου προσευχῆς κληθήσεται πᾶσιν τοῖς ἔθνεσιν; ὑμεῖς δὲ πεποιήκατε αὐτὸν σπήλαιον λῃστῶν.

My house shall be called a house of prayer for all the nations? But you *have made* it a den of robbers.[135]

[Luke 17:10] οὕτως καὶ ὑμεῖς, ὅταν ποιήσητε πάντα τὰ διαταχθέντα ὑμῖν, λέγετε ὅτι δοῦλοι ἀχρεῖοί ἐσμεν, ὃ ὠφείλομεν ποιῆσαι πεποιήκαμεν.

So you also, when you have done all that you were commanded, say, "We are unworthy servants; we *have* only *done* what we ought to have done."[136]

[John 13:12] εἶπεν αὐτοῖς· γινώσκετε τί πεποίηκα ὑμῖν;

When he had washed their feet and put on his garments and resumed his place, he said to them, "Do you understand what I *have done* to you?"

The perfects in these texts express a current situation coming from the past. After Jesus Christ healed a demon-possessed man in Mark 5:19, πεποίηκεν indicates his current state of being healed, which results from the previous state of being demon-possessed. Buth and Bentein regard πεποίηκα as a current relevance perfect. They state that πεποίηκα denotes *continuing an achieved state*, "I have done it."[137] In Classical Greek and the Septuagint, similar usages of πεποίηκα are present.[138]

---

135. Bock states that the usage of the perfect πεποιήκατε "stresses the temple's appalling state" (Bock, *Luke*, 1579). Cirafesi critiques Bock, saying that the perfect rather denotes "the complex state of affairs in which the buyers and sellers are portrayed" (Cirafesi, *Synoptic Parallels*, 92). However the debate may end, πεποιήκατε delivers a current state resulting from a past event.

136. In Luke 17:10, McKay describes πεποιήκαμεν as a state. Campbell says, however, it is somewhat forced (Campbell, *Indicative Mood*, 168).

137. Buth, "Perfect Greek Morphology," 422; Bentein, "Periphrastic Perfect," 178. In contrast, the aorist ἐποίησεν expresses an action that occurred in the past: in Matt 27:23, Pilate asks a question of Jesus, τί γὰρ κακὸν ἐποίησεν; ("What evil did he do?").

138. Plato, *Apology* 20d, τί ποτ᾽ ἐστὶν τοῦτο ὃ ἐμοὶ πεποίηκεν τό τε ὄνομα ("what it is that has brought about my reputation"). See Lysias, *Lysias* 12.34, οὕτως δὲ ὡμολόγηκεν ἀδίκως συλλαβεῖν, ὥστε ῥᾳδίαν ὑμῖν τὴν διαψήφισιν περὶ αὐτοῦ πεποίηκε ("But he has admitted that he laid hands on him unjustly, so that he has made your verdict on himself

A bewildering case is 2 Corinthians 11:25: ἐν τῷ βυθῷ πεποίηκα ("I was adrift at sea"). In this text it is difficult to see πεποίηκα as a current relevance perfect. Paul is speaking of his experience of a shipwreck in the past. Thus, πεποίηκα is not able to convey a current state here. It points out a past event without current relevance. Most cases of πεποίηκα express current relevance, but in 2 Corinthians 11:25 it carries a preterite notion.

Ἑώρακα

In many cases ἑώρακα delivers the same nuance of the English perfect, that of current relevance.[139] Many passages demonstrate this nuance:

> [John 1:18] Θεὸν οὐδεὶς ἑώρακεν πώποτε· μονογενὴς θεὸς ὁ ὢν εἰς τὸν κόλπον τοῦ πατρὸς ἐκεῖνος ἐξηγήσατο.
>
> No one has ever seen God; the only begotten God, who is in the bosom of the Father, he has made him known.[140]
>
> [John 9:37] εἶπεν αὐτῷ ὁ Ἰησοῦς· καὶ ἑώρακας αὐτὸν καὶ ὁ λαλῶν μετὰ σοῦ ἐκεῖνός ἐστιν.
>
> Jesus said to him, "You have seen him, and it is he who is speaking to you."
>
> [John 15:24] νῦν δὲ καὶ ἑωράκασιν καὶ μεμισήκασιν καὶ ἐμὲ καὶ τὸν πατέρα μου.
>
> But now they have seen and hated both me and my Father.

---

an easy matter") (This example is from Bentein, "Periphrastic Perfect," 178); LXX Gen 27:45, καὶ τὴν ὀργὴν τοῦ ἀδελφοῦ σου ἀπὸ σοῦ καὶ ἐπιλάθηται ἃ πεποίηκας αὐτῷ ("Until your brother's anger turns away from you, and he forgets what you have done to him"); Gen 34:30, μισητόν με πεποιήκατε ὥστε πονηρόν με εἶναι πᾶσιν τοῖς κατοικοῦσιν τὴν γῆν ("you have done trouble on me by making me stink to the inhabitants of the land"); see Gen 44:5; 1 Sam 12:20, μὴ φοβεῖσθε ὑμεῖς πεποιήκατε τὴν πᾶσαν κακίαν ταύτην πλὴν μὴ ἐκκλίνητε ἀπὸ ὄπισθεν κυρίου καὶ δουλεύσατε τῷ κυρίῳ ἐν ὅλῃ καρδίᾳ ὑμῶν ("Do not be afraid; you have done evil. Yet do not turn aside from following the Lord, but serve the Lord with all your heart"); 1 Sam 13:11, καὶ εἶπεν Σαμουηλ τί πεποίηκας ("But Samuel said, 'What have you done?'"); 1 Kgs 19:20, ἀνάστρεφε ὅτι πεποίηκά σοι ("Go back again, for what have I done to you?").

139. Gerö and Stechow, "Tense in Time," 281–82.

140. Cf. 1 John 4:12, θεὸν οὐδεὶς πώποτε τεθέαται ("No one has ever seen God"); 1 John 4:14, τεθεάμεθα καὶ μαρτυροῦμεν ("And we have seen and bear witness").

[Col 2:1] Θέλω γὰρ ὑμᾶς εἰδέναι ἡλίκον ἀγῶνα ἔχω ὑπὲρ ὑμῶν καὶ τῶν ἐν Λαοδικείᾳ καὶ ὅσοι οὐχ ἑόρακαν τὸ πρόσωπόν μου ἐν σαρκί.

For I want you to know how great a struggle I have for you and for those at Laodicea and for all who have not seen me face to face.

[LXX Gen 26:28] καὶ εἶπαν ἰδόντες ἑωράκαμεν ὅτι ἦν κύριος μετὰ σοῦ.

And they said, "We surely have seen that the Lord has been with you."[141]

All the employments of ἑώρακα show an anterior (current relevance) nuance. Especially in John 1:18, the adverb πώποτε stresses that the event of seeing God has never occurred, from the past until now. The background of John 15:24 is the end of Jesus Christ's life, in which the unbelieving Jews have observed Jesus' public ministry so far. Nevertheless, the conclusion is that they hate Jesus Christ and God the Father now. Thus, the perfects ἑωράκασιν and μεμισήκασιν summarize the Jews's final rejection of Jesus Christ since they saw his ministry in the beginning.

In John 9:37, the blind man has just met Jesus Christ for the first time after he gained his sight. Campbell renders ἑώρακας as "You now see," instead of "having seen."[142] However, his assertion is not persuasive because the formerly blind man's action of seeing Jesus has already passed in the moment of Jesus' speaking to him.[143] The perfect ἑώρακα points out the anterior event, not the present time ("You now see"). In Colossians 2:1, in the same vein, the apostle Paul speaks of those who have never seen his face so far, implying a time period between now and the past. In Genesis 26:28, finally, Abimelech and his general have seen God be with Abraham for a period of time from the past. Now they have decided to make a covenant with Abraham lest they become enemies against him and God.

Many other texts in the NT show ἑώρακα as a current relevance perfect.[144] Nevertheless, difficult passages also exist. The texts below reveal the

141. LXX Gen 31:12, ἑώρακα γὰρ ὅσα σοι Λαβαν ποιεῖ ("for I have seen all that Laban is doing to you"); Gen 46:30, ἀποθανοῦμαι ἀπὸ τοῦ νῦν ἐπεὶ ἑώρακα τὸ πρόσωπόν σου ("Now let me die, since I have seen your face").

142. Campbell, *Indicative Mood*, 195.

143. Sicking and Stork, *Two Studies*, 151–55.

144. John 3:11, ὃ ἑωράκαμεν μαρτυροῦμεν ("we testify what we *have seen*"); John 5:37, καὶ ὁ πέμψας με πατὴρ ἐκεῖνος μεμαρτύρηκεν περὶ ἐμοῦ. οὔτε φωνὴν αὐτοῦ πώποτε ἀκηκόατε οὔτε εἶδος αὐτοῦ ἑωράκατε ("And the Father who sent me has himself borne witness about me. His voice you have never heard, his form you *have* never *seen*"); John 6:36, Ἀλλ᾽ εἶπον ὑμῖν ὅτι καὶ ἑωράκατέ [με] καὶ οὐ πιστεύετε ("But I said to you that you

perplexity of deciding whether ἑώρακα signifies a current relevance (anterior) or a past event.

> [John 20:18] ἔρχεται Μαριὰμ ἡ Μαγδαληνὴ ἀγγέλλουσα τοῖς μαθηταῖς ὅτι ἑώρακα τὸν κύριον.
> Mary Magdalene went and announced to the disciples, "I *have seen* the Lord."

> [Acts 22:15] ὅτι ἔσῃ μάρτυς αὐτῷ πρὸς πάντας ἀνθρώπους ὧν ἑώρακας καὶ ἤκουσας.
> For you will be a witness for him to everyone of what you *have seen* and heard.

In John 20:18, Mary Magdalene has had an experience of seeing the Lord and is now delivering the message of the resurrection to the disciples. Because of the difficulty of precluding the past nuance, it is plausible that Mary is describing the past event of seeing the Lord that morning.[145] Nevertheless, it seems that Mary's use of ἑώρακα focuses more on current relevance of the past event (resurrection). After Mary met the risen Lord, she immediately ran to report the news to the disciples. This perfect connotes the connection of Mary's current statement with the preceding event of theophany rather than separating ἑώρακα from the present moment and limiting it to a past event.

---

have seen me and do not believe"); John 6:46, οὐχ ὅτι τὸν πατέρα ἑώρακέν τις εἰ μὴ ὁ ὢν παρὰ τοῦ θεοῦ, οὗτος ἑώρακεν τὸν πατέρα ("not that anyone *has seen* the Father except he who is from God; he *has seen* the Father"); John 8:38, ἃ ἐγὼ ἑώρακα παρὰ τῷ πατρὶ λαλῶ ("I speak of what I *have seen* with my Father"); John 8:57 καὶ Ἀβραὰμ ἑώρακας; ("You are not yet fifty years old, and *have you seen* Abraham?"); John 14:7, 9, εἰ ἐγνώκατέ με, καὶ τὸν πατέρα μου γνώσεσθε. καὶ ἀπ᾽ ἄρτι γινώσκετε αὐτὸν καὶ ἑωράκατε αὐτόν.... λέγει αὐτῷ ὁ Ἰησοῦς· τοσούτῳ χρόνῳ μεθ᾽ ὑμῶν εἰμι καὶ οὐκ ἔγνωκάς με, Φίλιππε; ὁ ἑωρακὼς ἐμὲ ἑώρακεν τὸν πατέρα ("If you had known me, you would have known my Father also. From now on you do know him and you *have seen* him.... Jesus said to him, 'Have I been with you so long, and you still do not know me, Philip? Whoever *has seen* me has seen the Father'"); 1 Cor 9:1, οὐχὶ Ἰησοῦν τὸν κύριον ἡμῶν ἑόρακα; ("*Have* I not *seen* Jesus our Lord?"); 1 John 4:20, ὁ γὰρ μὴ ἀγαπῶν τὸν ἀδελφὸν αὐτοῦ ὃν ἑώρακεν, τὸν θεὸν ὃν οὐχ ἑώρακεν οὐ δύναται ἀγαπᾶν ("for he who does not love his brother whom he *has seen* cannot love God whom he has not seen"); 3 John 1:11, ὁ κακοποιῶν οὐχ ἑώρακεν τὸν θεόν ("whoever does evil *has* not *seen* God").

145. Similarly, in John 11:34 (ποῦ τεθείκατε αὐτόν; "where have you laid him?") English Bible translates this phrase as following: (1) ESV, "Where have you laid him?"; (2) NASB, "Where have you laid him?"; (3) NIV, "Where have you laid him?"; and (4) KJV, "Where have ye laid him?" Mandilaras sees this perfect τεθείκατε as denoting past time (Mandilaras, *Non-Literary Papyri*, 218). However, I see it as a current relevance because laying him in the past still remains and this action's status continues in the present moment.

In Acts 22:15, secondly, ἑώρακας seems to express current relevance (anterior) in contrast to ἤκουσας denoting a past time event.[146] However, the possibility of ἑώρακας being a past event cannot be decisively excluded. Andrason and Locatell, importantly, note the existence of ambiguous perfects.[147] Difficulty truly exists in putting these perfects into either the specific category of a current relevance or of the preterite. Nevertheless, these perfects seem to be closer to current relevance than to a preterite nuance.

The beginning of 1 John is worth noting.

[1 John 1:1–3] Ὃ ἦν ἀπ' ἀρχῆς, ὃ **ἀκηκόαμεν**, ὃ **ἑωράκαμεν** τοῖς ὀφθαλμοῖς ἡμῶν, ὃ ἐθεασάμεθα καὶ αἱ χεῖρες ἡμῶν ἐψηλάφησαν περὶ τοῦ λόγου τῆς ζωῆς καὶ ἡ ζωὴ ἐφανερώθη, καὶ **ἑωράκαμεν** καὶ μαρτυροῦμεν καὶ ἀπαγγέλλομεν ὑμῖν τὴν ζωὴν τὴν αἰώνιον ἥτις ἦν πρὸς τὸν πατέρα καὶ ἐφανερώθη ἡμῖν—ὃ **ἑωράκαμεν** καὶ **ἀκηκόαμεν**.

That which was from the beginning, which we *have heard*, which we *have seen* with our eyes, which we looked upon and [have] touched with our hands, concerning the word of life—the life was made manifest, and we *have seen* it and testify to it and proclaim to you the eternal life, which was with the Father and was made manifest to us—that which we *have seen* and *heard*.

The first significant characteristic of 1 John 1:1–3 is the mixture of the perfect, the aorist, and the present in the text. The verbs of each tense express its own nuance well: the perfect as current relevance, the aorist as past events, and the present as ongoing action. The perfect ἑωράκαμεν in 1 John 1:2 is a tricky one as to whether it denotes current relevance or simple past.[148] Nevertheless, it still looks closer to the current relevance (anterior). Since ἑώρακα occurs with a past event in many places of the NT, the next chapter will handle this issue.

---

146. BDF §342.

147. Andrason and Locatell, "Perfect Wave," 39–40.

148. Andrason and Locatell regard ἑωράκαμεν in 1 John 1:2 as referring to a past event, "we *saw* it and testify to it and proclaim to you the eternal life (Andrason and Locatell, "Perfect Wave," 52). Köstenberger et al. consider ἀκηκόαμεν and ἑωράκαμεν in 1 John 1:1 as the anterior (current relevance) (Köstenberger et al., *Going Deeper*, 302–3).

Γέγονα

The previous chapter illustrated the cases of γέγονα delivering a resultative-stative. This chapter introduces the cases of γέγονα with current relevance. In the NT and the Septuagint, γέγονα shows the anterior nuance many times (perfects in bold).[149]

> [LXX Gen 38:14] εἶδεν γὰρ ὅτι μέγας **γέγονεν** Σηλωμ αὐτὸς δὲ οὐκ ἔδωκεν αὐτὴν αὐτῷ γυναῖκα.
>
> For she saw that Shelah himself was grown up, but he [Judah] did not give her as a wife to him.[150]

> [Matt 24:21] ἔσται γὰρ τότε θλῖψις μεγάλη οἵα οὐ **γέγονεν** ἀπ' ἀρχῆς κόσμου ἕως τοῦ νῦν οὐδ' οὐ μὴ γένηται.
>
> For then there will be great tribulation, such as has not occurred from the beginning of the world until now, nor ever shall.[151]

---

149. Mark 14:4, εἰς τί ἡ ἀπώλεια αὕτη τοῦ μύρου γέγονεν ("Why has this perfume been wasted?"); John 5:14, ἴδε ὑγιὴς γέγονας ("Behold, you have become well"); Rom 6:5, εἰ γὰρ σύμφυτοι γεγόναμεν τῷ ὁμοιώματι τοῦ θανάτου αὐτοῦ, ἀλλὰ καὶ τῆς ἀναστάσεως ἐσόμεθα ("For if we have been united with him in a death like his, we shall certainly be united with him in a resurrection like his"); Gal 4:16, ὥστε ἐχθρὸς ὑμῶν γέγονα ἀληθεύων ὑμῖν; ("Have I then become your enemy by telling the truth?"); 1 Cor 9:22, τοῖς πᾶσιν γέγονα πάντα ("I have become all things to all people"); 2 Cor 12:11, Γέγονα ἄφρων, ὑμεῖς με ἠναγκάσατε ("I have become foolish; you yourselves compelled me"); Gal 3:24, ὥστε ὁ νόμος παιδαγωγὸς ἡμῶν γέγονεν εἰς Χριστόν ("Therefore the law has become our tutor into Christ"); Heb 3:14, μέτοχοι γὰρ τοῦ Χριστοῦ γεγόναμεν ("For we have come to share in Christ"); Rev 16:17, καὶ ἐξῆλθεν φωνὴ μεγάλη ἐκ τοῦ ναοῦ ἀπὸ τοῦ θρόνου λέγουσα· γέγονεν ("and a loud voice came out of the temple, from the throne, saying, 'It is done!'"); Rev 21:6, γέγοναν ("It is done!").

150. LXX Gen 32:11, νῦν δὲ γέγονα εἰς δύο παρεμβολάς ("but now I have become two camps"); Gen 47:9, μικραὶ καὶ πονηραὶ γεγόνασιν αἱ ἡμέραι τῶν ἐτῶν τῆς ζωῆς μου ("Few and evil have been the days of the years of my life"); Exod 2:14, ἐφοβήθη δὲ Μωυσῆς καὶ εἶπεν εἰ οὕτως ἐμφανὲς γέγονεν τὸ ῥῆμα τοῦτο ("Then Moses was afraid, and thought, 'Surely the matter has become known'").

151. See (perfect in bold) Matt 19:8, Μωϋσῆς πρὸς τὴν σκληροκαρδίαν ὑμῶν ἐπέτρεψεν ὑμῖν ἀπολῦσαι τὰς γυναῖκας ὑμῶν, ἀπ' ἀρχῆς δὲ οὐ **γέγονεν** οὕτως ("Because of your hardness of heart, Moses permitted you to divorce your wife, but from the beginning it has not been this way"); Matt 26:56, τοῦτο δὲ ὅλον **γέγονεν** ἵνα πληρωθῶσιν αἱ γραφαὶ τῶν προφητῶν ("But all this has taken place that the Scriptures of the prophets might be fulfilled"); Mark 13:19, ἔσονται γὰρ αἱ ἡμέραι ἐκεῖναι θλῖψις οἵα οὐ **γέγονεν** τοιαύτη ἀπ' ἀρχῆς κτίσεως ἣν ἔκτισεν ὁ θεὸς ἕως τοῦ νῦν καὶ οὐ μὴ γένηται ("For in those days there will be such tribulation as has not been from the beginning of the creation that God created until now, and never will be"); Acts 4:16, ὅτι μὲν γὰρ γνωστὸν σημεῖον **γέγονεν** δι' αὐτῶν πᾶσιν τοῖς κατοικοῦσιν Ἰερουσαλὴμ φανερὸν ("For the fact that a noteworthy miracle has taken place through them is apparent to all who live in Jerusalem"); The Didache 16.4, καὶ ποιήσει ἀθέμιτα ἃ οὐδέποτε **γέγονεν** ἐξ αἰῶνος ("and he will commit

[Mark 9:21] καὶ ἐπηρώτησεν τὸν πατέρα αὐτοῦ· πόσος χρόνος ἐστὶν ὡς τοῦτο **γέγονεν** αὐτῷ;

And Jesus asked his father, "How long has it happened to him?"

[Luke 14:22] καὶ ὁ δοῦλος· κύριε, **γέγονεν** ὃ ἐπέταξας, καὶ ἔτι τόπος ἐστίν.

And the slave said, "Master, what you commanded has been done, and still there is room."

[John 6:25] καὶ εὑρόντες αὐτὸν πέραν τῆς θαλάσσης εἶπον αὐτῷ· ῥαββί, πότε ὧδε **γέγονας**;

When they found him on the other side of the see, they said to him, "Rabbi, when did you come here?"

[John 12:30] ἀπεκρίθη Ἰησοῦς καὶ εἶπεν· οὐ δι' ἐμὲ ἡ φωνὴ αὕτη **γέγονεν** ἀλλὰ δι' ὑμᾶς.

Jesus answered, "This voice has not come for my sake, but for your sakes."

[2 Cor 5:17] ὥστε εἴ τις ἐν Χριστῷ, καινὴ κτίσις· τὰ ἀρχαῖα παρῆλθεν, ἰδοὺ **γέγονεν** καινά.

Therefore if anyone is in Christ, he is a new creation. The old has passed away; behold, the new has come.

[Heb 5:11] Περὶ οὗ πολὺς ἡμῖν ὁ λόγος καὶ δυσερμήνευτος λέγειν, ἐπεὶ νωθροὶ **γεγόνατε** ταῖς ἀκοαῖς.

About this we have much to say, and it is hard to explain, since you have become dull of hearing.[152]

[1 John 2:18] Παιδία, ἐσχάτη ὥρα ἐστίν, καὶ καθὼς ἠκούσατε ὅτι ἀντίχριστος ἔρχεται, καὶ νῦν ἀντίχριστοι πολλοὶ **γεγόνασιν**, ὅθεν γινώσκομεν ὅτι ἐσχάτη ὥρα ἐστίν.

Children, it is the last hour, and as you have heard that antichrist is coming, even now many antichrists have come. Therefore we know that it is the last hour.

All usages of γέγονεν above show a current relevance nuance. First of all, γέγονεν in Genesis 38:14 denotes a period of time between now and the past

---

abominations the likes of which have never happened before") (Holmes, *Apostolic Fathers*, 368–69).

152. See Heb 12:8, εἰ δὲ χωρίς ἐστε παιδείας ἧς μέτοχοι γεγόνασιν πάντες, ἄρα νόθοι καὶ οὐχ υἱοί ἐστε ("If you are left without discipline, of which all have become partakers, then you are illegitimate children and not sons").

in which Shelah has grown. In Matthew 24:21, γέγονεν similarly indicates the present time continuing from the beginning of the creation. The adverbial phrases ἀπ' ἀρχῆς κόσμου ἕως τοῦ νῦν ("from the beginning of the world until now") bolster our detection of this nuance. It is the same case in Mark 9:21 that Jesus Christ asks the father the question of *how long* his son has been possessed by a demon. Andrason and Locatell state that γέγονεν in Mark 9:21 refers to a present condition continuing from a specific past moment.[153]

With respect to the translation in John 6:25, many English Bibles render it, "Rabbi, when did you come here?"[154] However, the literal translation is, "when have you been (γέγονας) here?" Runge also points out that γεγόνατε in Hebrews 5:11 clearly correlates to the current state that has resulted from the preceding sluggishness.[155] The cases of γέγονα communicating past time will be introduced in the next chapter.

Perfect Middle with Anterior Sense

The last issue is the occurrence of the perfect middle conveying an anterior nuance. The previous chapter explored the origin of the perfect middle. Many perfect-middle forms express a resultative-stative nuance in Homer and the Greek New Testament (as well as in selected texts from Classical Greek). However, not all of them embrace a resultative-stative notion. The perfect middle forms also show the anterior (current relevance) nuance in the NT. Surprisingly, many of them are so-called "deponent" verbs.[156]

---

153. Andrason and Locatell, "Perfect Wave," 44.

154. ESV, "Rabbi, when did you come here?"; NASB, "Rabbi, when did You get here?"; NIV, "Rabbi, when did you get here?"; and KJV, "Rabbi, when camest thou hither?"

155. Runge, "Discourse Function," 468.

156. See Pennington's "Deponency in Koine Greek," 55–76. Interestingly, the same case is found in Classical Greek (perfects in bold): Plato, *Timeo* 47a, **δεδώρηται**, μετὰ τοῦτο ῥητέον. ὄψις δὴ κατὰ τὸν ἐμὸν λόγον αἰτία τῆς μεγίστης ὠφελίας γέγονεν ἡμῖν, ὅτι τῶν νῦν λόγων περὶ τοῦ παντὸς λεγομένων οὐδεὶς ἄν ποτε ἐρρήθη μήτε ἄστρα μήτε ἥλιον μήτε οὐρανὸν ἰδόντων. νῦν δ' ἡμέρα τε καὶ νὺξ ὀφθεῖσαι μῆνές τε καὶ ἐνιαυτῶν περίοδοι καὶ ἰσημερίαι καὶ τροπαὶ **μεμηχάνηται** μὲν ἀριθμόν, χρόνου δὲ ἔννοιαν περί τε τῆς τοῦ παντὸς φύσεως ζήτησιν ἔδοσαν ("benefit effected by them, for the sake of which God *bestowed* them upon us. Vision, in my view, is the cause of the greatest benefit to us, inasmuch as none of the accounts now given concerning the universe would ever have been given if men had not seen the stars or the sun or the heaven. But as it is, the vision of the day and night and of months and circling years *has created* the art of number and has given us not only the notion of time but also means of research into the nature of the universe").

[Acts 16:10] ὡς δὲ τὸ ὄνομα εἶδεν, εὐθέως ἐζητήσαμεν ἐξελθεῖν εἰς Μακεδονίαν συμβιβάζοντες ὅτι **προσκέκληται** ἡμᾶς ὁ θεὸς εὐαγγελίσασθαι αὐτούς.

And when Paul saw the vision, immediately we sought to go on into Macedonia, concluding that God *has called* us to preach the gospel to them.[157]

[Acts 17:7] οὓς **ὑποδέδεκται** Ἰάσων· καὶ οὗτοι πάντες ἀπέντατι τῶν δογμάτων Καίσαρος πράσσουσιν βασιλέα ἕτερον λέγοντες εἶναι Ἰησοῦν.

Jason *has received* them, and they are all acting against the decrees of Caesar, saying that there is another king, Jesus.

[Acts 23:1] Ἀτενίσας δὲ ὁ Παῦλος τῷ συνεδρίῳ εἶπεν· ἄνδρες ἀδελφοί, ἐγὼ πάσῃ συνειδήσει ἀγαθῇ **πεπολίτευμαι** τῷ θεῷ ἄχρι ταύτης τῆς ἡμέρας.

And looking intently at the council, Paul said, "Brothers, I *have lived* my life before God in all good conscience up to this day."

[Acts 27:24] λέγων· μὴ φοβοῦ, Παῦλε, Καίσαρί σε δεῖ παραστῆναι, καὶ ἰδοὺ **κεχάρισταί** σοι ὁ θεὸς πάντας τοὺς πλέοντας μετὰ σοῦ.

He said, "Do not be afraid, Paul; you must stand before Caesar. And behold, God *has granted* you all those who sail with you."

[1 Cor 9:15] Ἐγὼ δὲ οὐ **κέχρημαι** οὐδενὶ τούτων. Οὐκ ἔγραψα δὲ ταῦτα, ἵνα οὕτως γένηται ἐν ἐμοί.

But I *have made* no use of any of these things. And I am not writing these things that it may be done so in my case.

[Phil 4:12] οἶδα καὶ ταπεινοῦσθαι, οἶδα καὶ περισσεύειν· ἐν παντὶ καὶ ἐν πᾶσιν **μεμύημαι**, καὶ χορτάζεσθαι καὶ πεινᾶν καὶ περισσεύειν καὶ ὑστερεῖσθαι.

---

157. ESV, "God had called us to preach"; NASB, "God had called us to preach"; NIV, "God had called us to preach"; and KJV, "the Lord had called us for to preach." Similarly, Acts 13:2, ἀφορίσατε δή μοι τὸν Βαρναβᾶν καὶ Σαῦλον εἰς τὸ ἔργον ὃ προσκέκλημαι αὐτούς ("Set apart for me Barnabas and Saul for the work to which I have called them"); Acts 25:12, Καίσαρα ἐπικέκλησαι, ἐπὶ Καίσαρα πορεύσῃ ("To Caesar you have appealed; to Caesar you shall go"). The perfect form (from ἐπικαλέω) delivers a current relevance nuance.

I know how to be brought low, and I know how to abound. In any and every circumstance, I *have learned* the secret of facing plenty and hunger, abundance and need.

[2 Cor 2:10] ᾧ δέ τι χαρίζεσθε, κἀγώ· καὶ γὰρ ὃ **κεχάρισμαι**, εἴ τι **κεχάρισμαι**, δι' ὑμᾶς ἐν προσώπῳ Χριστοῦ.

Anyone whom you forgive, I also forgive. Indeed, what I *have forgiven*, if I *have forgiven* anything, has been for your sake in the presence of Christ.

[2 Cor 7:14] ὅτι εἴ τι αὐτῷ ὑπὲρ ὑμῶν **κεκαύχημαι**, οὐ κατῃσχύνθην.

For if in anything I *have boasted* to him about you, I was not put to shame.

[2 Pet 1:4] δι' ὧν τὰ τίμια καὶ μέγιστα ἡμῖν ἐπαγγέλματα **δεδώρηται**, ἵνα διὰ τούτων γένησθε θείας κοινωνοὶ φύσεως ἀποφυγόντες τῆς ἐν τῷ κόσμῳ ἐν ἐπιθυμίᾳ φθορᾶς.

By which he *has granted* to us his precious and very great promises, so that through them you may become partakers of the divine nature, having escaped from the corruption that is in the world because of sinful desire.

In the texts above, many of the perfect middle verbs with anterior meaning have their lexical forms with middle endings: ὑποδέδεκται (ὑποδέχομαι); πεπολιτεύμαι (πολιτεύομαι); κεχάρισται (χαρίζομαι); κέχρημαι (χράομαι); μεμύημαι (μυέω); κεκαύχημαι (καυχάομαι); and δεδώρηται (δωρέομαι).[158] First Corinthians 9:15 indicates that from the past up to now the apostle Paul has not utilized various rights that he could have employed.

These examples show the perfect middle conveying current relevance in the Greek New Testament:

CONCLUSION

In Classical Greek, a great number of perfects express the anterior (current relevance) nuance, similar to the English perfect. The most prominent

---

158. See Acts 13:47, οὕτως γὰρ ἐντέταλται ἡμῖν ὁ κύριος· τέθεικά σε εἰς φῶς ἐθνῶν ("For so the Lord *has commanded* us, saying 'I have made you a light for Gentiles'") (from ἐντέλλομαι); 1 Tim 5:8, τὴν πίστιν ἤρνηται ("he has denied the faith") (from ἀρνέομαι); and Heb 12:5, καὶ ἐκλέλησθε τῆς παρακλήσεως, ἥτις ὑμῖν ὡς υἱοῖς διαλέγεται; ("And *have you forgotten* the exhortation that addresses you as sons?") (from ἐκλανθάνομαι).

change in this era is the increase of transitive perfects. Due to the rise of the transitive perfect, the perfect in the Classical era expanded the scope of expression. Wackernagel and Chantraine argue for the notion of the "resultative perfect," indicating that the perfect does not convey the state of the subject but that of the object. Despite being refuted by McKay, their works are meaningful for studying the semantic change of the perfect during the Classical period. Wackernagel and Chantraine sensed the critical changes to the perfect that occurred in Classical Greek. Although their arrows miss the target, their contribution has value for stimulating further study.

The purview of the ancient perfect was limited because they were intransitive and resultative-stative. In Classical Greek, the perfect expanded its scope by taking transitive forms. These transitive perfects occur many times in Classical Greek as well as in the Greek New Testament. IITSC also supports the possibility of the semantic change of the perfect. By employing an increased number of transitive perfects, speakers may have expanded the scope of the expression. For example, if the perfect middle form of a certain verb, such as κέκληται or γέγραπται, denotes a resultative-stative, its transitive active form, like κέκληκεν and γέγραφε, conveys the anterior meaning. This explanation might not perfectly reveal the detailed process, but it does give some hint about how the semantic change of the perfect may have occurred.

A great number of the transitive active perfects occur in Classical literatures. Many scholars show that they are well attested in the fourth and fifth centuries BC. These occurrences support the semantic change of the perfect during Classical period because the Homeric perfect expressed the resultative-stative with intransitivity. The transitive perfect active also occurs frequently in the Septuagint as well as in the Greek New Testament. With hundreds of cases in the NT, these perfects demonstrate an anterior nuance.

Therefore, the perfect went through a semantic change in Classical Greek, from resultative to anterior. Looking at the diachronic development of the perfect clarifies its current relevance nuance in the Greek New Testament. Moreover, this explanation is not opposed to the traditional interpretation of the perfect.

4

THE THIRD STAGE
PERFECT AS SIMPLE PAST

IN THE POST-CLASSICAL PERIOD, the perfect emerges as a simple past with no relevance to the present time. This so-called "aoristic perfect" occurs in the Greek New Testament in some places. This peculiar behavior of the perfect has perplexed scholars, entailing difficulties as to how to analyze these verbs.

> [Rev 8:5] καὶ **εἴληφεν** ὁ ἄγγελος τὸν λιβανωτὸν καὶ ἐγέμισεν αὐτὸν ἐκ τοῦ πυρὸς τοῦ θυσιαστηρίου.
> And the angel *took* the censer and filled it with fire from the altar.

In Revelation 8:5, the perfect does not deliver a typical anterior (current relevance) nuance.[1] Haspelmath identifies εἴληφεν here as an example of the perfect of simple past. This usage becomes more frequent in Koine Greek.[2] Perfects denoting simple past are found occasionally even in Classical literature.

---

1. A general case of the opposition between the perfect and the aorist is Mark 11:21: ἴδε ἡ συκῆ ἣν κατηράσω ἐξήρανται ("the fig tree you cursed has withered"). See Plato, *Charmides* 163a 10–12, ἐγὼ γὰρ που, ἦ δ' ὅς, τοῦθ' ὡμολόγηκα, ὡς οἱ τὰ τῶν ἄλλων πράττοντες σωφρονοῦσιν, εἰ τοὺς ποιοῦντας ὡμολόγησα ("And have I, pray, he said, admitted that those who do others' business are temperate? Or was my admission of those who make things?") (Plato, *Charmides*, 42–43). The example is from Sicking and Stork, *Two Studies*, 157.

2. Haspelmath, "From Resultative to Perfect," 218.

Traditional scholars such as Burton and Wallace state that the perfect sometimes expresses a simple past.[3] However, it is insufficient to merely introduce these cases as exceptions. Elucidating this peculiar characteristic of the Greek perfect is necessary. This chapter will argue that in Koine Greek the perfect went through the semantic change from the anterior to simple past, as illustrated by related texts from the Greek New Testament.[4]

SEMANTIC CHANGE FROM THE ANTERIOR TO SIMPLE PAST

Many scholars acknowledge the semantic change of the Greek perfect from the anterior to simple past.[5] Beginning in the Hellenistic period, the functional merger of the aorist and the perfect occurred, as seen in the increasing use of the perfect as a simple past.[6] Scholarly consensus holds that the perfect was confused with the aorist, with the end result that the perfect was no longer distinguished from the aorist.[7] Bentein notes that the merger

---

3. Burton, *Syntax*, 39; Jannaris, *Historical Greek Grammar*, 439; Wallace, *Beyond the Basics*, 578.

4. Selective examples from the Septuagint and Classical literatures will be introduced as well.

5. Moulton, *Prolegomena*, 141–45; Chantraine, *Parfait grec*, 233; Mandilaras, *Studies in the Greek Language*, 11–21; Mandilaras, *Non-Literary Papyri*, 224–25; Moser, "Perfect Periphrases," 223–25; Haspelmath, "From Resultative to Perfect," 217–20; Slings, "Geschiedenis van het perfectum," 245; Willi, *Languages of Aristophanes*, 232; Haug, "From Resultatives to Anteriors," 285–305; Horrocks, *Greek*, 176–78; Crellin, "Gothic Eyes," 10; Bentein, "Ecological-Evolutionary Account," 206; Bentein, "Perfect," 46–49; Bentein, *Verbal Periphrasis*, 153; Andrason and Locatell, "Perfect Wave," 79–80; Allan, "Tense and Aspect," 112–14; Fanning, "Greek Tenses in John's Apocalypse," 347–48. Contra Sicking and Stork, *Two Studies*, 167.

6. Horrocks, *Greek*, 131, 176–77. This phenomenon may partly reflect the influence of the Latin in which the perfect conveys a simple past, not the current relevance (anterior) nuance like English perfect, according to Horrocks. However, he adds, "But its origins can be traced already in the usage of authors such as Menander, and Latin can have done no more than promote a trend that was already under way."

7. Chantraine, *Parfait grec*, 183–84, 239–44; Moulton, *Prolegomena*, 142–45; Moulton and Turner, *Syntax*, 81; Haspelmath, "From Resultative to Perfect," 218–19; Burton, *Syntax*, 42; Moser, "Perfect Periphrases," 223–25; Caragounis, *New Testament Language and Exegesis*, 158–59; Aubrey, "Greek Perfect," 113; Dickey, "Greek and Latin Languages in the Papyri," 155; Horrocks, *Greek*, 178; Mandilaras, *Non-Literary Papyri*, 221; Duhoux, *Le verbe grec ancien*, 430; Drinka, "Development of the HAVE Perfect," 111; Trotter, "Perfect Tenses," 97; Kavčič, "Decline of the Aorist Infinitive," 287; Runge, "Discourse Function," 483. In Byzantine times, says Mandilaras, it is likely that the perfect was replaced by the aorist to a great extent (Mandilaras, *Studies in the Greek Language*, 20; Mandilaras, *Non-Literary Papyri*, 221). Andrason states, "During the

had already begun in the early post-classical period (between the third and first centuries BC).[8] Similarly, Caragounis maintains that the confusion of the perfect and the aorist became more frequent in the early Hellenistic period and following.[9]

The merger of the perfect and the aorist became even more common from the first to the third century AD.[10] In the Greek New Testament, this usage occurs eighty-nine times, according to my research. Duhoux argues that the semantic change of the perfect into the simple past was completed in the second century AD, while Porter asserts that the traditional sense of the perfect survived up to fourth or fifth century.[11] Afterwards, the κ-perfect dies out. Bentein says,

> Perhaps the most important development for our present purposes is the disappearance of the synthetic perfect. This development is generally attributed to the functional overlap between the aorist and the perfect when the latter became an anterior perfect. While initially the synthetic perfect indicated the current relevance of a past event, its use seems to have been extended, whereby it came to be employed as a perfective past.[12]

The confusion of the perfect and aorist triggered the decay and gradual disappearance of the perfect. By the Byzantine period, the aorist had replaced the perfect because they were not distinguished in terms of meaning.[13]

---

conversion of a present anterior into a definite past, it is possible to detect a gradual weakening of the relevance of a previously performed action for the present state of affairs. This means that as the present anterior (old resultative) evolves, its original current relevance character first diminishes and finally is entirely lost" (Andrason, "From Resultatives to Present Tenses," 5).

8. Bentein, "Ecological-Evolutionary Account," 206n2; Bentein, "HAVE-Perfects," 152–53; Bentein, "Perfect," 48; Bentein, *Verbal Periphrasis*, 155; Andrason and Locatell, "Perfect Wave," 79–80. Mandilaras states that the perfect and the aorist occur side by side in post-classical texts (Mandilaras, *Non-Literary Papyri*, 221).

9. Caragounis, *Development of Greek*, 154–55.

10. Bentein, *Verbal Periphrasis*, 168.

11. Duhoux, *Le verbe grec ancien*, 430–31; Porter, *Verbal Aspect*, 273. Wackernagel states that the perfect gradually becomes out of use from AD 500 (Wackernagel, "Studien zum griechischen Perfektum," 23). See Allan, "Tense and Aspect," 112.

12. Bentein, *Verbal Periphrasis*, 153.

13. Chantraine, *Parfait grec*, 245; Mandilaras, *Studies in the Greek Language*, 20; Mandilaras, *Non-Literary Papyri*, 221. According to Mandilaras, the lexicographer Hesychius (fifth century AD) often interprets perfects with the corresponding aorists: ἀγήοχα (ἤνεγκα), ἀνατέταλκεν (ἀνέτειλεν), ἀνηρήμεθα (ἠρωτήθημεν), ἀπῆρκεν (ἀπεδήμησεν), βεβίωκα (ἔζησα), etc.

The confusion of the perfect with the aorist is also observed in papyri.[14] Moulton explains,

> The perfect was increasingly used, as the language grew older, as a substitute for what would formerly have been a narrative aorist. A cursory reading of the papyri soon shows us how much more the vernacular tends to use this tense; and the inference might be drawn that the old distinction of aorist and perfect was already obsolete.[15]

Mandilaras surveys a great number of perfects and aorists in 1,194 texts from private and official documents between the third century BC and the eighth century AD. He finds that the use of the perfect in papyri surpasses that of the aorist between the third and first centuries BC. After that point, the proportions reverse. The perfect decreases greatly in the post-Ptolemaic papyri while the aorist increases in the same period (the ratio of the perfect to the aorist is one-to-two).[16] Mandilaras points out that the perfect continually decreases until the third and fourth centuries AD. For instance, the perfect occurs only twelve times in twenty-eight letters from the third century AD.[17] In the same period there are eighty-four aorists, making the ratio of perfects to aorist one-to-seven.[18] In Mandilaras' research, the total ratio of the perfect to the aorist between the second and the eighth centuries AD is about one-to-three.[19]

---

14. Chantraine, *Parfait grec*, 240–41; Moulton and Turner, *Syntax*, 81; Mandilaras, *Studies in the Greek Language*, 47; Duhoux, *Le verbe grec ancien*, 431; Porter, *Verbal Aspect*, 272. Porter notes that in private letters the perfect is employed abundantly from the third century BC to the first century AD.

15. Moulton, *Prolegomena*, 141.

16. Mandilaras, *Studies in the Greek Language*, 19; Mandilaras, *Non-Literary Papyri*, 218. In contrast, Mandilaras states that in the third century BC, the ratio of the perfect and the aorist is almost equal in papyri (91 perfects and 78 aorists in 42 letters). In the official letters, 45 perfects and 66 aorists occur in 43 documents. In the second century BC, 66 perfects and 20 aorists are found in 24 letters while 56 perfects and 93 aorists in 46 official documents. In the first century BC, there are 26 perfects along with 17 aorists in 14 letters (27 perfects and 16 aorists in 20 official documents).

17. See Mandilaras, *Studies in the Greek Language*, 19n18.

18. Mandilaras, 19–20. Out of 44 letters of Christian papyri by the third and fourth centuries AD (by G. Ghedini), the perfect occurs only eight times: (παρα-)δέδωκα, εἴρηκα, ἐνήνοχα, ἀπέσταλκα, ἠπάντηκα, προστέθεικα, and ἐτόλμηκα. In the *Abinnaeus Archive* (the fourth century AD), Mandilaras notes that 28 perfects occur with 113 aorists in 44 letters; 22 perfects and 44 aorists in 14 petitions; 17 perfects and 35 aorists in 8 contracts.

19. Mandilaras, *Non-Literary Papyri*, 219–20. See the table for the occurrences of the perfect and the aorist in 1,194 texts between the third century BC and eighth century AD.

In the end, the x-perfect became extinct. In Byzantine and Medieval epoch (AD 300–1450), the x-perfect no longer occurs.[20] Bentein, Gerö and Stechow suppose that the fate of the synthetic perfect resulted from morphology. Gerö and Stechow state,

> During this era [Byzantine and Medieval] the morphology of the Perfect and the Aorist become more and more similar: reduplication is used instead of augmentation in Aorist forms and the suffix -k-, typical of the Perfect (but also earlier found in some Aorists, the so-called kappa-Aorists), spreads more generally within the Aorist paradigm; also the Perfect and Aorist personal endings get to be more alike.[21]

The perfect and the aorist are not distinguished morphologically during the Byzantine and Medieval era. The suffix x and reduplication appear within aorist forms, whose personal endings become similar to the perfect's. The perfect does not have the same meaning as the aorist but conveys a similar meaning. Therefore, the morphological confusion of the two tenses led to the loss of one of them.[22]

With extinction of the x-perfect, periphrastic constructions are employed in order to express a prior event with resulting state. Dickey describes,

> The loss of the perfect was particularly complex. It began in the Ptolemaic period with a loss of the distinction in meaning between aorist and perfect, so that either tense could be used in place of the other. For a while this merger resulted in an increased use of the perfect, but eventually the aorist, which had always been more common, prevailed, and the perfect largely disappeared from use. A periphrastic formation using a perfect or an aorist participle and the verb "be" came to fill the function originally performed by the old perfects, and the beginnings of that development are evident in some papyri.[23]

20. Chantraine, *Parfait grec*, 245; Mandilaras, *Studies in the Greek Language*, 20.

21. Gerö and Stechow, "Tense in Time," 283. See Bentein, *Verbal Periphrasis*, 156; Chantraine, *Parfait grec*, 255; Moser, "Perfect Periphrases," 216–18.

22. Bentein, "Perfect." According to Bentein, it is unclear why the perfect passes away, despite its increase in post-classical period. A possible reason why the perfect died out is that seemingly the aorist form was established more firmly. Contra Moser, "Perfect Periphrases," 282. Horrocks states that the falling together of aorist and perfect in popular varieties of the Koine led to confusion between aorist and perfect. For example, due to the confusion between the aorist ἦκα and the perfect εἶκα, the perfect/aorist form is sometimes spelled wrong ἶκα (from ἵημι "send"). Besides, this morphological merger is also found in augmented perfect ἐπλήρωκα and aorist with reduplication πεπλήρωσα, "I filled" in the third and fourth centuries AD (Horrocks, *Greek*, 168, 177).

23. Dickey, "Greek and Latin Languages," 155.

The use of periphrastic formations already occurred in Classical Greek.[24] Smyth notes that ἔχω with an aorist participle was sometimes employed in place of perfect active, while εἰμί with perfect participle delivered "stativity."[25] Examining these periphrastic constructions, however, Bentein maintains that in Classical Greek εἰμί with a perfect participle was fully developed as an expression of anterior nuance with retention of resultative usages.[26] Interestingly, Bentein demonstrates that εἰμί with a perfect participle similarly went through a semantic change from resultative to anterior, just like the synthetic perfect did.[27] According to Bentein, the constructions of ἔχω and εἰμί with aorist participle are employed to express the anterior nuance in the Koine period.[28] The aim of this book is not to pursue the study of periphrastic formations in detail. Moser notes that periphrastic constructions played only a marginal role until they took over when the synthetic perfects disappeared in the fourth century AD.[29]

---

24. Chantraine, *Parfait grec*, 246–49; Burton, *Syntax*, 42; McKay, "Ancient Greek Perfect," 1–2, 17; Bentein, "Periphrastic Perfect," 200. Bentein notes that the form εἰμί with perfect participle is found in Homer, *Odyssey* 17.163, τετελεισμένον εἴη (Bentein, "Transitivity, Ecology, and the Emergence," 289). See Mocciaro, "Auxiliaries," 218–21.

25. Smyth, *Greek Grammar*, 182. Smyth adds, "especially when a perfect active form with transitive meaning is lacking," such as στήσας ἔχω ("I have placed"). Moser argues that εἶμαι (εἰμί) plus participle form is not "a perfect periphrasis, but a predicational construction consisting of a copula and an adjective" while the ἔχω plus participle construction "can be seen as a perfect, albeit in a very early stage of development" (Moser, "Perfect Periphrases," 167–68, 173). Rijksbaron regards this construction as stative (Rijksbaron, *Syntax and Semantics*, 129). However, Bentein rejects these claims (Bentein, *Verbal Periphrasis*, 125; Bentein, "Transitivity, Ecology, and the Emergence," 305).

26. Bentein, *Verbal Periphrasis*, 139–40. In Classical Greek, the construction of εἰμί with the perfect participle occurs much more frequently than that of ἔχω with the aorist participle (Bentein, *Verbal Periphrasis*, 132). In early Byzantine time, the ratio is reversed, so that εἰμί with an aorist participle occurs more than εἰμί with a perfect participle (Bentein, "Ecological-Evolutionary Account," 257).

27. Bentein, "Periphrastic Perfect," 196–99, 208; Bentein, "Transitivity, Ecology, and the Emergence," 295; Bentein, *Verbal Periphrasis*, 132–45, 160–71, 201–22, 307. In Koine period, εἰμί with perfect participle shows both resultative and anterior nuance. Bentein shows that in early post-Classical period εἰμί with a perfect participle was mainly employed as resultative in biography and hagiography (81 percent; 167 out of 206), and in scientific prose (82 percent; 92 out of 116) while it is used slightly more often as anterior in historiography and in the papyri (Bentein, *Verbal Periphrasis*, 160, 184).

28. Bentein, *Verbal Periphrasis*, 124, 166–68, 179. Between the first and third centuries AD, Bentein notes that εἰμί with aorist participle is predominantly used to denote the anterior perfect nuance (Bentein, *Verbal Periphrasis*, 171).

29. Moser, "Perfect Periphrases," 118, 221. Bentein describes periphrastic constructions in the Koine and early Byzantine period, "εἰμί with the perfect participle became used in less transitive contexts (that is, as a resultative perfect), while a new periphrasis,

In Modern Greek, the perfect formation uses the auxiliary ἔχω with an infinitive.[30] It is said that in Modern Greek these Modern Greek periphrastic perfect formations with ἔχω replace the ancient κ-perfect.[31] However, Moser opposes this argument that directly connects the synthetic κ-perfect with the Modern Greek that was formulated ten centuries later. She says,

> The important fact from the point of view taken here is the eventual loss of the perfect stem, which, as pointed out above, must signal the loss of the category it expressed. Not only is the new periphrasis based on a perfective form, but it does not appear until 13th century AD. The gap of several centuries makes it possible that, despite the label allotted to it, the new periphrasis is not necessarily an exponent of the original category. . . . I would like to stress again the importance of the fact that the perfect was not to be replaced by the modern periphrases for about ten centuries to come.[32]

The synthetic κ-perfect forms were replaced by periphrastic constructions with ἔχω or εἰμί in the Byzantine and Medieval era.[33] According to Bentein, in the Byzantine period (the fourth to eighth centuries AD), constructions of εἰμί with an aorist participle express an anterior nuance.[34] The

εἰμί with the aorist participle, became used in more transitive ones (that is, as an anterior perfect)" (Bentein, *Verbal Periphrasis*, 202).

30. Haspelmath, "From Resultative to Perfect," 219; McKay, "Ancient Greek Perfect," 17; Moser, "Perfect Periphrases," 1, 122, 131, 153–58, 242–57; Moser, "From Aktionsart to Aspect," 74. See Drinka, "Development of the HAVE Perfect," 101–21. Drinka maintains that the "have" periphrastic construction of Greek was calqued into Latin.

31. Chantraine, *Parfait grec*, 251–55; Mandilaras, *Studies in the Greek Language*, 14; Gerö and Stechow, "Tense in Time," 252–54; Duhoux, *Le verbe grec ancien*, 431; Haspelmath, "From Resultative to Perfect," 218–19. Haspelmath says, "But Greek was not without a perfect for a long time. A New Perfect was created in Modern Greek using the auxiliary *éxo* 'I have' plus an Aorist infinitive form in *-i*." See Moser, "Tense and Aspect," 554.

32. Moser, "Tense and Aspect," 554, 559. Moser regards the beginning of the Modern Greek period as the first half of the eleventh century (Moser, "Perfect Periphrases," 209).

33. Gerö and Stechow, "Tense in Time," 283–85; Dickey, "Greek and Latin Languages," 155; Bentein, *Verbal Periphrasis*, 185, 307; Drinka, "Evolution of Grammar," 125. In early Byzantine time, the form ἔχω with aorist participle was seemingly lumped together with κ-perfects, equivalent to the aorist. Moser states that "the construction seems to fall out of use during early Byzantine times, and was virtually absent from the texts; this is probably due to the loss from the system of the Aorist and the Active Perfect Participle; this obviously took place before the complete grammaticalization of the forms" (Moser, "Perfect Periphrases," 239).

34. Bentein, *Verbal Periphrasis*, 182–88. Between the first and third centuries AD, the merger of the perfect and the aorist also affected the periphrastic constructions.

Modern Greek perfect form, ἔχω with the infinitive, did not emerge until the end of thirteenth or the beginning of the fourteenth century.³⁵ Moser points out that "the replacement of synthetic forms by periphrases" took place over a long period of time, so that modern periphrastic formations with ἔχω plus infinitive first appeared in the thirteenth to fourteenth centuries.³⁶

Finally, comparative linguistics can be helpful. The phenomenon of the shift of the perfect from "anterior" to "indefinite past" is observed in other languages.³⁷ The transition from the anterior to simple past is found in French, Italian, Rumanian, German, and Dutch.³⁸ Haspelmath states,

> The developments described here antedate the common European developments by more than thousand years. While the perfects and their development in Romance, Germanic, and Slavic are so similar that it is hard to imagine that areal convergence has played no role, the Greek Perfect is clearly an independent case.³⁹

As in Greek, European languages show similarities and varieties in regard to auxiliary constructions, such as the German perfect formation having both *sind* ("be") and *haben* ("have").⁴⁰ The development of the Greek

---

Bentein states, "the aorist primarily took over the anterior perfect function, and this influence can also be felt in the development of the periphrasis tenses" (Bentein, *Verbal Periphrasis*, 171).

35. Slings, "Geschiedenis van het perfectum," 246; Moser, "Perfect Periphrases," 98, 123, 210. See *Chronicles of Morea* 4900–4901, ὁ κάποιος φράγκος εὐγενής, ἄνθρωπος παιδευμένος ἀπό τήν πόλιν ἔχει ἐλθεῖ ἀπό τόν βασιλέαν ("some Frankish gentleman, an educated man has come from Constantinople, (sent) by the King") (this example is from Moser, "Perfect Periphrases," 98). Moser and Horrocks state that only perfect passive participle constructions survived during Byzantine period up to Modern Greek (Moser, "Perfect Periphrases," 100; Horrocks, *Greek*, 178).

36. Moser, "Perfect Periphrases," 210–17; Moser, "Tense and Aspect," 554. Moser says, "After the loss of the synthetic perfect, Greek, while having as its disposal a perfectly acceptable, indeed typical, participial construction with the auxiliary *exo*, failed to develop it into a fully-fledged perfect, or even a fully-fledged periphrasis, despite the powerful reinforcement from the parallel developments in Vulgar Latin and later the Romance languages. The speakers of the language were clearly quite happy to live without a typical perfect for several centuries" (Moser, "Tense, Aspect, and the Greek Perfect," 248).

37. Lindstedt, "Perfect–Aspectual," 369. Moser states that "the loss of synthetic forms and their replacement by periphrases is a generalised phenomenon in the Indo-European, as well as other groups of languages" (Moser, "Perfect Periphrases," 273).

38. Bybee et al., *Evolution of Grammar*, 52, 81, 86. See Lindstedt, "Perfect–Aspectual," 369–71.

39. Haspelmath, "From Resultative to Perfect," 221.

40. See Drinka, *Language Contact in Europe*, 1–10.

perfect is peculiar and very interesting. The diachronic development of the perfect independently occurred thousands of years earlier than that within other languages. Even in ancient Greek, the perfect had already undergone semantic changes from the resultative-stative to the anterior nuance, and from the anterior to simple past. Before the decay and disappearance of the κ-perfect, the Greek New Testament preserves the footprints of its development—three different nuances.

AORISTIC PERFECT PROBLEM AND REMEDY FROM THE TRADITIONAL APPROACH

We have so far explored the semantic change of the perfect from the anterior to the simple past. Many so-called "aoristic perfects" occur in the Greek New Testament. Fanning regards perfects of this sort as exceptional cases.[41] However, these "exceptional cases" appear more frequently than expected. Occurrences of this kind of perfects make up 89 out of 839 total usages in the Greek New Testament (11 percent) according to my research. We will briefly look at several examples.

Selected Texts from the Book of Revelation

The book of Revelation is notorious for its shifting tenses.[42] The perfect in Revelation shows peculiar behaviors in parallel with other tenses.

Revelation 2:28

In Revelation 2:28, the perfect εἴληφα occurs alongside a future tense verb.

> [Rev 2:28] ὡς κἀγὼ εἴληφα παρὰ τοῦ πατρός μου καὶ δώσω αὐτῷ τὸν ἀστέρα τὸν πρωϊνόν.
> As I also *received* from my Father, I will give him the morning star.

---

41. Fanning, *Verbal Aspect*, 112n74. Fanning says, "On the other hand, there are a few perfects in the NT which display a tendency to become virtual equivalents of the aorist in denoting simply a past action without reference to its present consequence (e.g., εἴληφα, εἴρηκα, ἔσχηκα). This tendency is clearly documented in later Greek."

42. See Mathewson, *Verbal Aspect in Revelation*, 117–23.

According to Blass and Debrunner, εἴληφα is used in the same way as the aorist (denoting a past event).[43] The perfect εἴληφα indicates that Jesus Christ received the authority from the Father in the past. Scholars such as Porter and Mathewson oppose this interpretation, arguing that the authority of Jesus Christ stands out, highlighted by the use of the perfect form ("Jesus Christ *is in the state of* possessing it").[44]

Revelation 5:7–8

The same phenomenon occurs in Revelation 5:7–8. The difficulty is that the apostle John locates the perfect in the middle of multiple aorists.

> [Rev 5:7–8] καὶ ἦλθεν καὶ εἴληφεν ἐκ τῆς δεξιᾶς τοῦ καθημένου ἐπὶ τοῦ θρόνου καὶ ὅτε ἔλαβεν τὸ βιβλίον, τὰ τέσσαρα ζῷα καὶ οἱ εἴκοσι τέσσαρες πρεσβύτεροι ἔπεσαν ἐνώπιον τοῦ ἀρνίου.
>
> And he went and *took* the scroll from the right hand of him who was seated on the throne. And he had taken the scroll, the four living creatures and the twenty-four elders fell down before the Lamb.

Many commentators argue that εἴληφεν here is aoristic.[45] Dougherty claims that the perfect can be also employed as a past tense in Revelation (Rev 5:7; 7:14; 8:5; 19:3).[46] Aune notably states that the author employs perfect in order to highlight the action, in contrast to the aorists.[47]

To merely categorize these examples as "exceptional" provides a very superficial explanation. Stating that the perfect behaves like the aorist from time to time is not very meaningful unless the underlying reasons for this behavior are examined. Mathewson attempts to solve this issue by arguing that the author selects the perfect form for the sake of emphasis

---

43. BDF §343. Fanning states that the aoristic use of the perfect is rare in the NT (Fanning, *Verbal Aspect*, 112n74).

44. Mathewson, *Verbal Aspect in Revelation*, 97; Porter, *Verbal Aspect*, 251–59.

45. Chantraine, *Parfait grec*, 239; BDF §343; Fanning, *Verbal Aspect*, 299–300; Wallace, *Beyond the Basics*, 579; Thompson, *Apocalypse and Semitic Syntax*, 44; Mussies, *Morphology of Koine Greek*, 348; Zerwick, *Biblical Greek*, 290; Beale, *Book of Revelation*, 357; Charles, *Revelation of St. John*, 144.

46. Dougherty, "Syntax of the Apocalypse," 425. Mathewson critiques Dougherty's view, saying that Dougherty does not develop semantically consistent implication of the perfect and does not still get out of the "traditional" box (Mathewson, *Verbal Aspect in Revelation*, 11, 17).

47. Aune, *Revelation 1–5*, 354. Mounce also notes that the perfect here dramatizes the action of the Lamb taking the scrolls (Mounce, *Book of Revelation*, 134).

or prominence. According to Mathewson, εἴληφεν should not be confused with the surrounding aorists because it functions to highlight the action in the text.[48] The next section will handle this matter in detail.

The Dramatic Historical Present Perfect

We have briefly introduced the merger of perfect and aorist using two key texts. In order to solve this conundrum of the confusion of the perfect with the aorist, Robertson introduces the category of "Dramatic Historical Present Perfect." He characterizes this category as when "an action completed in the past is conceived in terms of the present time for the sake of vividness."[49] Moulton and Robertson illustrate the concept with an example from Plato:

> [Plato, Crito 44a] τεκμαίρομαι ἔκ τινος ἐνυπνίου, ὃ ἑώρακα ὀλίγον πρότερον ταύτης τῆς νυκτός.
>
> I design/purpose from any dream that I *saw* a little ago this night.[50]

The speaker (Socrates) employs a vivid present perfect, says Moulton: "where the point of time in the past would have εἶδον, as inevitable as the aorist in English, had not Socrates meant to emphasize the present vividness of the vision."[51] Mandilaras also affirms this perspective from Plato's text.[52]

---

48. Mathewson, *Verbal Aspect in Revelation*, 95, 98. Mathewson quotes Zerwick, "The choice between aorist and perfect is not determined by the objective facts, but the writer's wish to connote the special nuance of the perfect; if this be not required, the aorist will be used" (Zerwick, *Biblical Greek*, 97).

49. Robertson, *Grammar*, 896.

50. Some functional overlap between aorist and perfect is found even in Classical Greek (Bentein, "Transitivity, Ecology, and the Emergence," 302). See Lysias, *Lysias* XII, 83, ἀλλὰ εἰ τὰ χρήματα τὰ φανερὰ δημεύσαιτε, καλῶς ἂν ἔχοι ἢ τῇ πόλει ἧς οὗτοι πολλὰ εἰλήφασιν, ἢ τοῖς ἰδιώταις ὧν τὰς οἰκίας ἐξεπόρθησαν; ("Or again, if you confiscated their material property, would this be compensation either to the city for all that they have taken from her, or to individuals for the houses that they pillaged?").

51. Moulton, *Prolegomena*, 141.

52. Mandilaras, *Studies in the Greek Language*, 16. Mandilaras says, "The statement of the definite point of time in the past (ὀλίγον πρότερον) would have required the use of the aorist according to the rules of syntax. In fact Socrates meant to emphasize the present vividness of the vision by using the perfect; he is not interested in '*when*' this happened, but it is of great importance for him that the vision is still alive in his memory. Such a use of the perfect occurs often in Attic with verbs denoting 'seeing' or 'hearing.' The situation in the text of the NT is similar." Mandilaras still views this perfect as aoristic (Mandilaras, *Studies in the Greek Language*, 47).

Several scholars consider ἑώρακα in this text simple past.⁵³ Bentein regards it as the perfect of recent past, saying, "a past event that has just occurred, and thus implies a certain emphasis on account of its recency."⁵⁴ While the other views are also likely, Robertson's category is attractive, at least for this text.⁵⁵

Revelation 5:7–8

We have already seen several debatable texts of this kind in the Greek New Testament.

> [Rev 5:7–8] καὶ ἦλθεν καὶ **εἴληφεν** ἐκ τῆς δεξιᾶς τοῦ καθημένου ἐπὶ τοῦ θρόνου καὶ ὅτε ἔλαβεν τὸ βιβλίον, τὰ τέσσαρα ζῷα καὶ οἱ εἴκοσι τέσσαρες πρεσβύτεροι ἔπεσαν ἐνώπιον τοῦ ἀρνίου.
>
> And he went and *took* the scroll from the right hand of him who was seated on the throne. And when he had taken the scroll, the four living creatures and the twenty-four elders fell down before the Lamb.

Just as with the example of Plato, Robertson sees εἴληφεν in Revelation 5:7 as Dramatic Perfect for vividness.⁵⁶ It is notable that the perfect εἴληφεν is situated between the two aorists ἦλθεν and ἔλαβεν. The role of εἴληφεν in light of Porter's system is perplexing because the stative aspect (perfect) is positioned between two aorists (perfective aspect). Accepting Porter's markedness theory, Mathewson maintains that the perfect (εἴληφεν) plays the role of marking the action that takes the frontground while the aorist ἦλθεν functions as the background. After using the perfect to highlight

---

53. Mandilaras, *Non-Literary Papyri*, 224–25; Caragounis, *New Testament Language*, 154; Bentein, *Verbal Periphrasis*, 40.

54. Bentein, *Verbal Periphrasis*, 40. Bentein describes, "the adverbial phrase ὀλίγον πρότερον ταύτης τῆς νυκτός 'a little while ago in the course of this night' specifies a recent the occurrence of a recent past event—that is, Socrates having a dream."

55. Robertson, *Grammar*, 896–97. Robertson also illustrates this vivid nuance with κέκραγεν ([John the Baptist] "cried out") in John 1:15: Ἰωάννης μαρτυρεῖ περὶ αὐτοῦ καὶ κέκραγεν λέγων· οὗτος ἦν ὃν εἶπον ("John bore witness about him, and cried out, saying, 'This was he of whom I said'"). See Burton, *Syntax*, 39; Caragounis, *New Testament Language*, 162–63; Andrason and Locatell, "Perfect Wave," 52.

56. Robertson, *Grammar*, 897; Köstenberger et al., *Going Deeper*, 301. Köstenberger et al. regard it as dramatic perfect. Similarly, McKay notes that the usage of the perfect here conveys the effect of a historical present with much more emphasis (McKay, *New Syntax*, 50).

the crucial point, says Mathewson, the author reverts to the background by employing the aorist (ἔλαβεν).[57]

Mathewson critiques Robertson's Dramatic Perfect as a "temporally awkward and confusing label."[58] Mathewson criticizes Robertson incorrectly attributing "a temporal, rhetorical transfer of the assumed force of the perfect tense form."[59] Mathewson avers that the perfect does not grammaticalize the temporality but represents a state of affairs, so that it functions as the most heavily marked tense form to highlight a certain action.[60] In spite of this criticism, Mathewson acknowledges Robertson's correct observation with regard to the perfect changing the flow of a sentence.[61]

Revelation 8:3–5

This is another bewildering passage in which tense shifting occurs in Revelation. One perfect form occurs in the middle of the text, together with seven aorists. While many view εἴληφεν as the aoristic perfect, Robertson considers it Dramatic Perfect.[62]

> [Rev 8:3–5] Καὶ ἄλλος ἄγγελος <u>ἦλθεν</u> καὶ <u>ἐστάθη</u> ἐπὶ τοῦ θυσιαστηρίου ἔχων λιβανωτὸν χρυσοῦν, καὶ <u>ἐδόθη</u> αὐτῷ θυμιάματα πολλὰ ἵνα δώσει ταῖς προσευχαῖς τῶν ἁγίων πάντων ἐπὶ τὸ θυσιαστήριον τὸ χρυσοῦν τὸ ἐνώπιον τοῦ θρόνου. καὶ <u>ἀνέβη</u> ὁ καπνὸς τῶν θυμιαμάτων ταῖς προσευχαῖς τῶν ἁγίων ἐκ χειρὸς τοῦ ἀγγέλου ἐνώπιον τοῦ θεοῦ. καὶ **εἴληφεν** ὁ ἄγγελος τὸν λιβανωτὸν καὶ <u>ἐγέμισεν</u>

---

57. Mathewson, *Verbal Aspect in Revelation*, 128.

58. Mathewson, *Verbal Aspect in Revelation*, 99.

59. Mathewson refutes the labels "Dramatic Perfect" and "Aoristic Perfect," which are perhaps better abandoned because they misunderstand the perfect tense by depending on the temporality (Mathewson, *Verbal Aspect in Revelation*, 94). In this book, I argue that the Greek perfect conveys the temporality and Robertson's Dramatic Perfect is still helpful to understand the perfect.

60. Mathewson, *Verbal Aspect in Revelation*, 100.

61. Mathewson, *Verbal Aspect in Revelation*, 99–100.

62. Chantraine, *Parfait grec*, 239; Fanning, *Verbal Aspect*, 302–3; Dougherty, "Syntax of the Apocalypse," 425; Smalley, *Revelation to John*, 217; Osborne, *Revelation*, 346n13; Beale, *Book of Revelation*, 460; Simcox, *Language of the New Testament*, 104; Robertson, *Grammar*, 896–97. Robertson offers more examples of Dramatic Perfect: Acts 21:28 (ἔτι τε καὶ Ἕλληνας εἰσήγαγεν εἰς τὸ ἱερὸν καὶ κεκοίνωκεν τὸν ἅγιον τόπον τοῦτον, "he even brought Greeks into the temple and has defiled this holy place"). Robertson regards εὑρήκαμεν in John 1:41 (εὑρήκαμεν τὸν Μεσσίαν, "We have found Messiah") as vivid, but it is unlikely. The perfect **εὑρήκαμεν** denotes the anterior nuance. See Caragounis, *New Testament Language*, 165.

> αὐτὸν ἐκ τοῦ πυρὸς τοῦ θυσιαστηρίου καὶ <u>ἔβαλεν</u> εἰς τὴν γῆν, καὶ <u>ἐγένοντο</u> βρονταὶ καὶ φωναὶ καὶ ἀστραπαὶ καὶ σεισμός.[63]
>
> Another angel holding a golden censer came and was stationed at the altar. A large amount of incense was given to him to offer up, with the prayers of all the saints, on the golden altar that is before the throne, and the smoke of the incense, with the prayers of the saints, rose before God from the hand of the angel. Then the angel *took* the censer and filled it with fire from the altar and threw it on the earth, and there were peals of thunder, rumblings, flashes of lightning, and an earthquake.

The lens of Porter's verbal aspect leaves it difficult to interpret this perfect in the middle of the aorists.[64] An attempt to understand the perfect εἴληφεν as stative is challenging because it is surrounded by the seven aorists, which generally denote completed actions. Utilizing Porter's markedness theory, Mathewson argues that the author intentionally placed the perfect in the middle of the aorist to make it stand out unexpectedly and stress the angel's action. Mathewson regards εἴληφεν as stative, depicting a state of affairs with implication of the past (using εἶδον).[65] Since he rejects the grammatical temporality of verbs such as the aorist, arguing against their conveying a past time, however, his interpretation of the aorist (εἶδον) with past time reference here in Revelation 8:5 is questionable in terms of consistency.[66] A discrepancy occurs if he accepts the usage of the aorist as past time selectively. Mathewson fails to solve the role of the perfect decisively among the seven aorists in the text.

---

63. Bold-font perfect with underlined aorists.
64. See Campbell, *Basics of Verbal Aspect*, 47.
65. Mathewson, *Verbal Aspect in Revelation*, 98.
66. Mathewson says, "If the aorist tense, however, does not grammaticalize absolute temporal reference, but verbal aspect" (Mathewson, *Verbal Aspect in Revelation*, 57). The issue actually grows bigger if he asserts that the aorist does not grammaticalize temporality—the augment issue. See Silva, "Response to Fanning and Porter," 77n1; Gentry, "Function of the Augment," in Runge and Fresch, *Greek Verb Revisited*, 353–78; Fresch, "Typology, Polysemy, and Prototypes," in Runge and Fresch, *Greek Verb Revisited*, 379–415; Galani, "Morphosyntax of Verbs in Modern Greek," 206–10; Evans, *Verbal Syntax*, 49. Evans says, "Porter fails to convince when he claims to have shown that the augment is not a temporal indicator. . . . He offers nothing to shake the normal understanding of this important morphological feature, though the onus is surely on him to disprove consensus opinion."

Unless one can elucidate the core issue of the stative, therefore, bringing another issue, such as "markedness theory," into the verbal system fails to provide a remedy. Resolving the problems of the perfect as "stative," as argued by Porter and Mathewson, is a prerequisite before adding another topic such as markedness theory. "Markedness theory" should not be used as a refuge to avoid coping with these baffling perfects. This tactic simply leads to producing another extended debate over markedness theory.[67]

In sum, Mathewson's approach does not satisfy the question of why the perfect as stative aspect is located between two aorists of perfective aspect. His acceptance of Porter's markedness theory does not offer a satisfactory explanation for these unique cases of the perfect, but only leads to a debate over markedness theory. Moreover, the perfect conveys past time like the aorist in many places (cf. Rev 2:28; 11:17; 19:3). These occurrences of the perfect are far from the stative. The methodology of Porter and Mathewson fails to explicate such behavior from the Greek perfect. Robertson's Dramatic Historical perfect has more cogency.

Colossians 2:13–15 and James 1:24

We will now consider more passages that show the perfect with a vivid nuance.

> [Col 2:13–15] συνεζωοποίησεν ὑμᾶς σὺν αὐτῷ, χαρισάμενος ἡμῖν πάντα τὰ παραπτώματα. ἐξαλείψας τὸ καθ' ἡμῶν χειρόγραφον τοῖς δόγμασιν ὃ ἦν ὑπεναντίον ἡμῖν, καὶ αὐτὸ **ἦρκεν** ἐκ τοῦ μέσου προσηλώσας αὐτὸ τῷ σταυρῷ· ἀπεκδυσάμενος τὰς ἀρχὰς καὶ τὰς ἐξουσίας ἐδειγμάτισεν ἐν παρρησίᾳ ἐν παρρησίᾳ.
>
> God made you alive together with him, having forgiven us all our trespasses, by canceling the record of debt that stood against us with its legal demands and he has taken it out of the way, nailing it to the cross. He disarmed the rulers and authorities and put them to open shame.

---

67. See Runge, "Markedness," 43–56. Fanning rightly evaluates the "stative" of Porter and Mathewson, saying, "One problem is that at a theoretical level the perfect aspect—described by Porter as 'stative'—should be expected to fall at the other end of the scale of prominence. In Stephen Wallace's 1982 treatment of foreground and background (followed by others since then), stativity occurs in the list of linguistic features that characterize *background*, while processes and events are expected to characterize *foreground*" (Fanning, "Greek Tenses in John's Apocalypse," 337; emphasis original).

[James 1:24] κατενόησεν γὰρ ἑαυτὸν καὶ **ἀπελήλυθεν** καὶ εὐθέως ἐπελάθετο ὁποῖος ἦν.
For he looked at himself and has gone away, he has immediately forgotten what kind of person he was.

Since the perfect ἦρκεν in Colossians 2:14 points out the past from Paul's perspective, the aorist form would fit here. Nevertheless, the perfect is employed instead in order to emphasize the vivid nuance. It is notable that ἀπελήλυθεν occurs between the aorists in James 1:24. Robertson states that ἀπελήλυθεν expresses vividness. If the aorist was employed, says Robertson, it "would have been prosaic."[68]

Conclusion

Robertson's category of Dramatic Historical Present Perfect admittedly gives some insight into the unique behaviors of the perfect. Against the temporal notion within the Greek verbal system, Mathewson argues that this label would be better abandoned.[69] However, Robertson's Dramatic Perfect demonstrates that traditional Greek grammar can explain some cases of the perfects behaving like aorists. Nevertheless, the Dramatic Perfect is not without its shortcomings.[70] Not all perfects used together with aorists convey a vivid nuance. Rather, many of them denote a simple past, which the next section will introduce.

GREEK PERFECT AS SIMPLE PAST

Although Robertson's Dramatic Perfect is helpful for comprehending some perfects used alongside aorists, this sense of vividness is not the solution for every thorny case. For example:

68. Robertson, *Grammar*, 897.

69. Mathewson, *Verbal Aspect in Revelation*, 94. Mathewson critiques that Wallace merges two distinct categories of "Dramatic Historical Present Perfect" and "aoristic perfect" (Wallace, *Beyond the Basic*, 578). Wallace introduces both categories, identifying the former with the latter.

70. Fanning introduces the category of Dramatic Aorist, which expresses a present state of feeling or comprehension: ἐδεξάμην ("I welcome"), ἤσθην ("I am pleased"), ἐγέλασα ("I must laugh"), ἐπῄνεσα ("I approve"), συνῆκα ("I understand"), and ἔδοξα ("I think") (Fanning, *Verbal Aspect*, 275). See Gildersleeve, *Syntax of Classical Greek*, §262; Moorhouse, *Syntax of Sophocles*, 195–96; Rijksbaron, *Syntax and Semantics*, 28–30; Smyth, *Grammar* §1937. Smyth introduces category "Dramatic Aorist" in which "the first person singular of the aorist is used in the dialogue parts of tragedy and comedy to denote a state of mind or an act expressing a state of mind."

[John 1:32] Καὶ ἐμαρτύρησεν Ἰωάννης λέγων ὅτι **τεθέαμαι** τὸ πνεῦμα καταβαῖνον ὡς περιστερὰν ἐξ οὐρανοῦ.

And John bore witness: "I *saw* the Spirit descending from heaven like a dove."

[LXX Gen 31:38–40] ταῦτά μοι εἴκοσι ἔτη ἐγώ εἰμι μέτα σοῦ τὰ πρόβατά σου καὶ αἱ αἶγες σου οὐκ ἠτεκνώθησαν κριοὺς τῶν προβάτων σου οὐ κατέφανον θηριάλωτον οὐκ **ἀνενήνοχά** σοι ἐγὼ ἀπετίννυον παρ᾽ ἐμαυτοῦ κλέμματα ἡμέρας καὶ κλέμματα νυκτός ἐγινόμην τῆς ἡμέρας συγκαιόμενος τῷ καύματι καὶ παγετῷ τῆς νυκτός καὶ ἀφίσατο ὁ ὕπνος ἀπὸ τῶν ὀφθαλμῶν μου.

These twenty years I have been with you. Your ewes and your female goats have not miscarried, and I have not eaten the rams of your flocks. What was torn by wild beasts I *did* not *bring* to you. I bore the loss of it myself. From my hand you required it, whether stolen by day or stolen by night. There I was: by day the heat consumed me, and the cold by night, and my sleep fled from my eyes.

Robertson claims that the perfect τεθέαμαι in John 1:32 plays the role of expressing vividness.[71] Although it is a possible option, however, the vividness on the perfect is not inevitable. It is also likely that τεθέαμαι conveys a simple past action, corresponding with the aorist ἐμαρτύρησεν. In Genesis 31:38–40, ἀνενήνοχα appears in the middle of aorists. Although the perfect might be used to deliver a vivid nuance, ἀνενήνοχα indicates a past event from years ago in the text. In the Greek New Testament, many perfects convey a simple past nuance.

Εἴληφας

Here is a case of the perfect as simple past:

---

71. Robertson, *Grammar*, 897–902. Robertson acknowledges the category "aoristic perfect," introducing it with lengthy explanation. It is the same case as **ἑώρακεν** in Luke 1:22 (ἐξελθὼν δὲ οὐκ ἐδύνατο λαλῆσαι αὐτοῖς, καὶ ἐπέγνωσαν ὅτι ὀπτασίαν **ἑώρακεν** ἐν τῷ ναῷ, "And when he came out, he was unable to speak to them, and they realized that he saw [had seen] a vision in the temple"). Although Robertson claims that this perfect is for vivid nuance, it does not seem to be.

[Rev 3:3] μνημόνευε οὖν πῶς **εἴληφας** καὶ ἤκουσας καὶ τήρει καὶ μετανόησον.

Remember therefore what you have received and heard; and keep it, and repent.[72]

Revelation 3:3 is another tough passage to handle because the juxtaposition of perfect, aorist, and present would be bewildering for proponents of Porter's theory.[73] Verbal aspect theory would render, "How you are in a *state* of taking, completed hearing, and ongoing process of keeping." Mathewson asserts that the perfect is employed to stress the state of the church in Sardis which has received (εἴληφας) the truth.[74] However, without elucidating the state itself, he cannot evade the main point by importing the markedness theory to assert that the perfect is stressed as the most heavily marked.[75] In the text, the general "state" of εἴληφας does not accord very well with a perfective past event by the aorist ἤκουσας ("heard"), according to the verbal aspect perspectives.

Revelation 11:17 and Luke 1:36 create similar situations.

[Rev 11:17] εὐχαριστοῦμέν σοι, κύριε ὁ θεὸς ὁ παντοκράτωρ, ὁ ὢν καὶ ὁ ἦν, ὅτι **εἴληφας** τὴν δύναμίν σου τὴν μεγάλην καὶ ἐβασίλευσας.

We give thanks to you, Lord God Almighty, who is and who was, for you have taken your great power and begun to reign.

[Luke 1:36] καὶ ἰδοὺ Ἐλισάβετ ἡ συγγενίς σου καὶ αὐτὴ **συνείληφεν** υἱὸν ἐν γήρει αὐτῆς καὶ οὗτος μὴν ἕκτος ἐστὶν αὐτῇ τῇ καλουμένῃ στείρᾳ.

And behold, your relative Elizabeth in her old age has also conceived a son, and this is the sixth month with her who was called barren.

---

72. See Lysias, *Lysias* XII, 83, ἀλλὰ εἰ τὰ χρήματα τὰ φανερὰ δημεύσαιτε, καλῶς ἂν ἔχοι ἢ τῇ πόλει ἧς οὗτοι πολλὰ εἰλήφασιν, ἢ τοῖς ἰδιώταις ὧν τὰς οἰκίας ἐξεπόρθησαν; ("Or again, if you confisticated their material property, would this be compensation either to the city for all that they have taken from her, or to individuals for the houses that they pillaged?"). Chantraine says that the perfect εἰλήφασιν is employed along with the aorist ἐξεπόρθησαν and chosen by the author for emphasis of action taking (Chantraine, *Parfait grec*, 187–88).

73. Mathewson, *Verbal Aspect in Revelation*, 91.

74. Mathewson, *Verbal Aspect in Revelation*, 97–98.

75. For example, the perfect οἶδα occurs 210 times and γέγραπται 65 times in the NT (out of 839). But it is hard to claim that they denote a highlighting nuance in every occurrence as the most heavily markedness.

In Revelation 11:17, εἴληφας is best translated as "took" rather than "have taken." The subject of εἴληφας is the eternal Almighty God who already had great power before the Creation. Robertson's vivid perfect does not fit with the context. Chantraine and Caragounis consider εἴληφας as equivalent to the aorist ἔλαβες.[76] With regard to συνείληφεν in Luke 1:36, McKay sees it as a state.[77] However, this is unlikely because in the present moment of the angel's speaking to Mary, Elizabeth's having conceived is clearly a past event, which happened six months ago. The angel's saying "sixth month" marks the conception of the baby as a precedent event.

Not every use of εἴληφεν denotes a simple past, however. In 1 Corinthians 10:13, εἴληφεν denotes an anterior nuance, "no temptation has overtaken you that is not common to man."[78]

Πέπρακεν

Next, we will look at the perfect of πιπράσκω, which is a difficult case.

> [Matt 13:46] εὑρὼν δὲ ἕνα πολύτιμον μαργαρίτην ἀπελθὼν **πέπρακεν** πάντα ὅσα εἶχεν καὶ ἠγόρασεν αὐτόν.
>
> Who, on finding one pearl of great value, went and *sold* all that he had and bought it.

Perplexed by the nuance of πέπρακεν, scholars express variegated opinions. Smyth regards it as a perfect with emphasis.[79] Burton and Horrocks view πέπρακεν as a simple past.[80] Gerö and Stechow state that πέπρακεν here is not greatly distinguished from ἠγόρασεν, even though the perfect and the aorist do not have the same meaning.[81] Morris and McKay see the use of πέπρακεν as due to a stylistic variation.[82]

---

76. Chantraine, *Parfait grec*, 239; Caragounis, *New Testament Language*, 166. Mathewson asserts that εἴληφας refers here to highlight "God's reception of great power," but it is not persuasive (Mathewson, *Verbal Aspect in Revelation*, 98).

77. McKay, *New Syntax*, 32.

78. In Greek 1 Cor 10:13 is πειρασμὸς ὑμᾶς οὐκ εἴληφεν (ESV, "No temptation has overtaken you"; NASB, "No temptation has taken you"; NIV, "No temptation has overtaken you"; and KJV, "There hath no temptation taken you").

79. Smyth, *Greek Grammar*, 435.

80. Horrocks, *Greek*, 154; Burton, *Syntax*, 43.

81. Gerö and Stechow, "Tense in Time," 282. Chantraine maintains that it is not possible to distinguish πέπρακεν from the aorist in the text (Chantraine, *Parfait grec*, 238).

82. Morris, *Gospel according to Matthew*, 360; McKay, "Ancient Greek Perfect," 16. Moser also emphasizes the stylistic matter: "The choice between the Aorist and the

On the other hand, Dana and Mantey consider πέπρακεν a Dramatic Perfect for emphasis.[83] Similarly, Davies and Allison regard πέπρακεν as vivid perfect, appealing to Robertson.[84] This perfect also occurs in the Apostolic Fathers.

> [*The Shepherd of Hermas* 1.1]˚Ο θρέψας με πέπρακέν μέ˚Ρόδῃ τινὶ εἰς˚Ρώμην. μετὰ πολλὰ ἔτη ταύτην ἀνεγνωρισάμην καὶ ἠρξάμην αὐτὴν ἀγαπᾶν ὡς ἀδελφήν.
>
> The man who brought me up *sold* me to a woman named Rhoda in Rome. Many years later I met her again and I began to love her as a sister.

Caragounis sees πέπρακεν as a perfect confused with the aorist.[85] Although πέπρακεν conveying a vivid nuance is possible, the option that this perfect, parallel with the aorist, conveys a past event is better.

Εἴρηκα

In several cases, εἴρηκα behaves like English perfect with an anterior (current relevance) nuance in the NT.[86] However, more cases occur with simply a past time nuance. Firstly, this includes passages from Revelation:

> [Rev 7:14] καὶ εἴρηκα αὐτῷ· κύριέ μου, σὺ οἶδας. καὶ εἶπέν μοι· οὗτοί εἰσιν οἱ ἐρχόμενοι ἐκ τῆς θλίψεως τῆς μεγάλης.

Perfect is a question of stylistics rather than grammar. This kind of stylistically marked expression, because of its expressive power, is particularly popular in everyday speech; the frequent use . . . [causes them to] become banal and lose colour. This is what exactly happened with the Perfect, which approached so much the meaning of the Aorist, that it became superfluous and eventually disappeared" (Moser, "Perfect Periphrases," 117).

83. Dana and Mantey, *Manual Grammar*, 204. McKay claims that a writer can stress a point by using the perfect (McKay, "Ancient Greek Perfect," 16). McKay cites Chantraine, *Parfait grec*, 187.

84. Davies and Allison, *Gospel according to Saint Matthew*, 439–40.

85. Caragounis, *Development of Greek*, 154; Caragounis, *New Testament Language*, 157.

86. John 4:18, πέντε γὰρ ἄνδρας ἔσχες καὶ νῦν ὃν ἔχεις οὐκ ἔστιν σου ἀνήρ· τοῦτο ἀληθὲς εἴρηκας ("for you have five husbands, and the one you now have is not your husband. What you *have said* is true"); John 6:65, διὰ τοῦτο εἴρηκα ὑμῖν ὅτι οὐδεὶς δύναται ἐλθεῖν πρός με ἐὰν μὴ ᾖ δεδομένον αὐτῷ ἐκ τοῦ πατρός ("For this reason I *have said* to you, that no one can come to me, unless it has been granted him from the Father"); John 14:29, καὶ νῦν εἴρηκα ὑμῖν πρὶν γενέσθαι ("And now I have *told you* before it takes place"); John 12:50, καθὼς εἴρηκέν μοι ὁ πατήρ, οὕτως λαλῶ ("I say as the Father *has told* me").

I *said* to him, "My lord, you know." And he said to me, "These are the ones who come out of the great tribulation."

[Rev 19:3] καὶ δεύτερον εἴρηκαν· ἁλληλουϊά.
And a second time they *said*, "Hallelujah!"

Many commentators state that the use of εἴρηκα above is in place of the aorist.[87] Robertson maintains that εἴρηκα in Revelation 7:14 and 19:3 is more like a real preterite, not dramatic perfect.[88] Similarly, Chantraine notes that εἴρηκε substitutes the aorist form because the use of εἶπε would be banal.[89]

Referring to εἴρηκα as a "culprit," Mathewson opines that the usage of εἴρηκα implies more than a stylistic variation of εἶπεν.[90] In the background of Revelation 7:9–17 describing the heavenly scene and the speech of the elders and angels, Mathewson argues that εἴρηκα emphasizes the response of John, who was probably surprised at the question of the elder.[91]

> The use of the perfect, then, functions to highlight John's response, perhaps due to his surprise at the question of the elder, and throws the question back on the interrogating elder. The elder's response is then simply summarized with the less marked aorist form (εἶπεν). In 19.3 the εἴρηκα is again used to introduce a speech in a series of speeches from heavenly voices. . . . Here εἴρηκα seems to be used to highlight what is spoken, while the speeches introduce what was heard.

Mathewson avers that the perfect should mean the "state" with highlight connotation. However, this interpretation does not produce a satisfactory clarification. In Revelation 7:14, εἴρηκα denotes the past, appearing parallel with εἶπεν. Andrason and Locatell point out that "Mathewson seems to dismiss evidence of the semantic extension of the perfect into the perfective-past sense."[92] It is necessary to present more fundamental and nuanced reasons rather than lumping all the perfects together as state. The

---

87. Osborne, *Revelation*, 323n10; Swete, *Apocalypse of St. John*, 102; Aune, *Revelation 6–16*, 472; Dougherty, "Syntax of the Apocalypse," 425; Charles, *Revelation*, 212; BDF §343.

88. Robertson, *Grammar*, 902.

89. Chantraine, *Parfait grec*, 182–83, 239. According to Chantraine, the perfect replacing the aorist occurs in particular when expressing it with force.

90. Mathewson, *Verbal Aspect in Revelation*, 91, 101.

91. Mathewson, *Verbal Aspect in Revelation*, 101; Porter, *Verbal Aspect*, 279.

92. Andrason and Locatell, "Perfect Wave," 86.

perfect οἶδα occurs 210 times in the NT, for example, but it is hard to say that οἶδα conveys a highlighting nuance every time.

In the Koine Greek, εἴρηκα expresses past events many times.[93]

[Acts 8:24] δεήθητε ὑμεῖς ὑπὲρ ἐμοῦ πρὸς τὸν κύριον ὅπως μηδὲν ἐπέλθῃ ἐπ' ἐμὲ ὧν **εἰρήκατε**.

Pray for me to the Lord, that nothing of what you have said may come upon me.

[Acts 17:28] ἐν αὐτῷ γὰρ ζῶμεν καὶ κινούμεθα καὶ ἐσμέν, ὡς καὶ τινες τῶν καθ' ὑμᾶς ποιητῶν **εἰρήκασιν**· τοῦ γὰρ καὶ γένος ἐσμέν.

For in him we live and move and exit, as even some of your own poets have said, "For we are also his offspring."

[2 Cor 12:8-9] ὑπὲρ τούτου τρὶς τὸν κύριον παρακάλεσα ἵνα ἀποστῇ ἀπ' ἐμοῦ. καὶ **εἴρηκέν** μοι· ἀρκεῖ σοι ἡ χάρις μου, ἡ γὰρ δύναμις ἐν ἀσθενείᾳ τελεῖται.

Three times I pleaded with the Lord about this, that it should leave me. But he said to me, "My grace is sufficient for you, for my power is made perfect in weakness."

[Heb 1:13] πρὸς τίνα δὲ τῶν ἀγγέλων **εἴρηκέν** ποτε· κάθου ἐκ δεξιῶν μου, ἕως ἂν θῶ τοὺς ἐχθρούς σου ὑποπόδιον τῶν ποδῶν σου;

And to which of the angels has he ever said, "Sit at my right hand, until I make your enemies a footstool for your feet"?

[Heb 4:3-4] καθὼς **εἴρηκεν**· ὡς ὤμοσα ἐν τῇ ὀργῇ μου· εἰ εἰσελεύσονται εἰς τὴν κατάπαυσίν μου, καίτοι τῶν ἔργων ἀπὸ καταβολῆς κόσμου γενηθέντων. **εἴρηκεν** γὰρ που περὶ τῆς ἑβδόμης οὕτως· καὶ κατέπαυσεν ὁ θεὸς ἐν τῇ ἡμέρᾳ τῇ ἑβδόμῃ ἀπὸ πάντων τῶν ἔργων αὐτοῦ,

As he has said, "As I swore in my wrath, 'They shall not enter my rest,'" although his works were finished

---

93. See Heb 13:5, Ἀφιλάργυρος ὁ τρόπος, ἀρκούμενοι τοῖς παροῦσιν. αὐτὸς γὰρ εἴρηκεν· οὐ μή σε ἀνῶ οὐδ' οὐ μή σε ἐγκαταλίπω ("Keep your life free from love of money, and be content with what you have, for he has said, 'I will never leave you nor forsake you.'"). In the Septuagint, the perfect as a simple past nuance already exists: Gen 42:14, τοῦτό ἐστιν ὃ εἴρηκα ὑμῖν λέγων ὅτι κατάσκοποί ἐστε ("It is as I said to you: You are spies"); In Gen 31:16, νῦν οὖν ὅσα εἴρηκέν σοι ὁ θεὸς ποίει ("Now then, whatever God [has] said to you, do").

from the foundation of the world. For he has somewhere spoken of the seventh day in this way: "And God rested on the seventh day from all his works."

[*Didache* 9.5] καὶ γὰρ περὶ τούτου **εἴρηκεν** ὁ κύριος· Μὴ δῶτε τὸ ἅγιον τοῖς κυσί.

For the Lord has also spoken concerning this: "Do not give what is holy to dogs."[94]

All the usages of εἴρηκα above denote the past time.[95] In Acts 8:24, Simon pleads to Peter that what he cursed may not fall upon him. In Acts 17:28, the apostle Paul cites one of the Greek poets who spoke in the past. Similarly, εἴρηκεν in Hebrews 1:13 and 4:3-4 indicates past actions in the OT (quoted from Psalms 110 and 95).[96] The author of *Didache* also speaks of what the Lord *spoke* in the past.

Second Corinthians 12:9 is notable. Andrason and Locatell say,

> Paul is not saying that Jesus' statement has resulted in an ongoing state, nor that Jesus' utterance was continuing up to the present moment. Nor was Paul pointing out that Jesus now had the experience of having made the statement. Nevertheless, Paul is presenting this past event as having some level of current relevance for his present situation.[97]

As Andrason and Locatell state, the apostle Paul speaks of what he experienced with the Lord in the past—asking for healing of his physical suffering.[98] Moreover, παρακάλεσα confirms the past context, so that εἴρηκεν also indicates the past event, in parallel with the aorist.

With the compound form is observed the same trait.[99]

---

94. Holmes, *Apostolic Fathers*, 358-59. See *The Epistle of Barnabas* 9.4: Ἀλλὰ καὶ ἡ περιτομὴ ἐφ' ᾗ πεποίθασιν κατήργηται, περιτομὴν γὰρ εἴρηκεν οὐ σαρκὸς γενηθῆναι, "But the circumcision in which they have trusted has been abolished, for he declared that circumcision was not a matter of the flesh"; *The Shepherd of Hermas* 43.19: Πῶς, φημί, κύριε, δύναται ταῦτα γενέσθαι; ἀδύνατα γὰρ ἀμφότερα ταῦτα εἴρηκας, "'How,' I asked, 'can these things be, sir? For both of these things you just said are impossible'" (Holmes, *Apostolic Fathers*, 406-7, 544-45).

95. While acknowledging that εἴρηκας implies a prior event in Aeschylus and Sophocles, Stork suggests that εἴρηκας denotes a state. However, it is unlikely (Stork, "Fragments of Aeschylus and Sophocles," 19-20).

96. Cf. Ng, "Greek Perfect in Hebrews," 22-24.

97. Andrason and Locatell, "Perfect Wave," 46.

98. Robertson puts εἴρηκεν of 2 Cor 12:9 into the category of the vivid perfect, but it is not inevitable (Robertson, *Grammar*, 897).

99. See *The Epistle of Barnabas* 6.18: προειρήκαμεν δὲ ἐπάνω· Καὶ αὐξανέσθωσαν καὶ πληθυνέσθωσαν καὶ ἀρχέτωσαν τῶν ἰχθύων, "Now we have already said above: 'And

[Rom 9:29] καὶ καθὼς **προείρηκεν** Ἡσαΐας· εἰ μὴ κύριος σαβαὼθ ἐγκατέλιπεν ἡμῖν σπέρμα, ὡς Σόδομα ἂν ἐγενήθημεν καὶ ὡς Γόμορρα ἂν ὡμοιώθημεν.

And just as Isaiah foretold, "If the Lord of hosts had not left us offspring, we would have been like Sodom and become like Gomorrah."

[2 Cor 7:3] πρὸς κατάκρισιν οὐ λέγω· **προείρηκα** γὰρ ὅτι ἐν ταῖς καρδίαις ἡμῶν ἐστε εἰς τὸ συναποθανεῖν καὶ συζῆν.

I do not say this to condemn you, for I said before that you are in our hearts, to die together and to live together.

[2 Cor 13:2] **προείρηκα** καὶ προλέγω, ὡς παρὼν τὸ δεύτερον καὶ ἀπὼν νῦν, τοῖς προημαρτηκόσιν καὶ τοῖς λοιποῖς πᾶσιν, ὅτι ἐὰν ἔλθω εἰς τὸ πάλιν οὐ φείσομαι.

I have previously said when present the second time, and though now absent I say in advance to those who have sinned in the past and to all the rest as well, that if I come again, I will not spare.

[Gal 1:9] ὡς **προειρήκαμεν** καὶ ἄρτι πάλιν λέγω· εἴ τις ὑμᾶς εὐαγγελίζεται παρ' ὃ παρελάβετε, ἀνάθεμα ἔστω.

As we have said before and now I say again, if any man is preaching to you a gospel contrary to that which you received, let him be accursed.

[Heb 4:7] καθὼς **προείρηται**· σήμερον ἐὰν τῆς φωνῆς αὐτοῦ ἀκούσητε, μὴ σκληρύνητε τὰς καρδίας ὑμῶν.

Just as it has been said before, "Today, if you hear his voice, do not harden your hearts."

The perfect προείρηκα above indicates previous events. The preposition πρό ("before") strengthens the past-time indication of εἴρηκα. In Romans 9:29, Isaiah prophesied in the OT, which is clearly the past.[100] By using προείρηκα in 2 Corinthians 7:3 and 13:2, Paul describes what he *said*

---

let them increase and multiply and rule over the fish'" (Holmes, *Apostolic Fathers*, 400–401).

100. Longenecker says, "but also by the third-person singular perfect indicative verb προείρηκεν ("he has already [or 'earlier'] said [i.e., in the same writing or document]")—which expression was often set out in contrast to the present tense and functioned to highlight a further important summary statement that was meant to explicate some earlier concluding statement" (Longenecker, *Epistle to the Romans*, 823).

previously. Especially in Galatians 1:9, προειρήκαμεν is contrasted to the present verb λέγω.

Admittedly, difficult passages with προείρηκα also exist in the NT.

> [Mark 13:23] ὑμεῖς δὲ βλέπετε· **προείρηκα** ὑμῖν πάντα.
> But take heed; I *have told* you all things beforehand.[101]

> [John 15:14–15] ὑμεῖς φίλοι μού ἐστε ἐὰν ποιῆτε ἃ ἐγὼ ἐντέλλομαι ὑμῖν. οὐκέτι λέγω ὑμᾶς δούλους, ὅτι ὁ δοῦλος οὐκ οἶδεν τί ποιεῖ αὐτοῦ ὁ κύριος· ὑμᾶς δὲ **εἴρηκα** φίλους, ὅτι πάντα ἃ ἤκουσα παρὰ τοῦ πατρός μου ἐγνώρισα ὑμῖν.
> You are my friends if you do what I command you. No longer do I call you servants, for the servant does not know what his master is doing; but I *have called* you friends, for all that I have heard from my Father I have made known to you.

Seemingly an overlap exists in these texts between the anterior and simple past nuance. Drawing an exact line between them does not seem possible. Nevertheless, I propose that the perfects προείρηκα and εἴρηκα here lean toward conveying a simple past. A hint is that Jesus Christ called his disciples friends in the *previous* verse (John 15:14), so that he can consider his calling them friends as a past action in John 15:15. Notably, Andrason and Locatell point out this overlap, saying: "This leaves the sense of the present perfect indefinite, which refers to a past, but still relevant event (though its 'relevance' is not found in a resulting state, continuing action, or experiential value)."[102]

Ἑώρακα

The previous chapter explored the usage of ἑώρακα as an anterior nuance. The problematic cases are the usages of the verb with a simple past nuance in the NT.[103]

---

101. Matt 24:25 is the same: ἰδοὺ προείρηκα ὑμῖν ("Behold, I have told you in advance").

102. Andrason and Locatell, "Perfect Wave," 46.

103. In the Septuagint, ἑώρακα also occurs as simple past: Gen 41:15, ἐνύπνιον ἑώρακα καὶ ... ἐγὼ δὲ ἀκήκοα περὶ σοῦ ("I *saw* a dream ... and I have heard about you"); Dan 2:31, καὶ σύ βασιλεῦ ἑώρακας καὶ ἰδοὺ εἰκὼν μία καὶ ἦν ἡ εἰκὼν ἐκείνη μεγάλη σφόδρα καὶ ἡ πρόσοψις αὐτῆς ὑπερφερὴς ἐστήκει ἐναντίον σου καὶ ἡ πρόσοψις τῆς εἰκόνος φοβερά ("You *saw*, O king, and behold, a great image. This image, mighty and of exceeding brightness, stood before you, and its appearance was frightening"); Dan 2:45, καθάπερ ἑώρακας ἐξ ὄρους τμηθῆναι λίθον ἄνευ χειρῶν καὶ συνηλόησε τὸ ὄστρακον τὸν σίδηρον καὶ

THE THIRD STAGE   151

[Luke 1:22] ἐξελθὼν δὲ οὐκ ἐδύνατο λαλῆσαι αὐτοῖς, καὶ ἐπέγνωσαν ὅτι ὀπτασίαν **ἑώρακεν** ἐν τῷ ναῷ.

And when he came out, he was unable to speak to them, and they realized that he saw [had seen] a vision in the temple.

[Luke 9:36] καὶ ἐν τῷ γενέσθαι τὴν φωνὴν εὑρέθη Ἰησοῦς μόνος. καὶ αὐτοὶ ἐσίγησαν καὶ οὐδενὶ ἀπήγγειλαν ἐν ἐκείναις ταῖς ἡμέραις οὐδὲν ὧν **ἑώρακαν**.

And when the voice had spoken, Jesus was found alone. And they kept silent and told no one in those days anything of what they had seen.[104]

[John 1:33-34] κἀγὼ οὐκ ᾔδειν αὐτόν, ἀλλ' ὁ πέμψας με βαπτίζειν ἐν ὕδατι ἐκεῖνός μοι εἶπεν· ἐφ' ὃν ἂν ἴδῃς τὸ πνεῦμα καταβαῖνον καὶ μένον ἐπ' αὐτόν, οὗτός ἐστιν ὁ βαπτίζων ἐν πνεύματι ἁγίῳ· κἀγὼ **ἑώρακα** καὶ **μεμαρτύρηκα** ὅτι οὗτός ἐστιν ὁ υἱὸς τοῦ θεοῦ.

I myself did not know him, but he who sent me to baptize with water said to me, "He on whom you see the Spirit descend and remain, this is he who baptizes with the Holy Spirit." And I have seen and have borne witness that this is the Son of God.

[John 20:25] ἔλεγον οὖν αὐτῷ οἱ ἄλλοι μαθηταί· **ἑωράκαμεν** τὸν κύριον. ὁ δὲ εἶπεν αὐτοῖς· ἐὰν μὴ ἴδω ἐν ταῖς χερσὶν αὐτοῦ τὸν τύπον τῶν ἥλων καὶ βάλω μου τὴν χεῖρα εἰς τὴν πλευρὰν αὐτοῦ, οὐ μὴ πιστεύσω.

So the other disciples told him, "We have seen the Lord!" But he said to them, Unless I see in his hands the mark of the nails, and place my finger into the mark of the nails, and place my hand into his side, I will never believe.

In Luke 1:22, ἑώρακεν indicates the prior event of Zechariah seeing a vision in the temple. Interestingly, most English Bibles translate this phrase

---

τὸν χαλκὸν καὶ ἄργυρον καὶ τὸν χρυσόν ("Inasmuch as you *saw* that a stone was cut out of the mountain without hands and that it crushed the iron, the bronze, the clay, the silver, and the gold"). See *The Shepherd of Hermas* 14.2, τοὺς δὲ ἑτέρους οὓς ἑώρακας πολλοὺς κειμένους ("As for the others that you *saw* lying around in great numbers") (Holmes, *Apostolic Fathers*, 480-81).

104. Köstenberger et al. see ἑώρακαν as the dramatic perfect (Köstenberger et al., *Going Deeper*, 301).

as a past perfect.[105] Andrason and Locatell analyze ἑώρακα in Luke 1:22 and 9:36 as simple past, especially located beside the aorists which explicitly convey past events.[106] In John 20:25, English translation renders the verb "have seen," but in fact the disciples are describing to Thomas the past event of Jesus's appearance while Thomas was not there. John 1:33–34 is noteworthy. Using ᾔδειν and εἶπεν, John the Baptist describes his previous memory of when he was baptizing Jesus Christ.

A final example is:

[John 3:32] ὃ **ἑώρακεν** καὶ ἤκουσεν τοῦτο μαρτυρεῖ, καὶ τὴν μαρτυρίαν αὐτοῦ οὐδεὶς λαμβάνει.

He [John the Baptist] bears witness to what he *has seen* and heard, yet no one receives his testimony.

It is very difficult to determine which category would fit best for ἑώρακεν—the anterior (current relevance) or the simple past. According to Robertson, this passage proves that the co-occurrence of the perfect and the aorist does not always create confusion of tense, but each tense becomes distinct.[107] In contrast, Caragounis argues that ἑώρακεν located beside the aorist shows "the result of the loss of feeling for the meaning of tenses."[108] Although Robertson's explanation is plausible, Caragounis's viewpoint is hard to ignore. The combination of perfect and aorist verbs is especially noteworthy, due to the merger of these tenses. The difficulty is the present tense verb μαρτυρεῖ. The intention of the author might be to deliver variegated nuances of the events by employing three tenses—perfect, aorist, and present. Nevertheless, ἑώρακα shows the process or tendency of the perfect

---

105. ESV, NASB, NIV, KJV, RSV, CSB: "he had seen a vision"; NLT, "he must have seen a vision." Caragounis states that ἑώρακαν here denotes a past event (Caragounis, *New Testament Language*, 162).

106. Andrason and Locatell, "Perfect Wave," 47. Similarly, Porter says "past implicature of the Perfect" (Porter, *Verbal Aspect*, 261).

107. Robertson, *Grammar*, 901; Fanning, *Verbal Aspect*, 300. See the cases that the perfect and the aorist are distinct: Mark 5:19, ὕπαγε εἰς τὸν οἶκόν σου πρὸς τοὺς σοὺς καὶ ἀπάγγειλον αὐτοῖς ὅσα ὁ κύριός σοι πεποίηκεν καὶ ἠλέησέν σε ("Go home to your friends and tell them how much the Lord has done for you, and how he had mercy on you"); John 8:56–57, Ἀβραὰμ ὁ πατὴρ ὑμῶν ἠγαλλιάσατο ἵνα ἴδῃ τὴν ἡμέραν τὴν ἐμήν καὶ εἶδεν καὶ ἐχάρη. εἶπον οὖν οἱ Ἰουδαῖοι πρὸς αὐτόν· πεντήκοντα ἔτη οὔπω ἔχεις καὶ Ἀβραὰμ ἑώρακας; ("Your father Abraham rejoiced that he would see my day. He saw it and was glad. So the Jews said to him, 'You are not yet fifty years old, and have you seen Abraham?'"); and 1 Clement 23.3, Ταῦτα ἠκούσαμεν καὶ ἐπὶ τῶν πατέρων ἡμῶν, καὶ ἰδού, γεγηράκαμεν καὶ οὐδὲν ἡμῖν τούτων συνβέβηκεν ("We heard these things even in the days of our fathers, and look, we have grown old, and none of these things have happened to us") (Holmes, *Apostolic Fathers*, 78–79).

108. Caragounis, *New Testament Language*, 163.

to merge with the aorist. Therefore, I regard ἑώρακα in John 3:32 as conveying a simple past more than an anterior nuance, even though its behavior falls on a fine line between the anterior and simple past nuance.[109]

Importantly, Mandilaras stresses that it is not always easy to detect the perfect conveying a simple past nuance. Mandilaras says,

> The context alone . . . is not sufficient to permit us to take a given perfect as aoristic. The perfect can be thus regarded in the following situations: (a) when the perfect is connected with an aorist symbolization, (b) when the context denotes no relationship of the past action to present time, and (c) when there is indication of past time. Criterion (a) is not always valid; sentences where aorists and perfects are used side by side must be treated with caution because the writer may be indicating a special meaning; (b) is often uncertain because the context alone may mislead us. There remains criterion (c), which is strong enough to transfer the perfect to the sphere of the aorist. Indeed, the perfect tends to become a mere preterite when a definite point of time in the past is stated or otherwise implied.[110]

Mandilaras asserts that with no present time in context the existence of past time indicators implies that this case of perfect is strongly aoristic. In spite of criticisms, Mandilaras' criteria are somewhat helpful.[111] In order to discern "aoristic perfect," it is necessary to examine the context very carefully, search for the connection to the aorist, and find a past time indicator, if possible. However, even a past time indicator does not always finalize the aoristic perfect.[112] Although the perfect (ἐγήγερται) and the aorist (ἐτάφη) occur in parallel, and the past time indicator (τῇ ἡμέρᾳ τῇ τρίτῃ) exists in 1 Corinthians 15:4, ἐγήγερται does not convey a simple past.[113]

---

109. Not all usages of ἑώρακα this period (the first and second centuries AD) are simple past: 1 Clement 53.3, καὶ εἶπεν κύριος πρὸς αὐτόν· Λελάληκα πρός σε ἅπαξ καὶ δὶς λέγων,Ἑώρακα τὸν λαὸν τοῦτον, καὶ ἰδού ἐστιν σκληροτράχηλος ("And the Lord said to him: 'I have spoken to you time and again, saying, I have seen this people, and they are stiff-necked indeed!'") (Holmes, *Apostolic Fathers*, 114-15).

110. Mandilaras, *Non-Literary Papyri*, 225-26.

111. Bentein evaluates that most of Mandilaras' criteria are problematic (Bentein, *Verbal Periphrasis*, 48).

112. Mandilaras, *Studies in the Greek Language*, 17; Mandilaras, *Non-Literary Papyri*, 225-26. See Robertson, *Grammar*, 901.

113. Fanning, *Verbal Aspect*, 302. See chapter 2 above.

Interestingly, Burton states that the perfect as simple past is limited to ἔσχηκα, εἴληφα, ἑώρακα, εἴρηκα, and γέγονα.[114] In addition to them, we are able to find more cases such as λελάληκα, ἀπέσταλκα, and δέδωκα.

Ἀπέσταλκα

The perfect ἀπέσταλκα conveys a current relevance (anterior) nuance,[115] but it also denotes a past action.

> [John 5:33] ὑμεῖς ἀπεστάλκατε πρὸς Ἰωάννην, καὶ μεμαρτύρηκεν τῇ ἀληθείᾳ.
> You *sent* to John, and he has borne witness to the truth.

> [Acts 7:35] Τοῦτον τὸν Μωϋσῆν ὃν ἠρνήσαντο εἰπόντες· τίς σε κατέστησεν ἄρχοντα καὶ δικαιστήν; τοῦτον ὁ θεὸς [καὶ] ἄρχοντα καὶ λυτρωτὴν ἀπέσταλκεν σὺν χειρὶ ἀγγέλου τοῦ ὀφθέντος αὐτῷ ἐν τῇ βάτῳ.
> This Moses, whom they rejected, saying, "Who made you a ruler and a judge?"—this man God *sent* as both ruler and redeemer by the hand of the angel who appeared to him in the bush.[116]

> [2 Cor 12:17] μή τινα ὧν ἀπέσταλκα πρὸς ὑμᾶς, δι' αὐτοῦ ἐπλεονέκτησα ὑμᾶς;
> Did I take advantage of you through any of those whom I *sent* to you?

---

114. Burton, *Syntax*, 44. Cf. Mandilaras, *Non-Literary Papyri*, 226–27.

115. See Luke 4:18, πνεῦμα κυρίου ἐπ' ἐμὲ οὗ εἵνεκεν ἔχρισέν με εὐαγγελίσασθαι πτωχοῖς. ἀπέσταλκέν με ("The Spirit of the Lord is upon me, because he has anointed me to proclaim good news to the poor. He *has sent* me"); John 5:36, τὰ γὰρ ἔργα ἃ δέδωκέν μοι ὁ πατὴρ ἵνα τελειώσω αὐτά, αὐτὰ τὰ ἔργα ἃ ποιῶ μαρτυρεῖ περὶ ἐμοῦ ὅτι ὁ πατήρ με ἀπέσταλκεν ("For the works that the Father has given me to accomplish, the very works that I do, bear witness about me that the Father *has sent* me"); Acts 10:20, ἀλλ' ἀναστὰς κατάβηθι καὶ πορεύου σὺν αὐτοῖς μηδὲν διακρινόμενος ὅτι ἐγὼ ἀπέσταλκα αὐτούς ("But arise and go down and accompany them without hesitation, for I [the Spirit] *have sent* them"); Acts 16:36, ἀπήγγειλεν δὲ ὁ δεσμοφύλαξ τοὺς λόγους [τούτους] πρὸς τὸν Παῦλον ὅτι ἀπέσταλκαν οἱ στρατηγοὶ ἵνα ἀπολυθῆτε ("And the jailer reported these words to Paul, saying 'The magistrates *have sent* to let you go'"); Acts 15:27, ἀπεστάλκαμεν οὖν Ἰούδαν καὶ Σιλᾶν ("we *have* therefore *sent* Judas and Silas").

116. A variety of English Bibles translate this phrase as past tense: ESV, "this man God sent"; NASB, "the one whom God sent"; NIV, "He was sent to be their ruler and deliverer by God himself"; and KJV, "the same did God send *to be* a ruler and redeemer."

[1 John 4:9, 14] τὸν υἱὸν αὐτοῦ τὸν μονογενῆ ἀπέσταλκεν ὁ θεὸς εἰς τὸν κόσμον ἵνα ζήσωμεν δι' αὐτοῦ. . . . καὶ ἡμεῖς τεθεάμεθα καὶ μαρτυροῦμεν ὅτι ὁ πατὴρ ἀπέσταλκεν τὸν υἱὸν σωτῆρα τοῦ κόσμου.

God *sent* his only Son into the world, so that we might live through him. . . . And we have seen and testify that the Father has sent his Son to be the savior of the world.[117]

[LXX Gen 45:8] νῦν οὖν οὐχ ὑμεῖς με ἀπεστάλκατε ὧδε ἀλλ' ἢ ὁ θεός καὶ ἐποίησέν με ὡς πατέρα Φαραω καὶ κύριον παντὸς τοῦ οἴκου αὐτοῦ καὶ ἄρχοντα πάσης γῆς Αἰγύπτου.

So it was not you who *sent* me here, but God. He has made me a father to Pharaoh, and lord of all his house and ruler over all the land of Egypt.[118]

All the perfects present a simple past. In John 5:33, Jesus Christ is describing the prior event that occurred in John 1:19 in which the Jews sent John the Baptist to ask his identity.[119] In Acts 7:35, ἀπέσταλκεν denotes a simple past, placed beside two aorists. Robertson argues that ἀπέσταλκεν delivers a vivid sense.[120] It might be a possible option too, but ἀπέσταλκεν in the text appears to express past events. In Genesis 45:8, Joseph speaks of the clear past event when his brothers sold him. In terms of nuance, ἀπέσταλκεν is not that different from the aorist ἀπέστειλας.[121]

---

117. Moule and Andrason and Locatell regard ἀπέσταλκεν as a past action (Moule, *Idiom Book*, 14; Andrason and Locatell, "Perfect Wave," 53).

118. LXX Gen 38:23, ἀπέσταλκα τὸν ἔριφον τοῦτον σὺ δὲ οὐχ εὕρηκας ("I sent this young goat, and you did not find her"); 1 Kgs 21:5, καὶ εἶπον τάδε λέγει υἱὸς Αδερ ἐγὼ ἀπέσταλκα πρὸς σὲ λέγων τὸ ἀργύριόν σου καὶ τὸ χρυσίον σου καὶ τὰς γυναῖκάς σου καὶ τὰς γυναῖκάς σου καὶ τὰ τέκνα σου δώσεις ἐμοί ("Thus says Ben-hadad, 'Surely, I sent to you, saying "You shall give me your silver and your gold and your wives and your children."'").

119. In John 1:19, the aorist occurs: Καὶ αὕτη ἐστὶν ἡ μαρτυρία τοῦ Ἰωάννου, ὅτε ἀπέστειλαν [πρὸς αὐτὸν] οἱ Ἰουδαῖοι ἐξ Ἱεροσολύμων ἱερεῖς καὶ Λευίτας ἵνα ἐρωτήσωσιν αὐτόν· σὺ τίς εἶ; ("And this is the testimony of John, when the Jews sent priests and Levites from Jerusalem to ask him, 'Who are you?'").

120. Robertson, *Grammar*, 897.

121. See John 11:42, ἐγὼ δὲ ᾔδειν ὅτι πάντοτέ μου ἀκούεις, ἀλλὰ διὰ τὸν ὄχλον τὸν περιεστῶτα εἶπον, ἵνα πιστεύσωσιν ὅτι σύ με ἀπέστειλας ("I knew that you always hear me, but I said this on account of the people standing around, that they may believe that you sent me"). Mandilaras says, "In the epistolary perfect, as in the epistolary aorist, the writer imagines himself to be present when the letter is read. The perfect, however, stresses the presence of the writer more than the aorist. . . . In the post-Ptolemaic papyri the epistolary perfect does not appear as frequently as in earlier times; this is due to the general decay of the perfect" (Mandilaras, *Non-Literary Papyri*, 227–28).

Difficult passages are Acts 9:17 and John 20:21.

[Acts 9:17] Ἀπῆλθεν δὲ Ἀνανίας καὶ εἰσῆλθεν εἰς τὴν οἰκίαν καὶ ἐπιθεὶς ἐπ᾽ αὐτὸν τὰς χεῖρας εἶπεν· Σαοὺλ ἀδελφέ, ὁ κύριος **ἀπέσταλκέν** με, Ἰησοῦς ὁ ὀφθείς σοι ἐν τῇ ὁδῷ ᾗ ἤρχου.

So Ananias departed and entered the house. And laying his hands on him said, "Brother Saul, the Lord Jesus, who appeared to you on the road by which you came has sent me."

[John 20:21] εἰρήνη ὑμῖν· καθὼς **ἀπέσταλκέν** με ὁ πατήρ πέμπω ὑμᾶς.

Peace be with you. As the Father has sent me, I also send you.

The timeline of Acts 9:17 is that the Lord had appeared to Ananias in a vision, commanding his departure, after which Ananias left his place, and has now entered the house where Saul stays. Now Ananias is delivering the message to Paul. Hence, ἀπέσταλκεν indicates the previous moment when the Lord sent Ananias to Paul. Nevertheless, the author employs the perfect, so that it is difficult to obliterate the current relevance nuance completely. The aorist verb would have been employed if the author wanted to emphasize only the past event without the present time nuance. The fuzziness of the nuance is the same in John 20:21. The Father has sent the risen Lord just now, but the context implies that the Father already sent Jesus Christ, incarnation of the Son, in the past as well.

In the semantic change of the perfect from the anterior to simple past, some overlap is inevitable, concurring with Traugott's statement that the old meanings are not immediately terminated.[122]

---

122. Hopper and Traugott, *Grammaticalization*, 97. Horrocks's statement is helpful: "But the importance of the formal expression of this retrospective viewing of an event, and the consequential emphasis on its continued relevance at the viewing point, is easily downgraded, and the grammaticalized temporal focus then shifts immediately to the event itself, with the result that what was the viewing point becomes instead the temporal reference point for the location of that event: cf. the virtual equivalence, when uttered by someone who wants to start cooking at the time of utterance, of *have you got the chops out of the freezer?* (the point from which the past is viewed is 'now') and *did you get the chops out of the freezer?* (i.e., in the past vis-à-vis 'now', but still with inferable contemporary relevance). In this way the perfect may come to be understood not just as an alternative to the simple past when continued relevance at the time of utterance is to be emphasized" (Horrocks, *Greek*, 177).

Δέδωκα

Most usages of δέδωκα denote an anterior nuance like that of the English perfect.[123] For example:

---

123. The usages are as follows (perfects in bold): in Luke 10:19, ἰδοὺ **δέδωκα** ὑμῖν τὴν ἐξουσίαν τοῦ πατεῖν ἐπάνω ὄφεων καὶ σκορπίων ("Behold, I have given you authority to tread on serpents and scorpions"); John 3:35, πάντα **δέδωκεν** ἐν τῇ χειρὶ αὐτοῦ ("the Father has given the Son all things into his hand"); John 5:22, ἀλλὰ τὴν κρίσιν πᾶσαν **δέδωκεν** τῷ υἱῷ ("but the Father has given all judgment to the Son"); John 5:36, τὰ γὰρ ἔργα ἃ **δέδωκέν** μοι ὁ πατὴρ ἵνα τελειώσω αὐτά ("the works that the Father has given me to accomplish"); John 6:39, ἵνα πᾶν ὃ **δέδωκέν** μοι μὴ ἀπολέσω ἐξ αὐτοῦ ("that I should lose nothing of all that he has given me"); John 7:19, Οὐ Μωϋσῆς **δέδωκεν** ὑμῖν τὸν νόμον; ("Has not Moses given you the law?"); John 10:29, ὁ πατήρ μου ὃ **δέδωκέν** μοι πάντων μεῖζόν ἐστιν ("My Father, who has given them to me, is greater than all"); John 12:49, ὁ πέμψας με πατὴρ αὐτός μοι ἐντολὴν **δέδωκεν** τί εἴπω καὶ τί λαλήσω ("the Father who sent me has himself given me a commandment what to say and what to speak"); John 17:2, καθὼς ἔδωκας αὐτῷ ἐξουσίαν πάσης σαρκός, ἵνα πᾶν ὃ **δέδωκας** αὐτῷ δώσῃ αὐτοῖς ζωὴν αἰώνιον ("just as you gave him authority over all flesh, to give eternal life to all whom you have given him"); John 17:7, νῦν ἔγνωκαν ὅτι πάντα ὅσα **δέδωκάς** μοι παρὰ σοῦ εἰσιν ("Now they know that everything that you have given me is from you"); John 17:8–9, ὅτι τὰ ῥήματα ἃ ἔδωκάς μοι **δέδωκα** αὐτοῖς. . . . οὐ περὶ τοῦ κόσμου ἐρωτῶ ἀλλὰ περὶ ὧν **δέδωκάς** μοι ("For I have given them the words you gave me. . . . I am not praying for the world but for those whom you have given me"); John 17:11–12, πάτερ ἅγιε, τήρησον αὐτοὺς ἐν τῷ ὀνόματί σου ᾧ **δέδωκάς** μοι, ἵνα ὦσιν ἓν καθὼς ἡμεῖς. ὅτε ἤμην μετ' αὐτῶν ἐγὼ ἐτήρουν αὐτοὺς ἐν τῷ ὀνόματί σου ᾧ **δέδωκάς** μοι ("Holy Father, keep them in your name which you have given me, that they may be one, even as we are one. While I was with them, I kept them in your name, which you have given me"); John 17:14, ἐγὼ **δέδωκα** αὐτοῖς τὸν λόγον σου καὶ ὁ κόσμος ἐμίσησεν αὐτούς ("I have given them your word, and the world hated them"); John 17:22, κἀγὼ τὴν δόξαν ἣν **δέδωκάς** μοι **δέδωκα** αὐτοῖς, ἵνα ὦσιν ἓν καθὼς ἡμεῖς ἕν ("The glory that you have given me I have given to them, that they may be one even as we are one"); John 17:24, Πάτερ, ὃ **δέδωκάς** μοι, θέλω ἵνα ὅπου εἰμὶ ἐγὼ κἀκεῖνοι ὦσιν μετ' ἐμοῦ, ἵνα θεωρῶσιν τὴν δόξαν τὴν ἐμήν, ἣν **δέδωκάς** μοι ὅτι ἠγάπησάς με πρὸ καταβολῆς κόσμου ("Father, I desire that they also, whom you have given me, may be with me where I am, to see my glory that you have given me because you loved me before the foundation of the world"); John 18:9, ἵνα πληρωθῇ ὁ λόγος ὃν εἶπεν ὅτι οὓς **δέδωκάς** μοι οὐκ ἀπώλεσα ἐξ αὐτῶν οὐδένα ("This was to fulfill the word that he had spoken: 'Of those whom you have given me I have lost not one'"); John 18:11, βάλε τὴν μάχαιραν εἰς τὴν θήκην· τὸ ποτήριον ὃ **δέδωκέν** μοι ὁ πατὴρ ("Put your sword into its sheath; shall I not drink the cup that the Father has given me?"); 1 John 3:1, Ἴδετε ποταπὴν ἀγάπην **δέδωκεν** ἡμῖν ὁ πατὴρ ("See what kind of love the Father has given to us"); 1 John 4:13, ὅτι ἐκ τοῦ πνεύματος αὐτοῦ **δέδωκεν** ἡμῖν ("because he has given us of his Spirit"); 1 John 5:20, οἴδαμεν δὲ ὅτι ὁ υἱὸς τοῦ θεοῦ ἥκει καὶ **δέδωκεν** ἡμῖν διάνοιαν ("And we know that the Son of God has come and has given us understanding"); Rev 3:8, ἰδοὺ **δέδωκα** ἐνώπιόν σου θύραν ἠνεῳγμένην ("Behold, I have put before you an open door"); Rev 16:6, ὅτι αἷμα ἁγίων καὶ προφητῶν ἐξέχεαν καὶ αἷμα αὐτοῖς [δ]**έδωκας** πιεῖν, ἄξιοί εἰσιν ("For they have shed the blood of saints and prophets, and you have given them blood to drink").

[John 17:8] τὰ ῥήματα ἃ ἔδωκάς μοι δέδωκα αὐτοῖς, καὶ αὐτοὶ ἔλαβον.

For I *have given* them the words that you gave me and they have received.

John 17:8 shows a distinction between the perfect and aorist. The combination of the perfect and the aorist does not always bring forth an aoristic perfect; as Robertson points out, the confusion of tenses can make them rather distinct.[124] In this text, δέδωκα expresses an anterior nuance while the aorists denote past events. For the past three years Jesus Christ has given the words to the disciples during his ministry.[125]

The difficulty lies in the cases of expressing the simple past. Chantraine notes that δέδωκα seems to overlap in meaning with the aorist.[126]

[John 6:32] ἀμὴν ἀμὴν λέγω ὑμῖν, οὐ Μωϋσῆς δέδωκεν ὑμῖν τὸν ἄρτον ἐκ τοῦ οὐρανοῦ, ἀλλ' ὁ πατήρ μου δίδωσιν ὑμῖν τὸν ἄρτον ἐκ τοῦ οὐρανοῦ τὸν ἀληθινόν.

Truly, truly, I say to you, it was not Moses who *gave* you the bread from heaven, but my Father gives you the true bread from heaven.

[John 7:22] διὰ τοῦτο Μωϋσῆς δέδωκεν ὑμῖν τὴν περιτομήν—οὐχ ὅτι ἐκ τοῦ Μωϋσέως ἐστίν ἀλλ' ἐκ τῶν πατέρων—καὶ ἐν σαββάτῳ περιτέμνετε ἄνθρωπον.

On this account Moses *gave* you circumcision (not that it is from Moses, but from the fathers), and you circumcise a man on the Sabbath.

[John 17:4] ἐγώ σε ἐδόξασα ἐπὶ τῆς γῆς τὸ ἔργον τελειώσας ὃ δέδωκάς μοι ἵνα ποιήσω.

I glorified you on earth, having accomplished the work that you *gave* me to do.

In John 6:32 and 7:22, δέδωκα denotes a past nuance, pointing to the events that occurred in the OT when Moses gave the Israelites bread and circumcision.[127] Notably, the background of John 17:4 is the final moment

---

124. Robertson, *Grammar*, 901.

125. Duhoux, *Le verbe grec ancien*, 430–31. The perfects here, as the current relevance, make a contrast to the aorist ἔδωκάς, which implies that the Father already gave him the words. See Moser, "Tense and Aspect," 553–54.

126. Chantraine, *Parfait grec*, 231–32.

127. Andrason and Locatell note the usage of δέδωκα as past time (Andrason and Locatell, "Perfect Wave," 53).

of Jesus Christ in his ministry as he prays before he is arrested. The perfect δέδωκας expresses the past event in parallel with the aorist ἐδόξασα.[128]

Second Corinthians

In 2 Corinthians, the perfect as simple past occurs many times. These usages do not deliver an anterior nuance.

Ἔσχηκα

This perfect is noteworthy. The occurrences from the NT are:

> [2 Cor 1:9] ἀλλ' αὐτοὶ ἐν ἑαυτοῖς τὸ ἀπόκριμα τοῦ θανάτου ἐσχήκαμεν, ἵνα μὴ πεποιθότες ὦμεν ἐφ' ἑαυτοῖς ἀλλ' ἐπὶ τῷ θεῷ τῷ ἐγείροντι τοὺς νεκρούς.
>
> Indeed, we *had* the sentence of death within ourselves in order that we should not trust in ourselves, but in God who raises the dead.
>
> [2 Cor 2:13] οὐκ ἔσχηκα ἄνεσιν τῷ πνεύματί μου τῷ μὴ εὑρεῖν με Τίτον τὸν ἀδελφόν μου, ἀλλ' ἀποταξάμενος αὐτοῖς ἐξῆλθον εἰς Μακεδονίαν.
>
> I *had* no rest for my spirit, not finding Titus my brother; but taking my leave of them, I went on to Macedonia.[129]
>
> [2 Cor 7:5] Καὶ γὰρ ἐλθόντων ἡμῶν εἰς Μακεδονίαν οὐδεμίαν ἔσχηκεν ἄνεσιν ἡ σὰρξ ἡμῶν ἀλλ' ἐν παντὶ θλιβόμενοι· ἔξωθεν.
>
> For even when we came into Macedonia our flesh *had* no rest, but we were afflicted on every side.

---

128. ESV, "that you gave me to do"; NASB, "which Thou hast given Me to do"; NIV, "the work you gave me to do"; KJV, "which thou gavest me to do." In the Septuagint, δέδωκα is also found with a past meaning: Gen 16:5, ἐγὼ δέδωκα τὴν παιδίσκην μου ("I have given [gave] my servant to your embrace"); Gen 35:12, καὶ τὴν γῆν ἣν δέδωκα Αβρααμ καὶ Ισαακ σοὶ δέδωκα αὐτήν σοὶ ἔσται ("The land that I gave to Abraham and Isaac I will give to you"). See *The Shepherd of Hermas* 8.2, ἦλθεν ἡ πρεσβυτέρα καὶ ἠρώτησέν με εἰ ἤδη τὸ βιβλίον δέδωκα τοῖς πρεσβυτέροις ("The elderly woman came and asked me if I had already given the little book to the elders") (Holmes, *Apostolic Fathers*, 468–69).

129. ESV, "my spirit was not at rest"; NASB, "I had no rest for my spirit"; NIV, "I still had no rest of mind"; and KJV, "I had no rest in my spirit." Köstenberger, Merkle, and Plummer consider ἔσχηκα as dramatic perfect (*Going Deeper*, 300).

Robertson states that ἐσχήκαμεν in 2 Corinthians 1:9 and 7:5 conveys vividness as a Dramatic Perfect in order to deliver the dreadfulness of the memory.[130] Robertson comments regarding ἔσχηκα in 2 Corinthians 2:13,

> Paul may have wished to accent the strain of his anxiety up to the time of the arrival of Titus. The aorist would not have done that. The imperfect would not have noted the end of his anxiety. It was durative plus punctiliar. Only the past perfect and the present perfect could do both. The experience may have seemed too vivid to Paul for the past perfect. Hence he uses the (historical dramatic) present perfect.[131]

Although I do not preclude the possibility of the Dramatic Perfect for vividness, it seems more likely that ἔσχηκα denotes a past event in the texts above. Moulton and Caragounis consider ἔσχηκα in 2:13 as simple past, parallel to the aorist ἐξῆλθον.[132]

Not all usages of ἔσχηκα denote prior actions. In Romans 5:2, it conveys an anterior nuance: δι' οὗ καὶ τὴν προσαγωγὴν ἐσχήκαμεν ("through whom we also *have obtained* access by faith"). The access to God behind the second curtain, the Holy of Holies, was restricted to only the high priest. The access to God has now been allowed for us after the resurrection of Jesus Christ.[133]

Πεποίηκα

Another famous example for the aoristic perfect is πεποίηκα.

> [2 Cor 11:25] τρὶς ἐρραβδίσθην, ἅπαξ ἐλιθάσθην, τρὶς ἐναυάγησα, νυχθήμερον ἐν τῷ βυθῷ πεποίηκα.
>
> Three times I was beaten with rods, once I was stoned, three times I was shipwrecked; a night and a day I *was* adrift at sea.

---

130. Robertson, *Grammar*, 897.

131. Robertson, *Grammar*, 901.

132. Moulton, *Prolegomena*, 145; Chantraine, *Parfait grec*, 238; Caragounis, *New Testament Language*, 164; Moule, *Idiom Book*, 14.

133. Aubrey, "Greek Perfect," 98. Schreiner states that ἔσχηκα is not equivalent to the aorist (Schreiner, *Romans*, 254). See Plato, *Apology* 20δ, ἐγὼ γάρ, ὦ ἄνδρες Ἀθηναῖοι, δι' οὐδὲν ἀλλ' ἢ διὰ σοφίαν τινὰ τοῦτο τὸ ὄνομα ἔσχηκα ("The fact is, men of Athens, that I have acquired this reputation on account of nothing else than a sort of wisdom"). The example is from McKay, "Ancient Greek Perfect," 12.

In this passage, scholars regard πεποίηκα as denoting a past event.[134] Robertson and Moulton state that the role of πεποίηκα is to describe the vividness of the memory.[135] Both are possible in this text, but another case of πεποίηκεν in Hebrews 11:28 ("By faith he *kept* the Passover and the sprinkling of the blood") shows a clear previous event.[136] Interestingly, Crellin introduces Wulfia's Gothic translation of the passage which renders πεποίηκα as a past tense.[137] As we observed in the previous chapter, most occurrences of πεποίηκα show an anterior (current relevance) nuance.[138]

Book of Hebrews

The book of Hebrews shows strikingly many cases of the perfect as a simple past—more than twenty.[139] The beginning of Hebrews is:[140]

> [Heb 1:3–5] ἐκάθισεν ἐν δεξιᾷ τῆς μεγαλωσύνης ἐν ὑψηλοῖς, τοσούτῳ κρείττων γενόμενος τῶν ἀγγέλων ὅσῳ διαφορώτερον παρ' αὐτοὺς **κεκληρονόμηκεν** ὄνομα. Τίνι γὰρ εἶπέν ποτε τῶν ἀγγέλων· υἱός μου εἶ σύ, ἐγὼ σήμερον γεγέννηκά σε;
>
> He sat down at the right hand of the Majesty on high, having become as much superior to angels as the name he *has inherited* is more excellent than theirs. For to which of the angels did God ever say, "You are my Son, today I have begotten you"?

This text juxtaposes the perfect and the aorist. The letter was written after the crucifixion and the resurrection of Jesus Christ, implying

---

134. Burton, *Syntax*, 43; Chantraine, *Parfait grec*, 239; Caragounis, *New Testament Language*, 164.

135. Robertson, *Grammar*, 897; Moulton, *Prolegomena*, 144; Köstenberger et al., *Going Deeper*, 300.

136. The Greek text in Heb 11:28 is: Πίστει πεποίηκεν τὸ πάσχα καὶ τὴν πρόσχυσιν τοῦ αἵματος, ἵνα μὴ ὁ ὀλοθρεύων τὰ πρωτότοκα θίγῃ αὐτῶν. Chantraine states that πεποίηκεν in Heb 11:28 denotes an acquired result, but this interpretation is unlikely (Chantraine, *Parfait grec*, 235).

137. Crellin, "Gothic Eyes," 17.

138. See chapter 3 above.

139. Andrason and Locatell state that the book of Hebrews shows 22 percent of the perfective past sense, occurring in Hebrews 7:6 [2x], 7:14, 10:9, 11:17, and 11:28 (68 percent of present perfect, 9 percent of present and stative present) (Andrason and Locatell, "Perfect Wave," 52–63). My research shows that the percentage is even higher, almost half of all the perfects in Hebrews (24 out of 45). See the table in the Introduction.

140. Note the bold-font perfect.

that its context describes these past events as a background. The perfect κεκληρονόμηκεν denotes a simple past in the middle of the two aorists.[141] In Hebrews, cases like this one are numerous.[142]

Other examples are:

> [Heb 7:6] ὁ δὲ μὴ γενεαλογούμενος ἐξ αὐτῶν **δεδεκάτωκεν** Ἀβραὰμ καὶ τὸν ἔχοντα τὰς ἐπαγγελίας εὐλόγηκεν.
>
> But this man who does not have his descent from them *received* tithes from Abraham and blessed him who had the promises.[143]

> [Heb 7:11] Εἰ μὲν οὖν τελείωσις διὰ τῆς Λευιτικῆς ἱερωσύνης ἦν, ὁ λαὸς γὰρ ἐπ᾽ αὐτῆς **νενομοθέτηται**, τίς ἔτι χρεία κατὰ τὴν τάξιν Μελχισέδεκ ἕτερον ἀνίστασθαι ἱερέα.
>
> Now if perfection had been attainable through the Levitical priesthood, for under it the people *received* the law, what further need would there have been for another priest to arise after the order of Melchizedek.

> [Heb 7:13-14] ἐφ᾽ ὃν γὰρ λέγεται ταῦτα, φυλῆς ἑτέρας **μετέσχηκεν**, ἀφ᾽ ἧς οὐδεὶς **προσέσχηκεν** τῷ θυσιαστηρίῳ· πρόδηλον γὰρ ὅτι ἐξ Ἰούδα **ἀνατέταλκεν** ὁ κύριος ἡμῶν.
>
> For the one of whom these things are spoken *belonged* to another tribe, from which no one *has* ever *served* at the altar. For it is evident that our Lord *was descended* from Judah.

> [Heb 8:5-6] οἵτινες ὑποδείγματι καὶ σκιᾷ λατρεύουσιν τῶν ἐπουρανίων, καθὼς **κεχρημάτισται** Μωϋσῆς μέλλων ἐπιτελεῖν τὴν σκηνήν. . . . νυν[ὶ] δὲ διαφορωτέρας τέτυχεν λειτουργίας, ὅσῳ καὶ κρείττονός ἐστιν διαθήκης μεσίτης, ἥτις ἐπὶ κρείττοσιν ἐπαγγελίαις **νενομοθέτηται**.
>
> They serve a copy and shadow of the heavenly things. For when Moses was about to erect the tent, he *was instructed* by God. . . . But as it is, Christ has obtained a ministry that is as much more excellent than the old

---

141. For the argument of κεκληρονόμηκεν as present state, see Ng, "Greek Perfect in Hebrews," 12-14.

142. This usage of the perfect includes: εἴρηκεν "he said" (Heb 1:13; 4:3, 4); and καθὼς προείρηται, "as it has been said before" (Heb 4:7). See Heb 8:13, ἐν τῷ λέγειν καινὴν πεπαλαίωκεν τὴν πρώτην ("In speaking of a new covenant, he has made the first one obsolete"); Heb 10:9, τότε εἴρηκεν· ἰδοὺ ἥκω τοῦ ποιῆσαι τὸ θέλημά σου ("then he said, 'Here I am, I have come to do you will'").

143. Heb 7:9, Λευὶ ὁ δεκάτας λαμβάνων δεδεκάτωται ("Levi, who also received tithes, paid tithes through Abraham").

as the covenant he mediates is better, since it *has been enacted* on better promises.

[Heb 9:18] ὅθεν οὐδὲ ἡ πρώτη χωρὶς αἵματος **ἐγκεκαίνισται**.

Therefore not even the first covenant *was inaugurated* without blood.

[Heb 9:26] νυνὶ δὲ ἅπαξ ἐπὶ συντελείᾳ τῶν αἰώνων εἰς ἀθέτησιν [τῆς] ἁμαρτίας διὰ τῆς θυσίας αὐτοῦ **πεφανέρωται**.

But now once at the consummation of the ages he *has been manifested* to put away sin by the sacrifice of himself.

[Heb 11:17] Πίστει **προσενήνοχεν** Ἀβραὰμ τὸν Ἰσαὰκ πειραζόμενος.

By faith Abraham, when he was tested, *offered* up Isaac.

All these perfects speak of past time events.[144] Surprisingly, even the perfect middle forms express simple past. Chapter 2 examined a great number of perfect middles conveying the resultative-stative, and chapter 3 observed that less than thirty of these perfect middles show the anterior nuance, many of them being so-called "deponent."[145] The perfect middle forms above are νενομοθέτηται, κεχρημάτισται, νενομοθέτηται, ἐγκεκαίνισται, and πεφανέρωται.[146]

Finally, Hebrews 12:26 needs to be noted.

---

144. These events are: Melchizedek blessing Abram and receiving tithes (Heb 7:6), the giving of the Law (Heb 7:11), the priestly service at the altar (Heb 7:13), God's instruction to Moses (Heb 8:5), Jesus Christ's ministry (Heb 8:6), the inauguration of the first covenant (Heb 9:18), Jesus Christ's appearance (Heb 9:26), Enoch's witness before the ascension (Heb 11:5), Abraham's sacrifice of his son (Heb 11:17), and the observance of the Passover (Heb 11:28). In Hebrews 9:18, Porter states that the temporal deixis (ἡ πρώτη) indicates the past time for the perfect ἐγκεκαίνισται ("was inaugurated") (Porter, *Verbal Aspect*, 264).

145. Scholars agree that the term "deponency" is to be abolished. See Pennington, "Deponency in Koine Greek," 55–76; Campbell, *Advances in the Study of Greek*, 91–104.

146. Similarly, in Acts 8:14, Ἀκούσαντες δὲ οἱ ἐν Ἱεροσολύμοις ἀπόστολοι ὅτι δέδεκται (from δέχομαι) ἡ Σαμάρεια τὸν λόγον τοῦ θεοῦ ἀπέστειλαν πρὸς αὐτοὺς Πέτρον καὶ Ἰωάννην ("Now when the apostles at Jerusalem heard that Samaria received the word of God, they sent to them Peter and John"); Gal 3:18, τῷ δὲ Ἀβραὰμ δι' ἐπαγγελίας κεχάρισται (from χαρίζομαι) ὁ θεός ("God *gave* it to Abraham by a promise").

> [Heb 12:26] οὗ ἡ φωνὴ τὴν γῆν ἐσάλευσεν τότε, νῦν δὲ **ἐπήγγελται** λέγων· ἔτι ἅπαξ ἐγὼ σείσω οὐ μόνον τὴν γῆν ἀλλὰ καὶ τὸν οὐρανόν.
>
> And his voice shook the earth then, but now he has promised, saying, "Yet once more I will shake not only the earth, but also the heaven."

This text is a prophecy originally from Haggai 2:6 and 2:21. In the Hebrew Bible, God spoke what he was about to do—shake the heavens and the earth.[147] The author of Hebrews cites this passage from the Old Testament, employing the perfect ἐπήγγελται to describe the past event. In other places of the NT, surprisingly, ἐπήγγελται delivers a simple past as well (Rom 4:21; Gal 3:19).[148]

Μεμαρτύρηκα

With respect to μεμαρτύρηκα, many usages of it convey an anterior nuance.[149] However, some texts in the Greek New Testament contain its past nuance.

> [John 3:26] ῥαββί, ὃς ἦν μετὰ σοῦ πέραν τοῦ Ἰορδάνου, ᾧ σὺ **μεμαρτύρηκας**, ἴδε οὗτος βαπτίζει καὶ πάντες ἔρχονται πρὸς αὐτόν.
>
> Rabbi, he who was with you across the Jordan, to whom you bore witness, behold, he is baptizing, and all are coming to him.

---

147. LXX Hag 2:6, 21 says: ἔτι ἅπαξ ἐγὼ σείσω τὸν οὐρανὸν καὶ τὴν γῆν καὶ τὴν θάλασσαν καὶ τὴν ξηράν.... ἐγὼ σείω τὸν οὐρανὸν καὶ τὴν γῆν ("Yet once more, in a little while, I will shake the heavens and the earth and the sea and the dry land.... I am about to shake the heavens and the earth").

148. Rom 4:21, ὃ ἐπήγγελται ("what he had promised"); Gal 3:19, Τί οὖν ὁ νόμος; τῶν παραβάσεων χάριν προσετέθη, ἄχρις οὗ ἔλθῃ τὸ σπέρμα ᾧ ἐπήγγελται (from ἐπαγγέλλομαι), διαταγεὶς δι' ἀγγέλων ἐν χειρὶ μεσίτου ("Why then the Law? It was added because of transgression, until the offspring should come to whom the promise had been made, and it was put in place through angels by an intermediary").

149. See John 5:37, καὶ ὁ πέμψας με πατὴρ ἐκεῖνος μεμαρτύρηκεν περὶ ἐμοῦ. οὔτε φωνὴν αὐτοῦ πώποτε ἀκηκόατε οὔτε εἶδος αὐτοῦ ἑωράκατε ("And the Father who sent me, he has borne witness of me. You have neither heard his voice at any time, nor seen his form"); John 19:35, ὁ ἑωρακὼς μεμαρτύρηκεν ("He who saw it has borne witness"); 1 John 5:9, ὅτι αὕτη ἐστὶν ἡ μαρτυρία τοῦ θεοῦ ὅτι μεμαρτύρηκεν περὶ τοῦ υἱοῦ αὐτοῦ ("for this is the testimony of God that he has borne concerning his Son"); 3 John 1:12, Δημητρίῳ μεμαρτύρηται ὑπὸ πάντων ("Demetrius has received a good testimony from everyone").

[John 5:33] ὑμεῖς ἀπεστάλκατε πρὸς Ἰωάννην, καὶ **μεμαρτύρηκεν** τῇ ἀληθείᾳ.

You sent to John, and he [John the Baptist] has borne witness to truth.

[Heb 11:5] πρὸ γὰρ τῆς μεταθέσεως **μεμαρτύρηται** εὐαρεστηκέναι τῷ θεῷ.

For he [Enoch] obtained the witness that before his being taken up he was pleasing to God

The perfect μεμαρτύρηκα above expresses a simple past. The disciples of John the Baptist describe a past time event when John witnessed Jesus Christ before.[150] In Hebrews 11:5, the ascension of Enoch happened in the Old Testament era before the Flood.

Γεγέννηκα

The perfect γεγέννηκα contains uses difficult to evaluate. The difficulty lies in that this perfect is found as a simple past.

[John 8:41] ὑμεῖς ποιεῖτε τὰ ἔργα τοῦ πατρὸς ὑμῶν. Εἶπαν [οὖν] αὐτῷ· ἡμεῖς ἐκ πορνείας οὐ **γεγεννήμεθα**, ἕνα πατέρα ἔχομεν τὸν θεόν.

"You are doing the works your father did." They said to him [Jesus], "We *were* not *born* of fornication; we have one Father, even God."

[John 18:37] εἶπεν οὖν αὐτῷ ὁ Πιλᾶτος· οὐκοῦν βασιλεὺς εἶ σύ; ἀπεκρίθη ὁ Ἰησοῦς· σὺ λέγεις ὅτι βασιλεύς εἰμι. ἐγὼ εἰς τοῦτο **γεγέννημαι** καὶ εἰς τοῦτο ἐλήλυθα εἰς τὸν κόσμον, ἵνα μαρτυρήσω τῇ ἀληθείᾳ· πᾶς ὁ ὢν ἐκ τῆς ἀληθείας ἀκούει μου τῆς φωνῆς.

Then Pilate said to him, "So you are not a king?" Jesus answered, "You say that I am a king. For this purpose I *was born* and for this purpose I have come into this world—to bear witness the truth. Everyone who is of the truth listens to my voice."

[Acts 22:28] ἀπεκρίθη δὲ ὁ χιλίαρχος· ἐγὼ πολλοῦ κεφαλαίου τὴν πολιτείαν ταύτην ἐκτησάμην. ὁ δὲ Παῦλος ἔφη· ἐγὼ δὲ καὶ **γεγέννημαι**.

---

150. See John 1:34.

The tribune answered, "I bought this citizenship for a large sum." Paul said, "But I *was* actually *born* a citizen."

[Gal 4:23] ἀλλ᾽ ὁ μὲν ἐκ τῆς παιδίσκης κατὰ σάρκα **γεγέννηται**, ὁ δὲ ἐκ τῆς ἐλευθέρας δι᾽ ἐπαγγελίας.

But the son of the bondwoman *was born* according to the flesh, and the son by the free woman through the promise.[151]

In many texts, γεγέννηκα denotes a past event as shown above. The perfect γεγέννηκα shows that the perfect is employed to convey past events. The aorist appears in a great number of cases (e.g., in John 9:19, "Is this your son, who you say was born [ἐγεννήθη] blind?").[152]

However, not all usages indicate a simple past. In Hebrews 1:5, which cites LXX Psalm 2:7, γεγέννηκα appears.[153]

[Heb 1:5] Τίνι γὰρ εἶπέν ποτε τῶν ἀγγέλων· υἱός μου εἶ σύ, ἐγὼ σήμερον γεγέννηκά σε;

For to which of the angels did God ever say, "You are my son, today I have begotten you"?

It is very difficult to determine whether γεγέννηκα here is an anterior perfect or a simple past. The text offers hint, the adverb σήμερον ("today"). Hence, it seems in the text that γεγέννηκα stresses current relevance more than a possible nuance of the simple past, due to σήμερον.[154]

Γέγονα

The final perfect is a perplexing one, γέγονα. Chapters 2 and 3 have examined its usages as resultative-stative and anterior, respectively.[155] This section will introduce the cases of γέγονα as simple past.

[1 Cor 13:11] ὅτε **γέγονα** ἀνήρ **κατήργηκα** τὰ τοῦ νηπίου.

When I *became* a man, I *gave up* childish ways.

---

151. Chapter 2 introduced γεγέννηται as resultative-stative ("has been born," in 1 John 2:29, 3:9, 4:7, and 5:1).

152. The aorist forms of γεννάω are employed in the genealogy of Matt 1:2–20.

153. Heb 5:5 and Acts 13:33 cite this Psalm; LXX Psalm 2, υἱός μου εἶ σύ ἐγὼ σήμερον γεγέννηκά σε ("You are my son; today I have begotten you").

154. The aorist ἐγέννησα delivers a clear past event. See 1 Cor 4:15; Phlm 10; 1 John 1:13.

155. See Moulton, *Prolegomena*, 145.

Although Robertson considers γέγονα here as having a present sense, that understanding does not seem to fit the context.[156] For the sake of the Corinthians, Paul explains the gospel, reflecting his personal experience during his younger days. According to Moulton, it is not proved that γέγονα ever delivers the past time in the NT.[157] However, many texts demonstrate the opposite.

In the Greek New Testament, γέγονα expresses the simple past many times.[158]

> [Matt 1:22] τοῦτο δὲ ὅλον γέγονεν ἵνα πληρωθῇ τὸ ῥηθὲν ὑπὸ κυρίου διὰ τοῦ προφήτου.
>
> All this *took place* to fulfill the word by the Lord through the prophet.[159]
>
> [Mark 5:33] ἡ δὲ γυνὴ φοβηθεῖσα καὶ τρέμουσα, εἰδυῖα ὃ γέγονεν αὐτῇ, ἦλθεν καὶ προσέπεσεν αὐτῷ καὶ εἶπεν αὐτῷ πᾶσαν τὴν ἀλήθειαν.
>
> But the woman, knowing what *had happened* to her, came in fear and trembling and fell down before him and told him the whole truth.

---

156. Robertson, *Grammar*, 900. Andrason and Locatell see these perfects as a past sense (Andrason and Locatell, "Perfect Wave," 52).

157. Moulton, *Prolegomena*, 146. Robertson agrees with him (Robertson, *Grammar*, 900).

158. See 1 Clement 12.5–8, καὶ εἶπεν πρὸς τοὺς ἄνδρας· Γινώσκουσα γινώσκω ἐγὼ ὅτι κύριος ὁ θεὸς ὑμῶν παραδίδωσιν ὑμῖν τὴν γῆν ταύτην, ὁ γὰρ φόβος καὶ ὁ τρόμος ὑμῶν ἐπέπεσεν τοῖς κατοικοῦσιν αὐτήν. . . . καὶ εἶπαν αὐτῇ. Ἔσται οὕτως ὡς ἐλάλησας ἡμῖν. . . . καὶ προσέθεντο αὐτῇ δοῦναι σημεῖον, ὅπως ἐκκρεμάσῃ ἐκ τοῦ οἴκου αὐτῆς κόκκινον. . . . ὁρᾶτε, ἀγαπητοί, οὐ μόνον πίστις ἀλλὰ προφητεία ἐν τῇ γυναικὶ γέγονεν ("Then she said to the men: 'I am absolutely convinced that the Lord your God is handing this country over to you, for fear and terror of you have fallen upon all the inhabitants.' . . . And they said to her: 'It shall be exactly as you have said.' . . . And in addition they gave her a sign, that she should hang from her house something scarlet. . . . You see, dear friends, not only faith but also prophecy is [was] found in this woman"). Although Holmes renders γέγονεν as "is," I argue that γέγονεν here is closer to "was" as a simple past after a series of the aorists; *The Shepherd of Hermas* 60.3, Εἰ δέ τις, φημί, κύριε, γέγονεν ἄγνοια προτέρα πρὶν ἀκουσθῆναι τὰ ῥήματα ταῦτα, πῶς σωθήσεται ὁ ἄνθρωπος ὁ μιάνας τὴν σάρκα ἑαυτοῦ; ("But if, sir,' I said, 'there was any previous ignorance before these words were heard, how will the man who has defiled his flesh be saved?'") (*Apostolic Fathers*, 60–61, 580–81).

159. Andrason and Locatell regard Matt 21:4 as a past sense (Andrason and Locatell, "Perfect Wave," 52): Matt 21:4, τοῦτο δὲ γέγονεν ἵνα πληρωθῇ τὸ ῥηθὲν διὰ προφήτου ("This took place to fulfill what was spoken by the prophet"). See Caragounis, *New Testament Language*, 161.

[John 1:3] πάντα δι' αὐτοῦ ἐγένετο, καὶ χωρὶς αὐτοῦ ἐγένετο οὐδὲ ἕν. ὃ γέγονεν.

All things came into being by him, and apart from him nothing came into being that *was made*.

[John 6:25] καὶ εὑρόντες αὐτὸν πέραν τῆς θαλάσσης εἶπον αὐτῷ· ῥαββί, πότε ὧδε γέγονας;

When they found him [Jesus] on the other side of the sea, they said to him, "Rabbi, when *did* you *come* here?"[160]

[Rom 16:7] ἀσπάσασθε Ἀνδρόνικον καὶ Ἰουνίαν τοὺς συγγενεῖς μου καὶ συναιχμαλώτους μου, οἵτινές εἰσιν ἐπίσημοι ἐν τοῖς ἀποστόλοις, οἳ καὶ πρὸ ἐμοῦ γέγοναν ἐν Χριστῷ.

Greet Andronicus and Junia, my kinsmen and my fellow prisoners, who are outstanding among the apostles, and they *were* in Christ before me.[161]

[1 Thess 2:1] Αὐτοὶ γὰρ οἴδατε, ἀδελφοί, τὴν εἴσοδον ἡμῶν τὴν πρὸς ὑμᾶς ὅτι οὐ κενὴ γέγονεν.

For you yourselves know, brothers, that our coming to you *was* not in vain.

[1 Tim 2:14] ἡ δὲ γυνὴ ἐξαπατηθεῖσα ἐν παραβάσει γέγονεν.

And Adam was not deceived, but the woman was deceived and *became* a transgressor.

All the cases of γέγονα above indicate past events. In Romans 16:7, for instance, Paul talks about Christians in the church of Rome who became believers earlier than he did. In John 6:25, when the crowd asks Jesus about the time that he had come, he was already with the disciples on the other side of the sea. Burton considers γέγονεν in John 6:25 and Romans 16:7 as simple past.[162]

Matthew 25:5-7 is a difficult passage with γέγονα and is worth to examining.

[Matt 25:5-7] χρονίζοντος δὲ τοῦ νυμφίου ἐνύσταξαν πᾶσαι καὶ ἐκάθευδον. μέσης δὲ νυκτὸς κραυγὴ **γέγονεν**· ἰδοὺ ὁ νυμφίος, ἐξέρχεσθε εἰς ἀπάντησιν [αὐτοῦ]. τότε

---

160. See Andrason and Locatell, "Perfect Wave," 52.
161. Andrason and Locatell, "Perfect Wave," 52.
162. Burton, *Syntax*, 40.

ἠγέρθησαν πᾶσαι αἱ παρθένοι ἐκεῖναι καὶ ἐκόσμησαν τὰς λαμπάδας ἑαυτῶν.

As the bridegroom was delayed, they all became drowsy and slept. But at midnight there was a cry, "Here is the bridegroom! Come out to meet him." Then all those virgins rose and trimmed their lamps.

It is very difficult to decide which category γέγονεν should belong to. At first, it appears to belong to the resultative-stative, "there is a cry," because as a parable it is a story, not a real event. While Moulton regards γέγονεν here as a historic present, Burton maintains that γέγονεν is employed as simple past.[163] It is difficult to find necessary reasons to see γέγονεν as aoristic if we pay attention to γέγονεν alone. The whole context of the parable provides a hint. In this story, eleven aorists occur.[164] These occurrences make it likely that γέγονεν functions like an aorist in the text.[165]

CONCLUSION

The perfect went through another semantic change—from the anterior to the simple past—in the Koine period. The Greek New Testament preserves the cases of the perfect denoting the simple past (eighty-nine times). After the Koine period, the κ-perfect faded away probably due to its morphological similarity to the aorist. Periphrastic constructions replaced the synthetic κ-perfect until the Modern Greek perfect form with ἔχω plus aorist infinitive appeared in the thirteen and fourteenth centuries AD.

In order to solve the thorny matter of the perfect, Mathewson insightfully analyzes the book of Revelation using Porter's verbal aspect. Nevertheless, Mathewson regards all the perfects as stative in aspect, even though several perfects in Revelation express an obvious past nuance. In order to overcome this discrepancy, Mathewson applies the markedness theory to the perfects. He asserts that the perfects are stressed as the most heavily marked form. However, οἶδα and γέγραπται show the weakness of Porter and Mathewson's methodology because they do not always function to highlight. Because the perfect does not show the stative nuance only, Mathewson's approach makes the Greek perfect too simplistic.

---

163. Moulton, *Prolegomena*, 146; Burton, *Syntax*, 39.

164. In Matt 25:1–12, eleven aorists, two imperfects, two presents, and one perfect are used in this parable of ten virgins.

165. Blass and Debrunner and Caragounis note that γέγονεν here is equivalent to the aorist ἐγένετο (BDF §343; Caragounis, *New Testament Language*, 161). Köstenberger et al. view it as dramatic perfect (Köstenberger et al., *Going Deeper*, 301).

The category of "Dramatic Historical Present Perfect," introduced by Robertson, a traditional scholar, provides helpful tips for understanding this difficult case of the perfect. Robertson categorizes the dramatic perfect as employed to convey the vividness of the past event. This category from Robertson possibly correlates to Campbell's concept of the perfect as "heightened proximity" on the basis of the intensiveness of the perfect. This intensive notion for the perfect could accord with Robertson's Dramatic Perfect, which stresses the vividness of the perfect when used together with aorists.[166] Moreover, Porter and Mathewson's perfect as "highlight" may be conceptually in a similar line with Campbell's intensive perfect as "heightened proximity." Both Porter and Campbell sense that the perfect delivers a sort of highlighting nuance, so does Robertson who argues for the vividness of the dramatic perfect when used alongside aorists.[167]

Apart from accepting radical systems such as verbal aspect, Robertson's Dramatic Perfect could remain as an adequate category for solving several thorny cases of the prefect. However, this category of Robertson still lies outside the comprehensive solution. Although Robertson's Dramatic Perfect is fascinating and explains some of tough cases of the perfect, it does not clarify all the (aoristic) perfects. The historical development and the semantic change of the perfect can better explain these puzzling usages of the perfect in the Greek New Testament.

Some perfects present particular difficulty in determining to which category they belong. Several cases of εἴρηκα and ἑώρακα show overlap between the anterior and simple past nuance.[168] In the middle of the semantic change, they seem to be located on the fine line between the anterior and simple past. The semantic change did not immediately eliminate old meanings, just as in the previous chapters we have noted that the resultative perfects still occurred often in Classical Greek and some archaic perfect forms survived up to the Koine Greek.[169] The Greek New Testament preserves perfects conveying the simple past, as well as perfects of resultative-stative and anterior nuance.

---

166. Campbell appeals to Robertson's vivid perfects (Campbell, *Indicative Mood*, 209–10).

167. Olsen also compares the perfect tense to the past tense in English, pointing out the vividness of the perfect (Olsen, *Semantic and Pragmatic Model*, 233–34).

168. Chapter 3 also introduced the anterior perfects that occasionally express simple past, such as λελάληκα, πεποίηκα, and ἑώρακα.

169. Hopper and Traugott state, "Persistence of old meanings is a common phenomenon" (Hopper and Traugott, *Grammaticalization*, 97).

5

CONCLUSION

THE TRADITIONAL DEFINITION OF the Greek perfect has struggled to explain how to interpret irregular perfects. Many scholars have made studious efforts to explain these perplexing perfects—"stative" perfect (such as οἶδα and ἕστηκα) and "aoristic" perfect. Together with this issue, other weaknesses of the traditional understanding of the Greek verbal system remained unaddressed for decades, eventually resulting in the Greek verbal aspect debate of the early 1990s. During that period, Porter's and Fanning's verbal aspect theories made a groundbreaking contribution to Greek verb studies. The verbal aspect debate tremendously affected approaches to the Greek perfect.

Despite Porter's contributions, his rejection of grammatical temporality for Greek verbs is too radical. Moreover, Porter simplistically views all Greek perfects as stative. However, this view cannot explicate cases where the perfect behaves like an aorist. Fanning holds essentially the traditional view of the perfect but modifies it by combining three elements: (1) an anterior tense; (2) a stative *Aktionsart*; and (3) a summary viewpoint (perfective) aspect. However, Fanning's concept of the perfect suffers from its incohesive and indefensible combination of these elements.

Despite many efforts, scholars have failed to reach a consensus on the Greek perfect. Evans and Campbell argue that the perfect conveys an imperfective aspect. However, the Greek New Testament contains many examples where a perfect expresses the simple past, which is far from the imperfective aspect. These so-called "aoristic" perfects also undermine the view that the perfect is stative only, as argued by Porter, McKay, and Mathewson. The many examples of current relevance (anterior) perfects contradict their argument for the stative perfect.

Following the path set by Porter, Mathewson insightfully analyzes the book of Revelation through the lens of verbal aspect theory. Mathewson regards the perfect as having stative aspect, applying markedness theory to all of the perfects in Revelation. Mathewson asserts repeatedly that the perfect highlights events to show what belongs in the frontground. However, Porter's markedness theory is not applicable to all the cases of perfects in the Greek New Testament. For instance, οἶδα (210 occurrences) and γέγραπται (65 occurrences) do not always function as highlighting perfects in the NT. Mathewson's analysis of the Greek perfect is too simplistic. A common danger seems to be in a simplification of the Greek perfect by depending on a certain theory too much.

Horrocks summarizes his evaluation of these scholarly attempts.

> Previous attempts to describe the perfect as a verb form denoting a state of the subject, an acquired state of the subject, or a past action of the subject with continuing relevance have all run into difficulty precisely because each covers only a subset of cases; and forming an overarching pseudocategory, comprising stative perfects, nacto-stative perfects (i.e., denoting result states), experiential perfects etc., is really no more than an acknowledgement of defeat.[1]

In other words, not only the traditional understanding of the perfect but also the new approaches developed according to verbal aspect theory still suffer, lacking a comprehensive solution for explaining the perfect. Horrocks points out that the mere combination of each individual trait does not result in a synthetic and comprehensive apprehension of the Greek perfect. To simply combine the variegated characteristics of the perfect fails to expound its irregular behaviors. According to Horrocks, the Greek perfect is located outside the simple opposition between the perfective and imperfective aspects.

In the midst of this cacophony, Haspelmath and Allan argue for the diachronic development of the Greek perfect and its polysemous characteristics. Other scholars like Haug and Bentein also accept this diachronic approach. The historical development of the perfect elucidates why stative perfects such as οἶδα and ἕστηκα appear in the Greek New Testament. In ancient Greek, the perfect had a resultative-stative value and was intransitive. Many archaic perfects disappeared, but a "remnant" appear in the NT, after surviving throughout the Classical period.

It is noteworthy that perfect middle forms replaced archaic perfect actives. The ancient perfect was intransitive and subject-affected, like the

---

1. Horrocks, "Envoi," in Runge and Fresch, *Greek Verb Revisited*, 633.

middle voice. These traits of the archaic perfect active perhaps led to its successful replacement by the perfect middle because both convey a similar nuance—resultative-stative idea. A great number of perfect middle forms are found in Classical Greek. Many of them are also attested in the Greek New Testament, with most expressing a resultative-stative nuance. About a dozen cases deliver an anterior nuance. Most of them are so-called "deponent" (*medium tantum*) verbs. Fewer than twenty perfect middles denote the simple past. The perfect middle forms seem also to have been influenced by the diachronic semantic changes of the perfect.

In the Classical period, the perfect demonstrates a semantic change from the resultative-stative to the anterior (current relevance). A great number of anterior perfects are attested in Classical Greek and in the Greek New Testament. Transitive perfects also increased suddenly between the fifth and fourth centuries BC. This phenomenon was very peculiar because most perfects were intransitive in Homer. This radical increase in transitivity may provide a clue that something significant would have occurred enough to effect a semantic change of the perfect from resultative to anterior (current relevance).

In the Greek New Testament, a great number of perfects convey an anterior nuance. However, some perfects express the simple past. In the Koine period, the perfect went through another semantic change from the anterior to the simple past. This semantic change is also observed in other European languages. The perfect with a simple past nuance is found in the Apostolic Fathers, in the Septuagint occasionally, and even rarely in Classical Greek. By Hellenistic times, the merger of the perfect with the aorist had begun, so that the synthetic κ-perfect disappeared after Koine Greek.

The diachronic development of the perfect provide the key to understanding the "irregular" perfects in the Greek New Testament—the so-called "stative" perfect and "aoristic" perfect. The Greek New Testament preserves three nuances of the perfect—resultative-stative, anterior (current relevance), and simple past.[2] The three nuances of the perfect appear concurrently in the NT. The history of the development of the Greek perfect successfully explains its "exceptional" usages.

On the other hand, Robertson's category of Dramatic Historical Present Perfect is a traditional method that attempts to interpret bewildering perfects occurring alongside aorists. Robertson's dramatic perfect is employed in the middle of aorist verbs to emphasize the vividness of a past action. If the aorist had been simply employed again, it would have sounded

---

2. The Apostolic Fathers also retain and show the cases of three nuances of the perfect indicative.

"prosaic." Interestingly, Porter's theory of the perfect as the most heavily marked verb also points to a function of highlighting events. Campbell's "heightened proximity" for the perfect on the basis of its intensive notion seems to be in a similar line. Robertson's vivid perfect may have some overlap with both Porter's and Campbell's view of the perfect as functioning to highlight.

Robertson's Dramatic Perfect is able to clarify several perfects surprisingly placed in the middle of aorist verbs. His view that the perfect is used for vividness helps to untangle some knots. Therefore, Robertson's Dramatic Perfect is a usable tool from the traditional view for solving several thorny cases of the perfect. Moreover, it demonstrates that the traditional understanding of the perfect already acknowledges the perfect's highlighting role, especially when used among aorist verbs. Nevertheless, Robertson's vivid perfect is not satisfactory for all cases, such as for perfects conveying the simple past. It still falls short when it comes to explaining the perfect solely employed to denote past events. This kind of perfect still lays outside the purview of the Dramatic Perfect.

Allan concludes that the Greek perfect may be a "chain of related meanings, a polysemous network of family resemblances, a complex layering of variant meanings that resulted from a long historical process of semantic extensions."[3] This polysemy is not a collection of individual nuances randomly chosen apart from the diachronic time line. Andrason and Locatell say,

> In Archaic Greek, *léluka*'s prototypically resultative proper meaning could occasionally be extended pragmatically to a present perfect meaning, but not perfective past. It was not until it gained a prototypically present perfect meaning in Classical and Post-classical Greek that it could then be pragmatically extended in perfective past contexts.... That is why there is a very close conceptual relation between the present perfect resultative and the present perfect experiential, but not between the non-stative present and perfective past senses.[4]

In other words, a jump in the perfect's development from resultative-stative to simple past would have been impossible. A long period of time is prerequisite for the semantic change of the perfect. It is inappropriate to ignore the diachronic timeline when it comes to the polysemous perfect.

---

3. Allan, "Tense and Aspect," 113; Traugott and Dasher, *Regularity in Semantic Change*, 16.

4. Andrason and Locatell, "Perfect Wave," 91–92, 99.

Andrason and Locatell rightly state that "polysemy is not a collection of random values, but a coherent set."[5]

The Greek New Testament is a precious source that retains in one place many variegated nuances of the perfect throughout its different books. The diachronic and polysemous characteristics of the perfect will illuminate the solutions to handle the "exceptional perfects" in the NT and make us understand the Greek perfect better.

---

5. Andrason and Locatell, "Perfect Wave," 17.

APPENDIX 1

CHART OF THE PERFECT INDICATIVE WITH THREE NUANCES IN THE GREEK NEW TESTAMENT

	Resultative-Stative	**Anterior (Current Relevance)**	**Perfect as Simple Past**
Period	Ancient and Homeric Greek	Classical and Koine Greek	Koine Greek (rarely in Classical Greek)
Meanings	A present state implied from the past/pure state (or intensive)	A current relevance resulting from past events	A simple past (preterite)
Representatives	οἶδα, ἕστηκα, γέγραπται, τέθνηκα, πέποιθα, ἥγημαι	τετήρηκα, πεπλήρωκα, δεδούλευκα, εὕρηκα, πεπίστευκα, πεφίληκα, ἠγάπηκα, ἡμάρτηκα, πέπτωκα	εἴληφα, εὕρηκα, ἑώρακα, ἀπέσταλκα
Occurrence (Total 839)	461 (55%)	289 (34%)	89 (11%)

APPENDIX 2

PERFECT INDICATIVE WITH THREE NUANCES ACCORDING TO EACH BOOK IN THE NEW TESTAMENT

	Resultative-Stative	Anterior (Current Relevance)	Perfect as Simple Past	Pluperfect	Sum
Matthew	37	11	4	8	60
Mark	31	15	1	8	55
Luke	38	18	4	16	76
John	81	106	19	34	240
Acts	26	23	7	17	73
Romans	46	8	3	1	58
1 Cor	55	11	2		68
2 Cor	26	10	8		44
Galatians	11	3	4		18
Ephesians	1				1
Philippians	9	2			11
Colossians	4	2	1		7
1 Thess	10	2	1		13
2 Thess	3	1			4
1 Timothy	6	2	1		9
2 Timothy	7	5			12
Titus	2	1			3

PERFECT INDICATIVE WITH THREE NUANCES ACCORDING TO EACH BOOK

	Resultative-Stative	Anterior (Current Relevance)	Perfect as Simple Past	Pluperfect	Sum
Philemon	1				1
Hebrews	8	13	24		45
James	12	1	1		14
1 Peter	2	1			3
2 Peter	5	2			7
1 John	19	39	2	1	61
2 John		1			1
3 John	1	2			3
Jude	2	1			3
Revelation	18	9	7	1	35
	461	289	89	86 (Pluperfect)	Total 925 (839 Perfect)

BIBLIOGRAPHY

Anderson, Henning, ed. *Language Contacts in Prehistory: Studies in Stratigraphy.* Amsterdam: Benjamins, 2003.
Allan, Rutger J. "The Middle Voice in Ancient Greek: A Study in Polysemy." PhD diss., University of Amsterdam, 2002.
———. "Stative (and Middle/Medium) Verbs." In vol. 3 of *EAGLL*, edited by Georgios K. Giannakis, 316–18. Leiden: Brill, 2014.
———. "Tense and Aspect in Classical Greek: Two Historical Development; Augment and Perfect." In *The Greek Verb Revisited: A Fresh Approach for Biblical Exegesis*, edited by Steven E. Runge and Christopher J. Fresch, 81–121. Bellingham, WA: Lexham, 2016.
Anderson, Lloyd B. "The 'Perfect' as a Universal and Language-Specific Category." In *Tense-Aspect: Between Semantics and Pragmatics: Containing the Contributions to a Symposium on Tense and Aspect*, edited by Paul J. Hopper, 227–64. Amsterdam: Benjamins, 1982.
Andrason, Alexander. "From Resultatives to Present Tenses: Simultaneous Path of Resultative Constructions." *IJL* 26.1 (2014) 1–58.
Andrason, Alexander, and Christian Locatell. "The Perfect Wave: A Cognitive Approach to the Greek Verbal System." *BAGL* 5 (2016) 7–121.
Aristophanes. *The Lysistrata. The Thesmophoriazusae. The Ecclesiazusae. The Plutus.* Translated by Benjamin Bickley Rogers. LCL 180. Cambridge: Harvard University Press, 1924.
———. *Wealth*. Edited by Eugene O'Neill Jr. The Complete Greek Drama 2. New York: Random House, 1938. http://www.perseus.tufts.edu/hopper/text?doc=Perseus%3 Atext%3A1999.01.0040%3Acard%3D1003
Aubrey, Michael G. "The Greek Perfect and the Categorization of Tense and Aspect: Toward a Descriptive Apparatus for Operators in Role and Reference Grammar." MA thesis, Trinity Western University, 2014.
Aune, David E. *Revelation 1–5*. WBC 52a. Dallas: Word, 1997.
———. *Revelation 6–16*. WBC 52b. Dallas: Word, 1998.
Bakker, Egbert J., ed. *A Companion to the Ancient Greek Language*. Chichester, UK: Wiley & Sons, 2010.
Bakker, Stéphanie, and Gerry Wakker, eds. *Discourse Cohesion in Ancient Greek*. Leiden: Brill, 2009.
Barrett, C. K. *The Gospel according to St. John: An Introduction with Commentary and Notes on the Greek text*. Philadelphia: Westminster, 1978.

Beale, G. K. *The Book of Revelation: A Commentary on the Greek Text*. NIGTC. Grand Rapids: Eerdmans, 1999.

Beek, Lucien van. "The Etymology of Greek of πέπᾱμαι." In *Etymology and the European Lexicon*, edited by Bjarne Simmelkjær Sandgaard Hansen et al., 427–41. Wiesbaden: Reichert, 2016.

———. "The Perfect in Homeric Greek: Towards a Unitary View of its Semantics." Lecture at Leiden University, November 8, 2018. http://www.universiteitleiden.nl/en/events/2018/11/the-perfect-in-homeric-greek.

Beek, Lucien van, and Laura Migliori. "Active versus Middle Perfect in Homeric Greek: Synchrony and Diachrony." In *The Paths of Greek: Literature, Linguistics and Epigraphy Studies in Honour of Albio Cesare Cassio*, edited by Enzo Passa and Olga Tribulato, 71–106. Berlin: de Gruyter, 2019.

Beekes, Robert. *Etymological Dictionary of Greek*. 2 vols. Leiden: Brill, 2010.

Bentein, Klaas. "HAVE-Perfects in Post-Classical and Early Byzantine Greek." *Emerita* 81 (2013) 151–182.

———. "Perfect." In *EAGLL* 3:46–49.

———. "Perfect Periphrases in Post-Classical and Early Byzantine Greek: An Ecological-Evolutionary Account." *JGL* 12 (2012) 205–75.

———. "The Periphrastic Perfect in Ancient Greek: A Diachronic Mental Space Analysis." *TPS* 110.2 (2012) 171–211.

———. "Transitivity, Ecology, and the Emergence of Verbal Periphrasis in Ancient Greek." *CP* 108.4 (2013) 286–313.

———. *Verbal Periphrasis in Ancient Greek: Have- and Be- Constructions*. Oxford: Oxford University Press, 2016.

Bhat, D. N. Shankara. *The Prominence of Tense, Aspect, and Mood*. Amsterdam: Benjamins, 1999.

Blass, Friedrich, and Albert Debrunner. *A Greek Grammar of the New Testament and Other Early Christian Literature*. Translated by Robert W. Funk. Chicago: University of Chicago Press, 1960.

Blass, Friedrich, and Henry St. John Thackeray. *Grammar of New Testament Greek*. London: Macmillan, 1911.

Bock, Darrell L. *Luke*. Vol. 2. Grand Rapids: Baker, 1996.

Burton, Ernest Dewitt. *Syntax of the Moods and Tenses in New Testament Greek*. 2nd ed. 1900. Reprint, Ancient Language Resources. Eugene, OR: Wipf & Stock, 2003.

Buth, Randall. "Getting the Right Handles on the Greek Perfect." https://www.biblicallanguagecenter.com/handles-greek-perfect/.

———. "Perfect Greek Morphology and Pedagogy." In *The Greek Verb Revisited: A Fresh Approach for Biblical Exegesis*, edited by Steven E. Runge and Christopher J. Fresch, 379–429. Bellingham, WA: Lexham, 2016.

———. "Verbs Perception and Aspect: Greek Lexicography and Grammar, Helping Students to Think in Greek." In *Biblical Greek Language and Lexicography: Essays in Honor of Frederick W. Danker*, edited by Bernard A. Taylor et al., 177–98. Grand Rapids: Eerdmans, 2004.

Bybee, Joan L. *Morphology: A Study of the Relation between Meaning and Form*. Amsterdam: Benjamins, 1985.

Bybee, Joan, et al. *The Evolution of Grammar: Tense, Aspect, and Modality in the Language of the World*. Chicago: University of Chicago Press, 1994.

Campbell, Constantine R. *Advances in the Study of Greek: New Insights for Reading the New Testament*. Grand Rapids: Zondervan, 2015.

———. *Basics of Verbal Aspect in Biblical Greek*. Grand Rapids: Zondervan, 2008.

———. *Verbal Aspect and Non-Indicative Verbs: Further Soundings in the Greek of the New Testament*. New York: Lang, 2008.

———. *Verbal Aspect, the Indicative Mood, and Narrative: Soundings in the Greek of the New Testament*. New York: Lang, 2007.

Campbell, Constantine R., et al. *The Perfect Storm: Critical Discussion of the Semantics of the Greek Perfect Tense under Aspect Theory*. New York: Lang, 2021.

Caragounis, Chrys C. *The Development of Greek and the New Testament: Morphology, Syntax, Phonology, and Textual Transmission*. Tübingen: Mohr Siebeck, 2004.

———. *New Testament Language and Exegesis: A Diachronic Approach*. Tübingen: Mohr Siebeck, 2014.

Carson, D. A., and Robert W. Yarbrough, eds. *Understanding Times: New Testament Studies in the 21st Century*. Wheaton: Crossway, 2011.

Carson, D. A., and Stanley E. Porter, eds. *Biblical Greek Language and Linguistics: Open Questions in Current Research*. JSNTS 80. Sheffield: Sheffield Academic, 1993.

Chantraine, Pierre. *Grammaire Homerique: Phonetique et Morphologie*. Paris: Librairie C. Klincksieck, 1948.

———. *Histoire du parfait grec*. Paris: Librairie Ancienne Honoré Champion, 1926.

Charles, R. H. *The Revelation of St. John*. Vol. 1. CEC. New York: Scribner's Sons, 1920.

Cirafesi, Wally V. *Verbal Aspect in Synoptic Parallels: On the Method and Meaning of Divergent Tense-Form Usage in the Synoptic Passion Narratives*. Leiden: Brill, 2013.

Clackson, James. *Indo-European Linguistics: An Introduction*. Cambridge Textbooks in Linguistics. Cambridge: Cambridge University Press, 2007.

Collins, Raymond F. *1 & 2 Timothy and Titus*. NTL. Louisville: Westminster John Knox, 2002.

Comrie, Bernard. *Aspect: An Introduction to the Study of Verbal Aspect and Related Problems*. Cambridge: Cambridge University Press, 1976.

Crellin, Robert. "Basics of Verbal Aspect in Biblical Greek." *JSNT* 35 (2012) 196–202.

———. "The Greek Perfect Active System: 200 B.C.–A.D. 150." PhD diss., University of Cambridge, 2012.

———. "The Greek Perfect Active System: 200 B.C.–A.D. 150." *TB* 64 (2013) 157–60.

———. "The Greek Perfect through Gothic Eyes: Evidence for the Existence of a Unitary Semantic for the Greek Perfect in New Testament Greek." *JGL* 14 (2014) 5–42.

Curtius, Georg. *Greek Verb: Its Structure and Development*. Translated by A. S. Wilkins. London: Murray, 1880.

Dana, H. E., and Julius R. Mantey. *A Manual Grammar of the Greek New Testament*. New York: Macmillan, 1946.

Davies, W. D., and D. C. Allison. *The Gospel according to Saint Matthew*. Vol. 2. ICC. London: T&T Clark, 1991.

Decker, Rodney J. *Reading Koine Greek: An Introduction and Integrated Workbook*. Grand Rapids: Baker, 2014.

———. *Temporal Deixis of the Greek Verb in the Gospel of Mark with Reference to Verbal Aspect*. New York: Lang, 2001.

———. "Verbal Aspect in Recent Debate: Objections to Porter's Non-Temporal View of the Verb." Paper presented at the annual meeting of the Evangelical Theological

Society Eastern Region, Philadelphia Biblical University, Langhorne, PA, March 30, 2001.

Dibelius, Martin. *James: A Commentary on the Epistle of James*. Hermeneia. Philadelphia: Fortress, 1988.

Dickey, Eleanor. "The Greek and Latin Languages in the Papyri." In *The Oxford Handbook of Papyrology*, edited by Roger S. Bagnall, 149–69. Oxford: Oxford University Press, 2009.

Dougherty, Edward C. A. "The Syntax of the Apocalypse." PhD diss., Catholic University of America, 1990.

Drinka, Bridget. "The Development of the HAVE Perfect: Mutual Influences of Greek and Latin." In *Split Auxiliary Systems: A Cross-Linguistic Perspective*, edited by Raúl Aranovich, 101–21. Amsterdam: Benjamins, 2007.

———. "Development of the Perfect in Indo-European Stratigraphic Evidence of Prehistoric Areal Influence." In *Language Contacts in Prehistory: Studies in Stratigraphy*, edited by Henning Andersen, 77–105. Amsterdam: Benjamins, 2003.

———. "The Evolution of Grammar: Evidence from Indo-European Perfects." In *Historical Linguistics 1997: Selected Papers from the 13th International Conference on Historical Linguistics, Düsseldorf, 10–17 August 1997*, edited by Monika S. Schmid et al., 117–33. Current Issues in Linguistic Theory 164. Amsterdam: Benjamins, 1998.

———. *Language Contact in Europe: The Periphrastic Perfect through History*. Cambridge: Cambridge University Press, 2017.

Duhoux, Yves. *Le verbe grec ancien: éléments de morphologie et de syntaxe historiques*. Leuven: Peeters, 2000.

Dunn, James D. G. *The Epistles to the Colossians and to Philemon*. NIGTC. Grand Rapids: Eerdmans, 1996.

Ellis, Nicholas J., et al. "The Greek Verbal System and Aspectual Prominence: Revising Our Taxonomy and Nomenclature." *JETS* 59 (2016) 33–62.

Evans, T. V. *Verbal Syntax in the Greek Pentateuch*. Oxford: Oxford University Press, 2001.

Euripides. *Cyclops Alcestis Medea*. Edited by Jeffrey Henderson. LCL 12. 1994. Reprint, Cambridge: Harvard University Press, 2001.

Fanning, Buist M. "Approaches to Verbal Aspect in New Testament Greek: Issues in Definition and Mood." In *Biblical Greek Language and Linguistics: Open Questions in Current Research*, edited by Stanley E. Porter and D. A. Carson, 46–62. JSNTS 80. Sheffield: Sheffield Academic, 1993.

———. "Greek Tenses in John's Apocalypse." In *The Language and Literature of the New Testament: Essays in Honor of Stanley E. Porter's 60th Birthday*, edited by Lois K. Fuller Dow et al., 328–53. Leiden: Brill, 2017.

———. *Verbal Aspect in New Testament Greek*. Oxford: Clarendon, 1990.

Galani, Alexandra. "The Morphosyntax of Verbs in Modern Greek." PhD diss., University of York, 2005.

Garland. David E. *1 Corinthians*. Baker Exegetical Commentary on the New Testament. Grand Rapids: Baker Academic, 2003.

Gerö, Eva-Carin, and Arnim von Stechow. "Tense in Time: The Greek Perfect." In *Words in Time: Diachronic Semantics from Different Points of View*, edited by Regine Eckhardt et al., 251–94. Berlin: de Gruyter, 2003.

Gildersleeve, Basil Lanneau. "Stahl's Syntax of the Greek Verb." *American Journal of Philology* 29 (1908) 389–409.

———. *Syntax of Classical Greek from Homer to Demosthenes*. New York: American Book, 1906.

Goodwin, William W. *Greek Grammar*. Eugene, OR: Wipf & Stock, 1892.

———. *Syntax of the Moods and Tense on Greek Verbs*. Cambridge, MA: Sever and Francis, 1870.

Graham, Michael Todd, Jr. "The Discourse Function of Koine Greek Verb Forms in Narrative: Testing Current Proposals in the Book of Judith." PhD diss., Southern Baptist Theological Seminary, 2018.

Grosheide, F. W. *Commentary on the First Epistle to the Corinthians: The English Text with Introduction, Exposition and Notes*. Grand Rapids: Eerdmans, 1953.

Haspelmath, Martin. "Against Markedness (and What to Replace It With)." *Journal of Linguistics* 42 (2006) 25–70.

———. "From Resultative to Perfect in Ancient Greek." *Función* 11/12 (1992) 185–224.

Hatina, Thomas R. "The Perfect Tense-Form in Colossians: Verbal Aspect, Temporality and the Challenge of Translation." In *Translating the Bible: Problems and Prospects*, edited by Stanley E. Porter and Richard S. Hess, 224–52. JSNTS 173. Sheffield: Sheffield Academic, 1999.

———. "The Perfect Tense-Form in Recent Debate: Galatians as a Case Study." *Filologia Neotestamentaria* 8 (1995) 3–22.

Haug, Dag. "From Resultatives to Anteriors in Ancient Greek: On the Role of Paradigmaticity in Semantic Change." In *Grammatical Change and Linguistic Theory: The Rosendal Papers*, edited by Thórhallur Eythórsson, 285–305. Amsterdam: Benjamins, 2008.

Herodotus. *The Persian Wars, Volume I: Books 1–2*. Translated by A. D. Godley. LCL 117. Cambridge: Harvard University Press, 1920.

———. *The Persian Wars, Volume III: Books 5–7*. Translated by A. D. Godley. LCL 119. Cambridge: Harvard University Press, 1922.

Homer. *The Iliad, Volume I: Books 1–12*. Translated by A. T. Murray. LCL 170. Cambridge: Harvard University Press, 1924.

———. *The Iliad, Volume II: Books 13–24*. Translated by A. T. Murray. LCL 171. Cambridge: Harvard University Press, 1925.

———. *The Odyssey, Volume I: Books 1–12*. Edited by G. P. Goold. LCL 104. Cambridge: Harvard University Press, 1919.

———. *The Odyssey, Volume II: Books 13–24*. Edited by G. P. Goold. LCL 105. Cambridge: Harvard University Press, 1919.

Holmes, Michael W., ed and trans. *The Apostolic Fathers: Greek Texts and English Translations*. 3rd ed. Grand Rapids: Baker, 2007.

Hopper, Paul J., and Elizabeth Closs Traugott. *Grammaticalization*. 2nd ed. Cambridge: Cambridge University Press, 2003.

Horrocks, Geoffrey. *Greek: A History of the Language and Its Speakers*. 2nd ed. Oxford: Wiley-Blackwell, 2010.

Jannaris, A. N. *An Historical Greek Grammar: Chiefly of the Attic Dialect*. London: Macmillan, 1987.

Jasanoff, Jay H. *Hittite and the Indo-European Verb*. Oxford: Oxford University Press, 2003.

Josephus. *Jewish Antiquities, Volume I: Books 1-3*. Translated by H. St. J. Thackeray. LCL 242. Cambridge: Harvard University Press, 1930.

Kavčič, Jerneja. "The Decline of the Aorist Infinitive in Ancient Greek Declarative Infinitive Clauses." *JGL* 16 (2016) 266–311.

———. "Notes on the Transitivity of the Aorist and the Perfect in Classical Greek." In *The Greek Verb: Morphology, Syntax, and Semantics*, edited by Annamaria Bartolotta. Leuven: Peeters, 2014.

Kimball, Sara E. "The Origin of Greek κ-Perfect." *Glotta* 69 (1991) 141–53.

Kloekhorst, Alwin. "The Origin of the Hittite ḫi-Conjugation." In *Farnah: Indo-Iranian and Indo-European Studies in Honor of Sasha Lubotsky*, edited by Lucien van Beek et al., 89–106. Ann Arbor, MI: Beech Stave, 2018.

Köstenberger, Andreas J., et al. *Going Deeper with New Testament Greek: An Intermediate Study of the Grammar and Syntax of the New Testament*. Nashville: B&H Academic, 2016.

Kulikov, Leonid, and Nikolaos Lavidas. "Reconstructing Passive and Voice in Proto-Indo-European." In *Proto-Indo-European Syntax and its Development*, edited by Leonid Kulikov and Nikolaos Lavidas, 101–24. Amsterdam: Benjamins, 2015.

Kümmel, Martin Joachim. *Das Perfekt im Indoiranischen: Eine Untersuchung der Form und Funktion einer ererbten Kategorie des Verbums und ihrer Weiterentwicklung in den altindoiranischen Sprachen*. Wiesbaden: Reichert, 2000.

Lavidas, Nikolaos, and Leonid Kulikov. "Voice, Transitivity and Tense/Aspect: Directionality of Change in Indo-European (Evidence from Greek and Vedic)." In *Reconstructing Syntax*, edited by Jóhanna Barðdal et al., 289–313. Leiden: Brill, 2020.

Lea, Thomas D., and Hayne P. Griffin, Jr. *1, 2 Timothy and Titus*. NAC 34. Nashville: Broadman, 1992.

Levinsohn, Stephen H. "Functions of Copula-Participle Combinations ('Periphrastic')." In *The Greek Verb Revisited: A Fresh Approach for Biblical Exegesis*, edited by Steven E. Runge and Christopher J. Fresch, 307–26. Bellingham, WA: Lexham, 2016.

Lindstedt, Jouko. "The Perfect–Aspectual, Temporal and Evidential." In *Tense and Aspect in the Languages of Europe*, edited by Östen Dahl, 365–83. Berlin: de Gruyter, 2000.

Lockwood, Gregory J. *1 Corinthians*. CC. St. Louis: Concordia, 2000.

Longenecker, Richard N. *The Epistle to the Romans: A Commentary on the Greek Text*. NIGTC. Grand Rapids: Eerdmans, 2016.

Louw, J. P. "Die Semantiese Waarde van die Perfektum in Hellenistiese Grieks." *AC* 10 (1967) 23–32.

Lyons, John. *Semantics*. Cambridge: Cambridge University Press, 1977.

Lysias. *Lysias*. Translated by W. R. M. Lamb. LCL 244. Cambridge: Harvard University Press, 1930.

Madariaga, Nerea. "The Development of Indo-European Middle-passive Verbs: A Case Study in Ancient Greek and Old Church Slavic." *Indogermanische Forschungen* 115 (2010) 149–78.

Magni, Elisabetta. "Intensity, Reduplication, and Pluractionality in Ancient Greek." *Lexis* 10 (2017). https://journals.openedition.org/lexis/1117.

———. "Pluractionality and Perfect in Homeric Greek." In *Ancient Greek Linguistics: New Approaches, Insights, Perspective*, edited by F. Logozzo and P. Poccetti, 325–44. Berlin: de Gruyter, 2017.

Malden, Henry. "On Perfect Tenses in Greek, and Especially the First Perfect Active." *PS* 10 (1865) 168–79.
Mandilaras, Basil G. *Studies in the Greek Language*. Athens: Xenopoulos, 1972.
———. *The Verb in the Greek Non-Literary Papyri*. Athens: Hellenic Ministry of Culture and Sciences, 1973.
Maslov, Jurij S. "Resultative, Perfect, and Aspect." In *Typology of Resultative Constructions: Translated from the Original Russian Edition*, edited by Vladimir P. Nedjalkov, translated by Bernard Comrie, 63–86. Amsterdam: Benjamins, 1988.
Mathewson, David L. *Verbal Aspect in the Book of Revelation*. Leiden: Brill, 2010.
McCoard, Robert W. *The English Perfect: Tense-Choice and Pragmatic Inference*. Amsterdam: North-Holland, 1978.
McKay, Kenneth L. *A New Syntax of the Verb in New Testament Greek: An Aspectual Approach*. New York: Lang, 1994.
———. "On the Perfect and Other Aspects in the Greek Non-Literary Papyri." *BICS* 23 (1980) 23–49.
———. "On the Perfect and Other Aspects in NT Greek." *NovT* 23.4 (1981) 289–329.
———. "Time and Aspect in New Testament Greek." *NovT* 34.3 (1992) 209–28.
———. "The Use of the Ancient Greek Perfect down to the Second Century A. D." *BICS* 12 (1965) 1–12.
McKnight, Scot. *The Letters of James*. Grand Rapids: Eerdmans, 2011.
Melick, Richard R., Jr. *Philippians, Colossians, Philemon*. NAC 32. Nashville: Broadman, 1991.
Merkle, Benjamin L. "The Abused Aspect: Neglecting the Influence of a Verb's Lexical Meaning on Tense-Form Choice." *BBR* 26 (2016) 57–74.
Miller, Neva F. "A Theory of Deponent Verbs." In *Analytical Lexicon of the Greek New Testament*, edited by Timothy Friberg et al., 423–30. Grand Rapids: Baker, 2000.
Mocciaro, Egle. "Auxiliaries." In vol. 1 of *EAGLL*, edited by Georgios K. Giannakis, 218–21. Leiden: Brill, 2014.
Monro, D. B. *A Grammar of the Homeric Dialect*. Oxford: Clarendon, 1891.
Moo, Douglas J. *The Letter of James*. Grand Rapids: Eerdmans, 2000.
Moorhouse, A. C. *The Syntax of Sophocles*. Leiden: Brill, 1982.
Morris, Leon. *The Gospel according to Matthew*. Grand Rapids: Eerdmans, 1992.
Moser, Amalia. "From Aktionsart to Aspect: Grammaticalization and Subjectification in Greek." *Acta Linguistica Hafniensia: International Journal of Linguistics* 46 (2014) 64–84.
———. "The History of the Perfect Periphrases in Greek." PhD diss., University of Cambridge, 1988.
———. "Tense, Aspect, and the Greek Perfect." In *Perfect Explorations*, edited by Artemis Alexiadou et al., 235–52. Berlin: de Gruyter, 2003.
———. "Tense and Aspect after the New Testament." In *The Greek Verb Revisited: A Fresh Approach for Biblical Exegesis*, edited by Steven E. Runge and Christopher J. Fresch, 539–62. Bellingham, WA: Lexham, 2016.
Moule, C. F. D. *An Idiom Book of New Testament Greek*. Cambridge: Cambridge University Press, 1963.
Moulton, James Hope. *A Grammar of the New Testament Greek, Volume 1: Prolegomena*. Edinburgh: T. & T. Clark, 1908.
Moulton, James Hope, and Nigel Turner. *A Grammar of New Testament Greek, Volume 3: Syntax*. Edinburgh: T. & T. Clark, 1963.

Mounce, Robert H. *The Book of Revelation*. NICNT. Grand Rapids: Eerdmans, 1977.
Mounce, William D. *Basics of Biblical Greek*. 2nd ed. Grand Rapids: Zondervan, 2003.
———. *Pastoral Epistles*. WBC 46. Nashville: Nelson, 2000.
Mussies, Gerard. *The Morphology of Koine Greek*. Leiden: Brill, 1971.
Nedjalkov, Vladimir P. "Resultative Constructions." In *Language Typology and Language Universals*, edited by Martin Haspelmath, 928–40. Berlin: de Gruyter, 2001.
Nedjalkov, Vladimir P., ed. *Typology of Resultative Constructions: Translated from the Original Russian*. Amsterdam: Benjamins, 1988.
Nedjalkov, Vladimir P., and Sergej Je. Jaxontov. "The Type of Resultative Construction." In *Typology of Resultative Constructions: Translated from the Original Russian Edition*, edited by Vladimir P. Nedjalkov, translated by Bernard Comrie, 3–62. Amsterdam: Benjamins, 1988.
Ng, Siu Nam. "The Use of the Greek Perfect in Hebrews." ThM thesis, Dallas Theological Seminary, 2013.
Olsen, Mari B. *A Semantic and Pragmatic Model of Lexical and Grammatical Aspect*. New York: Garland, 1997.
Orriens, Sander. "Involving the Past in the Present: The Classical Greek Perfect as a Situating Cohesion Device." In *Discourse Cohesion in Ancient Greek*, edited by Stéphanie Bakker and Gerry Wakker, 221–39. Leiden: Brill, 2009.
Osborne, Grant B. *Revelation*. BECNT. Grand Rapids: Baker, 2002.
Pao, David W. *Colossians & Philemon*. ECNT. Grand Rapids: Zondervan, 2012.
Pennington, Jonathan T. "Deponency in Koine Greek: The Grammatical Question and the Lexicographical Dilemma." *Trinity Journal* 24 (2003) 55–76.
Perel'muter, Ilja A. "The Stative, Resultative, Passive and Perfect in Ancient Greek (Homeric Greek)." In *Typology of Resultative Constructions: Translated from the Original Russian Edition*, edited by Vladimir P. Nedjalkov, translated by Bernard Comrie, 277–87. Amsterdam: Benjamins, 1988.
Picirilli, Robert E. "The Meaning of the Tenses in New Testament Greek: Where Are We?" *JETS* 48.3 (2005) 533–55.
Pindar. *Nemean Odes Isthmian Odes Fragments*. Edited and translated by William H. Race. LCL 485. Cambridge: Harvard University Press, 1997.
Plato. *Charmides. Alcibiades I and II. Hipparchus. The Lovers. Theages. Minos. Epinomis.* Translated by W. R. M. Lamb. LCL 201. Cambridge: Harvard University Press, 1927.
———. *Cratylus. Parmenides. Greater Hippias. Lesser Hippias.* Translated by H. N. Fowler. LCL 167. Cambridge: Harvard University Press, 1926.
———. *Euthyphro. Apology. Crito. Phaedo. Phaedrus.* Translated by Harold North Fowler. LCL 36. Cambridge: Harvard University Press, 1914.
———. *Lysis. Symposium. Gorgias.* Translated by W. R. M. Lamb. LCL 166. Cambridge: Harvard University Press, 1925.
———. *Timaeus. Critias. Cleitophon. Menexenus. Epistles.* Translated by R. G. Bury. LCL 234. Cambridge: Harvard University Press, 1929.
Porter, Stanley E. "Greek Linguistics and Lexicography." In *Understanding the Times: New Testament Studies in the 21st Century*, edited by Andreas J. Köstenberger and Robert W. Yarbrough, 19–61. Wheaton, IL: Crossway, 2011.
———. *Idioms of the Greek New Testament*. Sheffield: JSOT Press, 1992.

———. "In Defence of Verbal Aspect." In *Biblical Greek Language and Linguistics: Open Questions in Current Research*, edited by Stanley E. Porter and D. A. Carson, 26–45. JSNTS 80. Sheffield: Sheffield Academic, 1993.

———. "Prominence: An Overview." In *The Linguist as Pedagogue: Trends in the Teaching and Linguistic Analysis of the Greek New Testament*, edited by Stanley E. Porter and Matthew Brook O'Donnell, 45–74. Sheffield: Sheffield Phoenix, 2009.

———. *Verbal Aspect in the Greek of the New Testament: With Reference to Tense and Mood*. New York: Lang, 1989.

Prior, Michael. *Paul the Letter-Writer and the Second Letter to Timothy*. JSNTS 23. Sheffield: Sheffield Academic, 1989.

Rau, Jeremy. "Greek and Proto-Indo-European." In *A Companion to the Ancient Greek Language*, edited by Egbert J. Bakker, 171–88. Chichester: Wiley & Sons, 2010.

Reed, Jeffrey T., and Ruth A. Reese. "Verbal Aspect, Discourse Prominence, and the Letter of Jude." *Filología Neotestamentaria* 9 (1996) 180–99.

Regier, Terry. *A Preliminary Study of the Semantics of Reduplication*. Technical Report TR-94-019. Berkeley: International Computer Science Institute, 1994.

Rijksbaron, Albert. "Het Griekse perfectum: subject contra object." *Lampas* 17 (1984) 403–19.

———. *Syntax and Semantics of the Verb in Classical Greek*. 3rd ed. Chicago: University of Chicago Press, 2002.

Robertson, A. T. *A Grammar of the Greek New Testament in the Light of Historical Research*. Nashville: Broadman, 1934.

Ropes, James Hardy. *A Critical and Exegetical Commentary on the Epistle of St. James*. ICC. Edinburgh: T. & T. Clark, 1991.

Ruijgh, Cornelis J. "Les valeurs temporelles des forms verbales en grec ancien." In *The Function of Tense in Texts*, edited by Jadranka Gvozdanović and Theo A. J. M. Janssen, 197–217. Amsterdam: North-Holland, 1991.

Runge, Steven E. "Contrastive Substitution and the Greek Verb: Reassessing Porter's Argument." *Novum Testamentum* 56.2 (2014) 154–73.

———. "Discourse Function of the Greek Perfect." In *The Greek Verb Revisited: A Fresh Approach for Biblical Exegesis*, edited by Steven E. Runge and Christopher J. Fresch, 458–85. Bellingham, WA: Lexham, 2016.

———. "Markedness: Contrasting Porter's Model with the Linguists Cited as Support." *BBR* 26 (2016) 43–56.

Runge, Steven E., and Christopher J. Fresch, eds. *The Greek Verb Revisited: A Fresh Approach for Biblical Exegesis*. Bellingham, WA: Lexham, 2016.

Sauge, André. *Les degrés du verbe: sens et formation du parfait en grec ancien*. New York: Lang, 2000.

Schrage, Wolfgang. *Der erste Brief an die Korinther: 1 Kor 15.1–16.24*. Evangelisch-Katholischer Kommentar zum Neuen Testament. Düsseldorf: Benziger, 2001.

Schreiner, Thomas R. *Romans*. BECNT. Grand Rapids: Baker, 1998.

Schwyzer, Eduard. *Griechische Grammatik: auf der Grundlage von Karl Brugmanns Griechischer Grammatik*. Vol. 1. München: Beck, 1953.

Sicking, C. M. J., and P. Stork. *Two Studies in the Semantics of the Verb in Classical Greek*. Leiden: Brill, 1996.

Sihler, Andrew L. *New Comparative Grammar of Greek and Latin*. New York: Oxford University Press, 1995.

Silva, Moisés. "A Response to Fanning and Porter on Verbal Aspect." In *Biblical Greek Language and Linguistics: Open Questions in Current Research Open Questions in Current Research*, edited by Stanley E. Porter and D. A. Carson, 74–82. JSNTS 80. Sheffield: Sheffield Academic, 1993.

Simcox, William Henry. *The Language of the New Testament*. London: Hodder and Soughton, 1889.

Slings, Simon R. "Geschiedenis van het perfectum in het oud-Grieks." In *Nauwe betrekkingen: Voor Theo Janssen bij zijn vijftigste verjaardag*, edited by Ronny Boogaart and Jan Noordegraaf, 239–47. Amsterdam: Stichting Neerlandistiek VU, 1994.

Smalley, Stephen S. *The Revelation to John: A Commentary on the Greek Text of the Apocalypse*. Downers Grove, IL: InterVarsity, 2005.

Smyth, Herbert Weir. *Greek Grammar*. Cambridge: Harvard University Press, 1984.

Sophocles. *Ajax. Electra. Oedipus. Tyrannus*. Edited and Translated by Hugh Lloyd-Jones. LCL 20. Cambridge: Harvard University Press, 1994.

Stagg, Frank. "The Abused Aorist." *JBL* 91.2 (1972) 222–31.

Stechow, Arnim von. "German *seit* 'since' and the Ambiguity of the German Perfect." In *More than Words: A Festschrift for Dieter Wunderlich*, edited by Ingrid Kaufmann and Barbara Stiebels, 393–432. Berlin: Akademie Verlag, 2002.

Stork, Peter. "The Use of the Perfect Stem in the Fragments of Aeschylus and Sophocles." In *Fragmenta Dramatica: Beiträge zur Interpretation der griechischen Tragikerframente und ihrer Wirkungsgeschichte*, edited by Heinz Hofmann and Annette Harder, 9–38. Göttingen: Vandenhoeck & Ruprecht, 1991.

Sumney, Jerry L. *Colossians*. NTL. Louisville: Westminster John Knox, 2008.

Swete, Henry Barclay. *The Apocalypse of St. John*. London: Macmillan, 1922.

Taylor, Bernard A., et al., eds. *Biblical Greek Language and Lexicography: Essays in Honor of Frederick W. Danker*. Grand Rapids: Eerdmans, 2004.

Thompson, Steven. *The Apocalypse and Semitic Syntax*. Cambridge: Cambridge University Press, 1985.

Thucydides. *History of the Peloponnesian War*. Translated by C. F. Smith. 4 Vols. LCL 108, 109, 110, 169. Cambridge: Harvard University Press, 1919–23.

Towner, Philip H. *The Letters to Timothy and Titus*. NICNT. Grand Rapids: Eerdmans, 2006.

Traugott, Elizabeth Closs, and Richard B. Dasher. *Regularity in Semantic Change*. Cambridge: Cambridge University Press, 2005.

Trotter, Julius Carroll, Jr. "The Use of the Perfect Tenses in the Pauline Epistles." ThD thesis, Southern Baptist Theological Seminary, 1951.

Veitch, William. *Greek Verbs: Irregular and Defective*. New ed. Oxford: Clarendon, 1879.

Vendler, Zeno. "Verbs and Times." *The Philosophical Review* 66 (1957) 143–60.

Wallace, Daniel B. *Greek Grammar beyond the Basics*. Grand Rapids: Zondervan, 1996.

Wackernagel, Jacob. "Studien zum griechischen Perfektum." In *Programm zur akademischen Preisverteilung*, 3–24. N.p., 1904.

———. *Vorlesungen über Syntax mit besonderer Berücksichtigung von Griechisch. Lateinisch und Deutsch* 1. Basel: Birkhäuser, 1926.

Weiss, Michael. "Morphology and Word Formation." In *A Companion to the Ancient Greek Language*, edited by Egbert J. Bakker, 104–19. Chichester: Wiley & Sons, 2010.

Willi, Andreas. *The Languages of Aristophanes: Aspects of Linguistic Variation in Classical Attic Greek*. Oxford: Oxford University Press, 2003.
———. *Origins of the Greek Verb*. Cambridge: Cambridge University Press, 2018.
Xenophon. *Memorabilia. Oeconomicus. Symposium. Apology*. Edited and revised by Jeffrey Henderson. Translated by E. C. Marchant and O. J. Todd. Loeb Classical Library 168. Cambridge: Harvard University Press, 2013.
Zerwick, Maximilian. *Biblical Greek*. Rome: Pontificium Institutum Biblicum, 1963.

www.ingramcontent.com/pod-product-compliance
Lightning Source LLC
Chambersburg PA
CBHW051738230426
43670CB00012B/2069